BEHIND
THE BALLOT BOX

BEHIND
THE BALLOT BOX

A Citizen's Guide to Voting Systems

DOUGLAS J. AMY

PRAEGER

Westport, Connecticut
London

Library of Congress Cataloging-in-Publication Data

Amy, Douglas J.
  Behind the ballot box : a citizen's guide to voting systems / Douglas J. Amy.
    p. cm.
  Includes bibliographical references and index.
  ISBN 0–275–96585–6 (alk. paper).—ISBN 0–275–96586–4 (pbk. : alk. paper)
    1. Elections. 2. Voting. 3. Representative government and representation. I. Title:
  Citizen's guide to voting systems. II. Title.
  JF1001.A47 2000
  324.6—dc21   00–029841

British Library Cataloguing in Publication Data is available.

Library of Congress Catalog Card Number: 00–029841
ISBN: 0–275–96585–6
    0–275–96586–4 (pbk.)

First published in 2000

Praeger Publishers, 88 Post Road West, Westport, CT 06881
An imprint of Greenwood Publishing Group, Inc.
www.praeger.com

Printed in the United States of America

The paper used in this book complies with the
Permanent Paper Standard issued by the National
Information Standards Organization (Z39.48–1984).

10 9 8 7 6 5 4 3 2 1

Copyright Acknowledgments

The author and publisher greatly acknowledge permission for use of the following material:

An earlier version of Appendix B was previously published as "The Forgotten History of the
Single Transferable Vote in the United States," in *Representation* 34, no. 1 (Winter 1996/7).
It is reprinted here with the kind permission of the McDougall Trust, a United Kingdom
charity that specializes in electoral studies.

There is not enough room on this page to list all the ways
you have made my life better.
So I will just say,
For Susan, with love, respect, and gratitude.

Supported by a grant from the Open Society Institute's
Individual Project Fellowship Program.

Contents

Illustrations

BALLOTS

Spotlights on the Debate

Preface

For almost a decade, I have been intrigued by voting systems—those seemingly innocuous election rules that turn out to have such wide-ranging political impacts. Until a few years ago, it was an obsession that I seemed to share only with some other political scientists and a handful of election reform advocates. But these days there is a burgeoning interest in voting systems and voting system reform in the United States, and that is why I wrote this book. I saw that as more politicians, election officials, activists, and citizens began to consider the issue of voting system reform, they were having trouble finding all the material they needed to make an informed and thoughtful choice among these systems. There was no one book that covered the entire range of available voting systems, described how they work, and discussed their political advantages and disadvantages. This book is intended to fill that gap.

When I was considering how to organize this book, one other book immediately came to mind: *The International IDEA Handbook of Electoral Design* by Andrew Reynolds and Ben Reilly. This excellent work discusses the criteria for designing election systems, describes a variety of voting systems, and explains their political consequences. It is intended primarily for an international audience, particularly emerging democracies. It occurred to me that a similar approach, aimed this time at an American audience, would be an effective way to present this material, and so I borrowed liberally from their work in developing the overall organization of this book.

Another book that informed the approach I took to this topic was *Smart Choices: A Practical Guide to Making Better Decisions* by John Hammond, Ralph Keeney, and Howard Raifa. It helped me to think about how to organize the steps involved in analyzing and choosing a good voting system. It also gave me the idea for including in the last chapter a section on the common pitfalls associated with choosing voting systems. I found two other books to be extremely useful sources of information about voting systems and their history: David M. Farrell, *Comparing Electoral Systems*, and Andrew McLaren Carstairs, *A Short History of Electoral Systems in Western Europe*.

I am particularly indebted to the Open Society Institute for providing a fellowship that allowed me to take time off from teaching during the spring of 1999 to write this book. I want to thank especially Gail Goodman and the other staff members in the Individual Project Program for their encouragement and their enthusiasm for this project. Their program has provided a uniquely supportive and nurturing atmosphere for a variety of scholars and activists, and I am very pleased that I was able to take part in it.

I also want to express my appreciation to all of those who were generous enough to take the time to read drafts of this manuscript and to offer corrections and advice, including Steve Chessin, Kathy Barber, Ray Bennett, John Gear, Sarah Grolnic-McClurg, Fred McBride, Mark Rush, Eric Olson, Rob Richie, and Andy Reynolds. This book benefited greatly from their suggestions, but of course any problems that remain are entirely my own responsibility. I also want to thank Joe Zimmerman, who was very helpful in my efforts to obtain support for this project and to find a publisher. And finally, particular thanks go to Ed Royce and Tom Wartenberg, who served as both good friends and thoughtful advisers throughout this project.

Introduction

Voting systems—the procedures by which we cast votes and elect our public officials—are a crucial part of the democratic election process. The decision to use one kind of voting system rather than another has far-reaching political consequences. Among other things, voting systems help to determine which officials are elected to run our governments, the variety of parties that voters have to choose from at the polls, how many citizens will turn out to vote, which citizens will or will not be represented in our legislatures, and whether the majority will rule. Ultimately, the choice of voting system has a profound effect not only on the process of elections, but also on the degree to which a political system is fair, representative, and democratic.

This book is designed to serve as a guide for people interested in learning more about voting systems and voting system reform in the United States. It will help you to evaluate your current voting system and compare it to other systems. Whether you are a government official considering changes to your voting system, a local citizen wanting to make your school board more representative of the community, a political activist concerned about improving American elections, a student studying voting procedures in a course, or simply someone curious about this topic—this book will help you develop a better understanding of this important political issue.

One goal of this book is to acquaint Americans with the various options available in the world of voting systems. In many other Western democracies, voting system reform has been a hot topic and so citizens and politicians in these countries have learned a great deal about these competing systems. But for many people in the United States, voting system reform is a new idea, and discussion has often been hampered by a lack of adequate information. In particular, many people are simply unfamiliar with the variety of possible voting systems. It is hard to have a good public debate over voting systems options if most people are unaware of their choices.

This book aims to remedy that problem. It will acquaint you with the three basic types of voting systems: plurality-majority systems, proportional representation systems, and semiproportional systems. It describes the workings of more than ten different voting systems, and it explains what the ballots look like, how votes are cast, and how the winners are determined. All the common voting systems used in the United States and other Western democracies are included, along with an Appendix that describes some lesser-used systems.

The primary aim of this book, however, goes beyond simply teaching you to recognize different voting systems, or enabling you to nod knowingly the next time someone mentions "cumulative voting." The main purpose is to help you find the best voting system in terms of your political values. The book is designed to give you all the basic information and analytical tools you need to search out the best system from among the alternatives. Unfortunately, finding the best set of voting procedures is not easy—it is certainly not something you can do over lunch. There are a confusing variety of systems to examine and a large number of political considerations that you must take into account. If you take a haphazard approach to this choice, you are very likely to make an ill-informed and misguided decision.

On the other hand, choosing a good voting system is not brain surgery either. You certainly don't have to be a trained psephologist—a scholar of electoral systems. All you need are a modest amount of time and energy to devote to the task, a source of reliable information about these systems, and a systematic approach to analyzing that information. If you provide the first of these, this book will furnish the second two. It will summarize all of the important political characteristics of voting systems, and it will guide you through a series of analytical steps that will help you to organize this information and to make an intelligent choice among these voting methods.

AN ORGANIZED APPROACH TO FINDING THE BEST SYSTEM

The four steps involved in investigating and selecting a good voting system—and around which this book is organized—are the following:

Step One: Develop Political Criteria for Judging Voting Systems

Before you begin to look at specific systems, you should think about what makes for a good voting system. How will you know a good system when you see one? To answer that question, you need to develop your own set of criteria that you can use to evaluate these systems.

Step Two: Compile a Broad Range of Alternative Voting Systems to Consider

You won't be able to find the best voting system if you aren't considering all the options. So you need to cast a wide net and examine a variety of voting methods.

Step Three: Examine the Alternatives and Identify Their Political Advantages and Disadvantages

To choose the best system, you need to know what the political effects of each system are. What are the political advantages and disadvantages of a particular voting system?

Step Four: Determine Which Voting System Best Meets Your Political Criteria

Once you know the political effects of the various options, you can compare them in a systematic way and decide which one best meets the criteria you set in the first step of your analysis.

This book is arranged to help you to go through these steps in order. The first chapter has introductory material intended especially for people who haven't thought much about voting procedures. It explains what voting systems are, why they are important, and why they have become the center of an increasing amount of political activity, both here and abroad. With these preliminaries out of the way, the book then turns to the process of helping you to analyze different voting systems. Chapter two covers the first step in this process: the need to develop criteria for judging voting systems. It gives you an extensive list of criteria that many scholars and reformers use to evaluate voting systems. These include such considerations as ensuring majority rule, producing fair representation for parties, encouraging voter turnout, being easy to use, and contributing to stable government. You are encouraged to use this chapter to decide which of these criteria are the most important. Several exercises are included to help you prioritize these criteria. By completing them, you will develop your own political yardstick for assessing voting system options.

Chapters three through six are where you will become acquainted with the actual voting systems themselves. All the most common and popular voting systems as well as some uncommon ones are included, so you should have no problem accomplishing the second step of the choice process: gathering a wide variety of voting system options to consider. Chapters three through five cover the various ways to elect legislative bodies: town councils, state legislatures, Congress, and so on. To make the analytic process easier, these voting systems are divided into three "families" of systems with a chapter devoted to each. Chapter three describes several kinds of plurality-majority voting systems, which include the systems most often used in U.S. elections. Chapter four addresses proportional representation voting systems, which are commonly used in most of the other advanced Western democracies. Finally, chapter five describes a somewhat less common variety of voting systems: semiproportional systems.

Each of these chapters explains the basic mechanics of these voting systems—how votes are cast, ballots are counted, and seats awarded to winners. But to make a good decision you need to know more than just how these systems work. You also need to know what their political consequences are—the third step in the choice process. Does a voting system encourage or discourage voter participation? Does it facilitate or hinder representation of political minorities? Does it maintain or undermine political stability? Does it invite or discourage gerrymandering and other forms of political manipulation?

To answer these kind of questions, each section on a particular voting system contains a description of its main political advantages and disadvantages. Fortunately, we don't have to speculate about these political effects. Nearly all of the voting systems covered in this book have been in use in the United States or some other Western country for many decades. This long track record has allowed political scientists to study these systems for years, and this book will include many of their findings. The existence of a great deal of historical evidence and a scholarly literature on this subject means that we can predict with some confidence many of the political advantages and disadvantages produced by each voting system.

Naturally, disagreements sometimes do arise over the alleged advantages or disadvantages of specific systems, even among political scientists, and these disputes will be covered as well. For example, there is some disagreement over whether proportional representation governments tend to be more unstable than those produced by plurality voting, and whether plurality systems really encourage close representative-constituent relationships. In such instances, I will describe the arguments and evidence offered by both the critics and the defenders of a particular system—so that you may decide for yourself which view seems most valid. Where appropriate, I will also try to give you an idea of where most experts come down on a particular issue. I will also highlight some of these disagreements in special sections of the text entitled "Spotlights on the Debate." These are designed to give you a better sense of the give and take of the arguments surrounding a particular issue.

Please keep in mind that just because I include a claim or criticism about a particular system does not necessarily mean it is valid. That is for you to decide. I have tried to include all the common claims made about each voting system, even if some of those may be based largely on myth or misinformation. I assume that people make the best decisions when they are exposed to all the arguments surrounding an issue—both the good and the bad arguments. I believe that if you have enough information and analysis available, you will be able to figure out for yourself which claims are dubious and which are sound.

Chapter six is a somewhat special case. Most of the current discussion over competing voting systems concerns legislative elections, and the analysis of these systems forms the heart of the book. But we also hold elections for single offices such as mayor and governor, and the way we do that is the topic of this chapter. In the United States, there is beginning to be debate about the voting systems used in fill these executive positions. In these elections, there are fewer options than in legislative elections. Obviously systems that require multimember districts, such as proportional and semiproportional systems, cannot be used to elect a single official. So we are left with several forms of plurality and majority voting. But even here there are significant enough differences between these options to merit a careful choice among them. However, if you are primarily interested in reforming your city council or state legislature, you can skip over this chapter and go on to the final chapter.

Chapter seven, the last chapter, addresses the fourth and final step in the choice process: selecting the best system. When you have learned about all the alternatives and their political consequences, it is time to choose the best one. To do this, you must decide which system best meets the criteria you developed in the first step of the analytic process. This chapter guides you through a method of organizing your criteria and all of the information you have collected about these systems, so that your final choice is easier. The chapter also contains a discussion of the some of the common pitfalls encountered in trying to choose a system and explains how to avoid them.

Following these chapters is a Selected Bibliography of books and articles on this topic. In an effort to keep this book to a reasonable length, I sometimes have been forced to summarize many of the arguments for and against each system and to leave out some of the finer points of the analysis. Similarly, I have also omitted some of the more esoteric details about the workings of some systems. If you want to go into some of these issues in more depth and detail—as I would encourage you to do if you have the time—then the works in this bibliography are the place to start. Following the bibliography is a section identifying some additional resources: web sites with additional information on voting systems and a list of organizations that are involved in voting system reform.

Additional information on various aspects of voting systems can also be found in a number of appendixes. One contains brief descriptions of little-used voting systems, those that are so uncommon that I felt that they did not merit prolonged analysis in the text but that may be of interest to some readers. Another appendix contains a description of the history of proportional representation elections in the United States. On the more practical side, another appendix contains sample statutory language for alternative systems such as instant runoff voting, choice voting, and cumulative voting.

At first, the large amount of material in this book might seem to be a bit overwhelming. You certainly should not feel that you must plow through it all in one sitting. Instead, feel free to dip into various parts and use them as they seem appropriate in whatever stage of the choice process you are in. In the end, my hope is that all the information and analysis in this book will enable you to think more clearly and critically about voting systems; allow you to engage in more intelligent discussions and debates about these systems; and ultimately, if you choose, help you to change what goes on "behind the ballot box."

Abbreviations

AV	Alternative Vote
FPTP	First Past the Post
IRV	Instant Runoff Voting
List PR	List Proportional Representation
LV	Limited Voting
MMP	Mixed-Member Proportional
PR	Proportional Representation
Semi-PR	Semiproportional Representation
SMDP	Single-Member District Plurality
SNTV	Single Nontransferable Vote
STV	Single Transferable Vote
TRS	Two-Round System

CHAPTER 1

What Are Voting Systems and Why Are They Important?

Before looking at voting systems in more detail, two preliminary questions need to be answered: What are voting systems, and why are they important? The first question is the easiest to answer. A voting system is the set of procedures that determine how people are elected to office. These procedures include how the ballot is structured, how people cast their votes, how those votes are counted, and how the winners are decided. Or as political scientists often put it: Voting systems are the means by which votes are translated into seats in the legislature.[1]

As an illustration, let's do a quick overview of two of the most common voting systems in Western democracies. The most prevalent system for legislative elections in the United States is the winner-take-all system—or in more formal parlance, the *single-member district plurality system*. That rather technical phrase captures the two basic attributes of this system. First, votes are cast in single-member districts—districts in which only one member of the legislature is elected. All the candidates are on the ballot and we cast a vote for only one of them. Second, the winner is determined by who receives the most votes—the plurality of the vote. This voting system has become so familiar to people in the United States that we hardly ever stop to think about it. You may even assume that this is just how democratic elections work.

But of course there are many different kinds of democratic voting systems. The main rival to the single-member plurality system is called *proportional representation*—the system used by most European democracies. As you will see later, there are many different forms of proportional representation, or "PR." They use different ballots and different ways of counting votes. But all PR systems do have two things in common—two ways they differ from our plurality voting system. First, proportional representation voting systems elect people in multimember districts. Instead of one member of the legislature being elected in a small district, PR uses much larger districts where five, ten, or more members are elected. So instead of only one winner, there are multiple winners of office in each district. The second difference is that these multiple seats are distributed according to the proportion of the vote won by particular parties or political groups. For example, if we had a ten-member PR district in which the Democratic candidates won 50% of the vote, they would receive five of those ten seats. With 30% of the vote, the Republicans would win three seats, and if a third party like the Reform party or the Libertarian party won 20% of the vote, it would get the remaining two seats. You can see even in this very brief description that the way votes are translated into seats in PR systems is very different from that in our plurality system.

WHY ARE VOTING SYSTEMS IMPORTANT?

The most obvious reason that voting systems are important is that they determine who is elected, and ultimately who runs our local, state, and federal governments. Who is elected directly affects what kinds of policies are passed and who benefits or suffers from those policies. Since it matters greatly who wins elections, voting systems matter as well, because different methods of voting can produce different winners. For example, it can make a difference whether a voting system requires a successful candidate for governor to get a plurality or a majority of the vote. Assume for instance, that candidate A receives 42% of the vote, candidate B 40%, and candidate C 18%. Under plurality rules, A is elected governor because the winner is the person with the most votes. But if the voting rules require a majority to win, then these results could force a runoff between the top two candidates in order to produce a winner with over 50% of the vote. In the preceding example, if most of C's supporters voted for candidate B in the runoff election, then B would be the winner, not A.

Voting procedures can also affect who wins in legislative elections. As you will see later, these systems help to determine which parties get representation in these bodies and which ones control policy-making. For instance, single-member district plurality systems usually produce legislatures controlled by a one-party majority. In contrast, proportional representation systems often result in a coalition of parties that forms the ruling majority, and this can change considerably the politics in these institutions.

But there are also other reasons why voting methods are important. In fact one of the main reasons there has been growing interest in voting system reform in the United States is the increasing perception that a link exists between voting rules and many of the problems that afflict American elections.

AMERICAN ELECTIONS IN TROUBLE

Elections are one of the basic foundations of a free and democratic society. They are the primary way that the public exerts control over government, influences public policy decisions, and holds officials accountable. But there are increasing signs that American elections are ailing. One of the most obvious symptoms is the unwillingness of many Americans even to show up at the polls. Our level of voter turnout is abysmally low. While many other Western democracies routinely enjoy turnout rates of 75%– 90%, we are lucky if half the eligible citizens vote. In the 1998 elections, only 36% of the electorate bothered to participate in choosing who would run Congress. Clearly something is wrong when most Americans don't vote most of the time.

There are other signs that elections are in trouble. Many Americans feel disillusioned about the choices they are offered at the polls. They have trouble finding candidates they really believe in and feel that they are often forced to vote for the lesser of two evils. Many are also fed up with races that emphasize negative campaigning and mudslinging, rather than a discussion of the issues. In a 1995 *Los Angeles Times* poll, nearly one-half of the respondents answered that they thought the two-party system in this country was basically unsound. Other recent polls have found that 75% of Americans feel that they are not well represented by the officials they elect, less than half (44%) think that elections are fair to voters, and only 26% believe that the federal government has the consent of the governed.

There is really nothing new about this kind of voter disillusionment, and over the years a number of different proposals have been made to try to reinvigorate American elections, including term limits, campaign finance reform, and voting by mail. But recently increasing attention has been paid to a different kind of election reform: changing the voting system. This approach is based on the growing realization that some of the causes of voter alienation may be traceable to problems in our voting system. Traditionally we have placed the blame for much of this election malaise on individual politicians or particular parties. But the source of many of our election problems may be much deeper. These may be systemic problems— located in the very system we use to vote for and elect candidates to office. One political commentator, Hendrik Hertzberg of *The New Yorker* magazine, has made this very point:

A lot of the political pathologies we worry about in this country—things like low voter turnout, popular alienation from politics, hatred of politicians and politics per se, the undue influence of special interests, the prevalence of negative campaigning and so on—are not caused by the usual suspects. They are not caused by the low moral character of our politicians. They are not caused by the selfishness of the electorate. They are not caused by the peculiarities of the American national character and the American political culture. They are not caused by television. They are not caused by money (although money certainly makes them worse). Instead, they are artifacts of a particular political technology. They are caused by our single-member district, geographically-based, plurality winner-take-all system of representation.[2]

But how could something as seemingly innocuous as voting system procedures be to blame for many of the common complaints that Americans have about politics and elections? To understand how this could be the case, let's look at two examples that are often used to illustrate the strong connection between voting rules and our election problems. The first example has to do with public dissatisfaction with our two-party system, and the second concerns the continuing frustrations surrounding the representation of racial and ethnic minorities.

VOTING SYSTEMS AND THE TWO-PARTY SYSTEM

Many of the complaints that Americans have about our elections center on our two-party system. It is no secret that many voters have become disillusioned with the system and the limited choices it offers. As noted earlier, polls reveal that almost half of American voters believe that the two-party system is basically unsound. It is also clear that most Americans do not feel a strong allegiance to either party. Only about one-third of the public see themselves as died-in-the-wool Republicans or Democrats, and an increasing number now define themselves as independents. In a 1995 CNN/USA Today poll, 43% of the respondents thought it "not too important" or "not at all important" for the president to be from one of the two major parties. In addition, more voters want to have a greater range of choices at the polls. They have grown more interested in independent candidates like Ross Perot and third parties like the Reform and Libertarian parties. Recent polls have shown that anywhere from one-half to two-thirds of Americans would like to see another party emerge to regularly challenge the Democrats and Republicans. But despite all of this, when most Americans go to the polls, the only choices they are presented with are from the two major parties.

Undoubtedly, part of the frustration that Americans feel with the two-party system is a result of the wide range of choices that we have come to expect in most other areas of life. When we walk into a supermarket, for example, we can find a wide variety of breakfast cereals designed to satisfy our various tastes. When we wander into a shoe store we find dozens of styles of shoes. But when we walk into a voting booth, we are instantly restricted to two choices—Republican or Democrat. So while Americans come in a wide variety of political stripes—from ultraconservative to ultraliberal—on election day many are faced with the uncomfortable task of trying to fit themselves into one of only two political categories.

So why don't Americans have more choices among parties and candidates? Voting system reformers have argued that much of the reason for the persistence of our two-party system can be found in the rules of our voting system. In fact, political scientists have long known that voting systems have a strong influence on the number of viable parties in a country.

In particular, they have found that our plurality voting system tends to reinforce a two-party system and to discourage a multiparty system. Plurality rules protect the two major parties from competition and discourage the efforts of third parties—or what political scientists refer to as "minor parties." It is easy to see why this is the case. Plurality rules require a party to win a majority or plurality of the vote in a district in order to win any representation. Since most third parties are relatively small, this requirement creates a barrier that few can overcome. Even if a third party wins a substantial amount of the vote in a single-member district—say 20%–30%—it still will not be able to elect anyone to office.

This plurality rule also discourages voters from supporting third-party candidates. People quickly learn that casting their ballots for these candidates is a waste of their vote. Worse yet, their vote may actually help to elect the candidate they dislike the most. Imagine, for example, a race between a Republican, a Democrat, and a Christian Coalition candidate. If a conservative votes for the Christian Coalition candidate, this takes a vote from the Republican candidate and helps the Democrat win office. Faced with this kind of dilemma, most supporters of third parties reluctantly cast their votes for the lesser of two evils in the major parties, and the result is that our legislatures are occupied exclusively by Democrats and Republicans. But as the political commentator Michael Lind has pointed out: "Because of our peculiar election law, the American government is divided between two parties. The American people are not."[3]

Contrast this with a proportional representation (PR) voting system, whose rules are much friendlier to minor party candidates. There is no plurality hurdle to overcome. As seen earlier, proportional representation voting allows minor party candidates with as little as 10% or 20% of the vote to get elected. For this reason, countries that use PR usually do not have two-party monopolies, but multiparty systems. If you went to the polls in Sweden, you would have seven parties in the legislature to choose from; in Germany, you would have five. It is clear then that the type of voting system a country uses has a strong effect on the range of party and candidate choices that voters have. And this is one reason why a number of political commentators have argued for a more serious consideration of alternative voting methods. One political scientist, Seymour Martin Lipset, has concluded that "the one way to assure more diversity on the ballot is to change the electoral system and adopt proportional representation."[4]

VOTING SYSTEMS AND REPRESENTATION OF RACIAL MINORITIES

Another example of the far-reaching political effects of voting rules can be seen in the area of minority voting rights. The question of how to ensure fair representation for racial and ethnic minorities is one of the most vexing problems surrounding American elections. Traditionally, African Americans, Latinos, and Asians have been underrepresented in our legislatures in comparison to their percentage of the population. For example, even though Latinos and blacks make up nearly a quarter of our population, they occupied none of the seats in the U.S. Senate in 1999. The main reason for this is that racial minorities—like third parties—have difficulty overcoming the plurality barrier in our voting system. Since they are usually numerical minorities in mostly white districts, they have had great trouble electing their own candidates. In many areas, the white majority continues to vote as a bloc against minority candidates, effectively preventing their election.

In an effort to remedy this problem, the federal government in the 1980s began encouraging the creation of so-called majority-minority districts. These districts, in which minorities make up a majority of the voters, did increase the number of minorities being elected to office. In North Carolina, for instance, even though African Americans are 23% of the population, they had never been able to elect an African American to fill any of the state's twelve congressional districts during the preceding ninety years. In the 1980s and 1990s, after the creation of several majority-minority districts, they were finally able to elect two representatives to Congress. However, the use of majority-minority districts has created a great deal of political controversy. Some whites have resented the creation of these special districts and have claimed reverse discrimination. They have mounted numerous suits to challenge these districts, and the Supreme Court handed down several decisions in the 1990s that found some districts unconstitutional. The Court maintained that this approach amounted to a form of racial segregation, and that it was wrong to use race as a major consideration in the districting process. Minorities have been very upset with these decisions and have complained that the elimination of majority-minority districts will lead to the "bleaching" of legislatures, as minority voters once again become submerged in predominantly white districts.

In the midst of this ongoing controversy, several prominent voting rights scholars and activists have begun to explore the role that voting system reform could have in solving this problem. Lani Guinier, a voting rights lawyer and professor at the Harvard Law School, has argued that if the plurality barrier in our current voting system is much of the cause of the underrepresentation of minorities, then it is only logical to consider other voting systems that could more fairly represent these voters.[5] She has proposed the use of proportional and semiproportional voting systems that would allow minorities to win some representation even if they were submerged in predominantly white districts. She cites a districting plan for North Carolina developed by the Center for Voting and Democracy that would divide the state into four three-seat districts that used proportional representation elections. In three of those districts, blacks would make up over 25% of the voters, a proportion that would allow them to elect one of the three representatives from that district. As Guinier explains, the appeal of this approach is that it allows both whites and minorities fair representation without resorting to the creation of special districts.

VOTING SYSTEMS HAVE WIDE-RANGING POLITICAL EFFECTS

The point of these examples about minority representation and our party system is not that multimember district voting systems are necessarily better than single-member district systems. As you will see later, there are plenty of people who would argue for the superiority of our current method of voting. Rather, the point of these examples is to show that voting systems can have consequences for the kind of party system we have and for the groups who get representation in our legislative bodies. And that is not all. Experts have suggested that voting procedures can have a significant impact on a wide variety of important political issues, including the level of voter turnout, the style of political campaigns, the relationship between constituents and their representatives, the ability of women to get elected to office, and the stability of government.

So although at first glance the study of voting procedures might seem to be a pretty dull and innocuous topic, it quickly becomes clear that these rules can have some very significant and wide-ranging political implications, as in a crime novel in which a detective takes on what appears to be a simple burglary only to see it quickly develop into a more elaborate case of blackmail and murder. Once you begin to investigate voting rules and to follow the trail of political effects emanating from them, you soon start to uncover some provocative links between voting procedures and a number of serious issues surrounding the American political system.

WORLDWIDE INTEREST IN VOTING SYSTEM REFORM

Although interest in voting system reform is relatively new in the United States, it has been a common political issue in many other democracies. One reason has been the recent rise in the number of new democracies—especially in Eastern Europe, the former Soviet Union, and Africa. These countries have had to choose the kind of voting processes they will use and this has led to heated debates. Interestingly, the vast majority of these countries ended up rejecting American-style plurality voting in favor of various forms of proportional or semiproportional systems.

In addition, in the last few years a number of established democracies have debated voting system change and adopted new systems. During the 1990s New Zealand abandoned single-member plurality elections for mixed-member proportional representation; Italy moved from a pure PR system to a mixed PR/plurality system; and Japan changed from its unique single nontransferable vote system to a mixed system. Even Great Britain, the original home of our single-member district system, has seen an intense political discussion of voting system options. In 1998, a commission appointed by Prime Minister Tony Blair completed a study of voting systems and recommended that a national referendum be held to choose between their traditional plurality voting system and a new system that included aspects of proportional representation. In fact, PR systems have already been introduced in some elections there. In 1999, when Scotland and Wales had elections for their newly created parliaments, they both chose to use forms of proportional representation instead of the traditional single-member plurality system. And in the most recent round of elections for representatives to the European Community, Great Britain switched to a PR voting system there as well.

VOTING SYSTEMS ARE IN CONSTANT EVOLUTION

Given these changes, it is clear that voting systems are not static elements of political systems. Throughout the history of democracy, voting systems have been in a state of constant evolution. New systems have been developed and old systems abandoned. Voting systems have changed in the United States as well. Our single-member district system is so pervasive today that we tend to assume that it has always been this way—but that is an illusion. The original framers of the Constitution did not specify how members of Congress would be elected and left the choice of voting systems to the states. Most of the original thirteen states used multimember districts to elect the first Congress. In fact, some states used multimember districts for their congressional elections as late as the early 1960s.

Single-member district voting systems have not always been the rule in state and local elections either. As recently as forty years ago, most members of state legislatures were elected in multimember districts. In municipal elections, over two dozen cities, including New York, Cleveland, and Cincinnati, used proportional representation voting systems for many years during the twentieth century. And even today, over half of American cities use at-large voting systems to fill at least some of their city council seats. In other words, even in the United States, voting systems have been evolving and changing over time. So there is no reason to think these procedures are written in stone. On the contrary, we have a moral and political obligation to take a critical look at our voting systems and to decide whether they can be improved.

NOTES

1. A point about terminology. Some people refer to voting systems as *electoral systems*—a term often found in the political science literature. But this term can

easily be confused with the term *election system*, which refers to **all** the procedures involved in elections, including ballot access rules and campaign finance laws. I believe the term *voting system* is the most clear and useful term for describing the specific procedures involved in voting for and electing candidates.

2. Hendrik Hertzberg, "Taxation Without Representation," The Irwin Mann Memorial Lecture on Proportional Representation, New York University, April 15, 1997.

3. Michael Lind, "A Radical Plan to Change American Government," *Atlantic Monthly* 270, no. 2 (August 1992): 77.

4. Seymour Martin Lipset, "Why Americans Refuse to Vote," *Insight* (February 7, 1994): 26.

5. See Lani Guinier, *The Tyranny of the Majority: Fundamental Fairness in Representative Democracy* (New York: Free Press, 1994) and *Lift Every Voice: Turning a Civil Rights Setback into a New Vision of Social Justice* (New York: Simon & Schuster, 1998), chapter nine.

CHAPTER 2

Criteria for Evaluating Voting Systems

Before beginning to examine the various voting system options, it is useful to spend some time thinking about how to evaluate them. How will you know a good voting system when you see one? And how will you judge whether one system is better or worse than another? Making these judgments is not as simple a task as it may sound. It is all too easy to take an off-the-cuff approach to this kind of political evaluation. Typically we already have one or two cursory ideas about what makes for a good voting system and we use those limited criteria to form quick judgments about the various voting options. For example, if you support a minor party, you may quickly conclude that proportional representation is the best voting system because it makes it easier for minor parties to win representation. But this kind of casual approach is a mistake. It practically guarantees that you will overlook some important considerations, and such oversights greatly increase the chances of making a bad decision.

It is very easy to miss important considerations when evaluating voting systems. As you saw in chapter one, these systems have a wide range of political implications, many of which are not readily apparent. It probably wouldn't occur to most people, for example, to judge these systems by how they affect the conduct of election campaigns, or by how they contribute to the management of political conflict, or by how prone they are to political manipulation. And yet all of these factors could play a role in your choice of systems.

Clearly what is needed is a systematic and comprehensive approach to evaluating voting systems: one that uses a broad and inclusive set of political criteria. A good set of criteria can guide your analysis and serve as a political yardstick against which you measure each of these systems. These criteria can also help you to think more clearly about exactly what it is you want to achieve—and avoid—through the choice of a voting system.

Fortunately, you do not have to develop this set of criteria from scratch. Political scientists, politicians, and political activists have spent a great deal of time thinking about what makes for a good voting system. Somewhat surprisingly, some consensus exists on the criteria for a good voting system. Virtually everyone agrees, for instance, that a good system should promote majority rule, fair representation, high voter turnout, and stable government. Most of the political disagreement about voting methods usually involves which criteria are most important or how well particular systems fulfill those criteria. For example, advocates of single-member district plurality elections tend to put local geographical representation near the top of their political list, while proponents of party list proportional representation are more likely to prioritize fair representation for political parties.

This chapter is designed to familiarize you with the various criteria that can be used to evaluate voting systems, and also to help you begin to arrive at your own priorities. The first part consists of a description of these criteria, presented in no particular order. These descriptions include an explanation of the importance of each criterion and the ways voting systems have an impact on them. You will notice that some of these criteria are interrelated and a few actually contradict each other. Keep in mind that although you should certainly consider seriously the criteria suggested by voting systems experts, you shouldn't assume that this list is complete or exhaustive. If there are some other considerations that you believe are important in evaluating these systems, add them to your list. At the end of the chapter, there are exercises that will help you or your group to prioritize these criteria. How you rank these criteria will have a large influence on what you decide is the best voting system, so it is useful to spend some time thinking about which criteria are the most important and why.

THE CRITERIA

Majority Rule

One characteristic of a good voting system is that it ensures majority rule. This decision-making principle is one of the cornerstones of democratic government. It justifies the use of governmental power, and it facilitates the peaceful transition of power from one political group to another. When officials or the government represent only a minority of citizens this greatly undermines their political legitimacy and increases the likelihood of public opposition to their policies.

Somewhat surprisingly, not all voting systems do a good job of assuring majority rule. Some systems, for instance, allow a candidate for office to win with less than majority support. Also, these same systems may allow a party to win a majority of the seats in the legislature while winning less than 50% of the vote. Other systems are explicitly designed to ensure that winning candidates and legislative majorities have the support of the majority of the electorate.

Minority Representation

Good voting systems also promote minority representation. This criterion is not incompatible with majority rule. A truly representative legislature can and must reflect the views of both the majority and significant minorities. Minority representation has several political benefits. It enhances the political legitimacy of legislatures; it promotes the protection of minority rights; and it fosters a greater sense of civic inclusion among political minorities. The presence of minority political views in our legislatures also creates a more healthy and vibrant political dialogue in these institutions and helps to introduce new political ideas into the policy-making process. No one political group has a monopoly on the truth, and a variety of political voices in our political institutions contributes to a more thorough search for the best policy ideas.

In the United States, the issue of minority representation usually arises in two forms. The first concerns the representation of minor political parties. Americans are displaying increasing interest in minor-party candidates. However, as you saw in chapter one, some methods of voting make it hard for minor parties to win any representation in legislatures, and some make it much easier.

The other concern over minority representation involves racial and ethnic minorities. We live in an increasingly racially diverse society. Many would argue that it is desirable for our legislatures to represent this racial and ethnic diversity accurately. However, voting systems differ greatly on how well they promote this political goal. Some voting methods make it difficult for minorities to be elected; others are specifically designed to facilitate the fair representation of such groups.

Geographical Representation

Many voters want someone to represent their geographical area: their neighborhood, city, or county. In part this is desirable because political concerns are sometimes specific to particular geographical regions. Rural areas and urban areas, for instance, may have very different policy problems. Some neighborhoods in a city may have more problems with crime than others. Environmental pollution may be a large concern in some regions and a small one in others. Having a representative accountable to a specific area ensures that local concerns have a voice in our governing bodies. Voting systems can have a strong effect on the extent of geographical representation. A few of them do away with local districts entirely.

Other voting systems put more emphasis on geographical representation and employ small districts in order to maximize this principle.

High Voter Turnout

Voter turnout is an important measure of the health of a democracy. Low voter turnout often indicates a high level of voter alienation from the electoral process. Also, when relatively few people vote in elections, this lack of participation casts doubt on the political legitimacy of elected officials. It becomes difficult for politicians to claim a mandate to govern when less than half of the electorate turns out to vote. Also, studies have shown that countries with higher voter turnout tend to have less political turmoil and experience fewer protests and riots.[1]

Many factors affect voter turnout, including registration procedures and whether elections take place during the week or on weekends. But political scientists have found that the voting system itself can also have a significant effect on turnout rates. As you will see, some systems give more incentives to voters than others, and this affects participation levels.

Sufficient Range of Voter Choice

American voters often complain that they lack real choices at the polls. Some find little difference between the candidates they usually see, and many would like to have more independent and third-party candidates on the ballot. When voters lack a sufficient range of choice, they often feel alienated from the election process, and unrepresented by elected officials.

The type of voting system has a very large effect on both the number of candidates and the variety of political parties present on the ballot. An obvious example of this effect is the presence or absence of minor parties on the ballot. Some voting systems—plurality-majority systems in particular—tend to discourage minor parties from running candidates because they stand so little chance of winning under those rules. In contrast, proportional representation systems make it easier for minor party candidates to get elected, and so more of them appear on the ballot.

Voting systems can also affect the range of choices among candidates of the same party. Some systems end up nominating only one candidate per party in the general election. Other systems that use multimember districts encourage each party to nominate several candidates for those seats. This allows a Republican voter, for instance, to choose between voting for a far Right Republican candidate and a moderate Republican candidate.

Of course while everyone wants a reasonable range of choice at the polls, there is disagreement over what "reasonable" is. One choice is obviously not enough and twenty choices may be too many for some people. But what is reasonable? Some people argue that having at least three or four parties to choose from is essential in democratic elections, and others maintain that a choice between two parties is sufficient in most cases. One point everyone can agree on: Which voting system you opt for will have a large impact on the range of candidate and party choices you have at the polls.

Resistance to Fraud and Political Manipulation

A good voting system should discourage fraud and political manipulation. Voters must have confidence that the results of the voting process are legal and fair. Most current voting systems have safeguards that make outright fraud unlikely, but political manipulation is another story. In some voting systems, it is easier for politicians to manipulate the rules and the way they are applied in order to give certain candidates or parties an unfair advantage. The most common example of this in the United States is the use of gerrymandering: the drawing of voting district lines to favor certain incumbents or parties. Voting systems differ dramatically in how much they allow or discourage gerrymandering and other kinds of political manipulation.

Fair and Accurate Party Representation

Democratically elected legislatures should reflect accurately the distribution of political views found among the public. We give these bodies the right to make laws for us in large part because they claim to mirror the views of the electorate. John Adams, one of our founding fathers, expressed this principle when he noted that legislatures in the United States "should be an exact portrait, in miniature, of the people at large, as it should think, feel, reason, and act like them."[2] In practical terms, this means that legislatures should give fair and accurate representation to political parties. The percentage of a party's seats in the legislature should reflect the strength of its support among voters. Legislatures that violate this principle cannot be relied on to produce public policies that reflect the will of the public.

Voting systems vary in how accurately they translate voter support for parties into seats in the legislature. Some systems routinely give the largest party more seats than it deserves and smaller parties fewer seats than they deserve. In some cases, a party with a significant part of the vote may receive no seats at all. Large deviations between a party's share of seats and its share of the vote raise questions about the fairness of the voting system and about how well the legislature represents the will of the people. A good voting system will do a reasonably good job of giving each party its fair share of seats.

Stable and Effective Government

Governments need enough stability and continuity to be able to act quickly and efficiently to address the pressing problems of society. But while most people agree on the need for stable and effective government, there is considerable disagreement on what exactly it is and what role various voting systems play in promoting this basic political value. For many people, an effective government is one that is able to prevent political gridlock and to act efficiently to pass policies in a timely manner. Several political factors have an effect on this—such as the design of checks and balances in these institutions—but voting systems do play a role in promoting or undermining this political goal. They can help to determine whether there is an effective working majority in the legislature and whether this majority is stable between elections. For example, some voting systems are more likely to produce one-party majorities in legislatures, while others tend to produce majorities made of coalitions of several parties. It is often argued that single-party majorities are more stable and more capable of passing their policy agenda.

Voting systems can also affect the degree of political continuity that exists from one election to the next, which is another way of looking at political stability. When one single-party majority is replaced with a completely different one, this can produce abrupt and radical changes in policies. A Republican Congress, for example, may have very different policy priorities than a Democratic one. However, elections using voting systems that encourage multiparty coalition governments often produce only a modification of the parties in the ruling coalition, not a complete replacement of the parties in power. Some argue that this outcome increases the continuity and stability of public policy over time.

Finally, the effectiveness and stability of government can also depend on its degree of support among the public. People must readily accept and obey the laws that the government passes. But this requires that the public see the government as legitimate and representative—a perception that can be directly affected by the operation of the voting system. Malfunctioning voting systems can easily undermine the political legitimacy of elected officials. Consider a situation in which a voting system allows a party that came in second at the polls to win a majority of the seats in the legislature. This threatens public confidence and support of that government and weakens its ability to rule effectively.

Maximum Effective Votes and Minimum Wasted Votes

Effective votes are those that actually contribute to the election of a candidate. Wasted votes are votes that do not elect someone. If your candidate loses, you have cast a wasted vote. Generally, a good voting system maximizes effective votes and minimizes wasted votes. Wasted votes are considered undesirable for several reasons. First, casting wasted votes can be very discouraging for voters and contributes to voter apathy. If your candidates always lose, why bother to vote? But more importantly, wasted votes mean that people come away from the voting booth with no representation. The more effective votes that are cast, the larger the number of people actually represented in the legislature. In this way, the number of effective votes is directly related to the quality and quantity of representation in a political system. If voters are to have not only the right to vote, but also the right to representation, then they must be able to cast an effective vote.

In the United States, we often assume that in all elections some voters must win and some must lose, and that large numbers of wasted votes are inevitable. But although this is usually true for single-office elections like that for governor, it is not necessarily true for legislative elections. In these elections, the amount of wasted votes depends very much on the voting system. Some systems for legislative elections routinely waste large numbers of votes, sometimes even a majority of them. In contrast, some other systems minimize wasted votes and ensure that upward of 80%–90% of voters cast effective votes.

Close Links between Constituents and Representatives

An important part of the job of legislators is to act on behalf of their constituents. A good voting system encourages close links between individual representatives and their local constituents. Officials should be in contact with their constituents and directly accountable to them. Also, constituents should feel free to contact their representatives about problems they are having with the government or its agencies.

All voting systems claim to foster these links, but they do so in very different ways. Some do it by utilizing small geographical districts where voters and officials may more easily interact. Other voting systems use larger multimember districts that are designed to ensure that most voters have an elected representative who is sympathetic to their particular political concerns and whom they would feel comfortable approaching.

Sincere Voting

Voters should be able to vote for their first choice candidate or party. This is called *sincere voting* and its desirability is obvious. For most people the whole point of voting is to support the candidate or party they like the most. But in practice, some voting systems create situations that actually penalize people for casting a sincere vote. For example, some voting rules tend to discourage potential supporters from voting for minor party candidates. If they do, they are likely to waste their vote or to inadvertently help elect the major party candidate they like the least. In response, voters often abandon their first preference and vote for the "lesser of two evils" among the major party candidates. Political scientists call this *strategic voting*, having to vote for a candidate other than your first choice in order to promote your political interests most effectively. As you will see, many systems are susceptible to strategic voting, but in general it is better to have a voting system that minimizes strategic voting and maximizes the opportunity for sincere voting.

Reinforcement of Two-Party System

Political parties play a crucial role in democracies. They are the main organizations that offer candidates and formulate policy alternatives. Voting systems can have large effects on party systems. Undoubtedly their most important and well-documented impact is on the size of the party system— whether it is a two-party system or a multiparty system. Experts have long known that winner-take-all systems, such as plurality voting, encourage a two-party system, while proportional representation voting usually promotes a multiparty system. Which voting system you think is best is going to be strongly affected by which kind of party system you prefer.

Some people prefer a two-party system. They argue that these systems offer voters clear and simple choices, promote more accountable government, and produce more effective legislative bodies. Two-party advocates also believe that this tradition is responsible for much of the long-term stability of the American political system. Any method of voting that helps to maintain this party system is highly valued by them.

Promotion of a Multiparty System

Others believe that multiparty systems—those consisting of a number of major and minor parties—are superior to two-party systems. They argue that multiparty democracies offer voters more choices at the polls, encourage more wide-ranging political debate, and produce legislatures that are much more representative of the variety of political views present in the electorate. So from this point of view, the best voting systems are those that encourage a multiparty system.

High-Quality Political Campaigns

Voters frequently complain about the poor quality of campaigns—campaigns that tend to emphasize mudslinging over a discussion of the issues. Campaigns that focus on personal attacks rather than policy substance tend to drive voters away from the polls and to increase voters' cynicism about elections and politics in general. Moreover, such campaigns make it much more difficult for voters to make an informed and intelligent choice among the candidates.

Voting systems can have an effect on the ways politicians campaign for office. Different voting rules create different requirements for victory, and these influence campaign strategies. For example, systems that require people to cast a vote for a party rather than a person seem to encourage less focus on individuals and more emphasis on issues and party platforms in campaigns. Also, voting schemes that use multiple votes or the ranking of candidates are often said to discourage mudslinging campaigns. Candidates may tend to be more civil to each other if they believe they might receive one of the votes of supporters of another candidate. If you are concerned about the current style of political campaigns in the United States, you will want to pay close attention to the influence of voting systems on campaign behavior.

Resistance to Extremism

A good voting system should discourage political extremism or extremist parties. However, we must be careful to make a distinction between fringe groups and extremist groups. Fringe groups may have radical political ideas—such as abolishing the income tax—but they usually pursue their goals in a peaceful and democratic manner. In contrast, extremist groups are those that advocate the violation of democratic rights, promote violence and disorder, or have racist ideologies. Neofascist or neo-Nazi parties are typical extremist groups.

There is some disagreement on how voting systems can best deal with the threat of extremism. Some voting systems erect high barriers to them— barriers that make it difficult for any minor party, not only extremist parties, to win representation. Other voting systems set lower barriers to representation, which are designed to allow some minor party representation but seek to exclude very small extremist parties. These systems would grant representation to extremist parties that have significant public support. Which approach is more desirable depends in part on how serious a threat you believe extremist groups are in your political system.

Competitive Elections

Many voters are concerned about the lack of competitive elections in the United States. In one typical example, 99% of the incumbents in the U.S. House who ran for reelection in 1998 won their contests. Without competitive elections, it is difficult for voters to hold politicians accountable.

Lack of competitiveness can have several causes. First, it may result from one or more parties' simply refusing to offer candidates. In 1998, for instance, in more than 40% of the races for state legislative seats, the smaller of the two major parties in the district did not even offer a candidate to challenge the other major party nominee: not much of a contest in those elections. Second, races may be uncompetitive even when several parties offer candidates, if one party has such a large majority of supporters in the district that their candidate is a shoo-in.

The competitiveness of elections can be directly affected by the choice of voting system. It can make a large difference, for example, whether a voting system uses single or multimember districts. In a single-member district, one party may be so dominant that other parties have little chance of winning the seat. This discourages those other parties from fielding candidates and devoting resources to campaigns in that district. Voting systems that use multimember districts can have a very different effect. It is easier for several parties to win representation in those districts, so many parties are likely to vie for office. Races become more competitive both in the sense that more parties offer candidates and in the sense that it is more possible for several parties actually to win seats.

Ease of Use and Administration

A good voting system also should allow citizens to cast their votes easily and understand the outcomes of elections. Overly complex voting systems may discourage some people from going to the polls. In addition, people who don't understand clearly how a voting system works may be unable to use it effectively to promote their political interests. In some multiple-vote systems, for instance, casting a vote for more than one candidate may hurt your chances of electing your favorite one.

Although experts agree that voting methods should be as user-friendly as possible, they disagree about how well various systems meet this criterion. For instance, some are concerned that American voters could be confused by the new ballot structures associated with some alternative voting systems. But others note that voters using these ballots in other countries have experienced little confusion.

A related concern involves the ease and expense of administering various voting systems. Some systems, for example, involve two rounds of voting or a process of transferring votes, and this adds to their administrative complexity. Also, switching to some alternative systems may require a change in voting machines, which is an added expense.

Fair Gender Representation

Despite gains over the last several decades, women continue to be severely underrepresented in many legislatures in this country. In the United States Congress, for example, women still hold only about 11% of the seats. For some, this means that a distinctive voice and set of political concerns is underrepresented in these bodies—a deficiency that ultimately undermines the legitimacy of these institutions.

At first glance, it might seem that voting systems would have little to do with this situation. But numerous cross-national studies have shown a strong correlation between voting systems and the percentage of women in legislatures.[3] In particular, it seems that in voting systems where slates of party candidates are nominated to fill seats in multimember districts, women tend to be nominated more often and go on to win office more often. People concerned with fair gender representation should therefore take a careful look at how different voting systems affect the achievement of this political goal.

Effective Management of Conflict

Elections are one of the main ways that we manage political conflict in our society. A good voting system should not intensify the discord between different political, religious, economic, and racial groups. Instead, it should promote dialogue, negotiation, and compromise among these groups—essential elements in any peaceful and democratic society.

All voting systems claim to aid in this process, but they attempt to do so in very different ways. Some tend to produce large and inclusive political parties, in which a considerable amount of negotiation between groups takes place before elections in an attempt to create an effective electoral coalition. Other methods of voting concentrate on encouraging dialogue and compromise after elections by ensuring that all significant political groups are adequately represented in legislatures and thus have a seat at the political table when policy is being discussed and decided.

THE NEED TO PRIORITIZE YOUR CRITERIA

Ideally you could choose the best voting system by simply finding the one that maximizes all of these criteria. But of course nothing in life is that simple. No voting system is good at everything. Each fulfills some criteria better than others. For instance, party list proportional representation maximizes the number of effective votes but does less well at geographical representation. Single-member district plurality systems tend to do just the opposite. To make matters even more complicated, sometimes the criteria themselves are in conflict. The goal of having a system that is easy to administer may conflict with a desire to have one that ensures minority representation. And an effort to emphasize geographical representation may conflict with the goal of fair representation for parties.

All of this should not be taken to mean that all voting systems are equally problematic—only that no voting system is perfect. Nor does it imply that you can't say that one system is better than another. It simply means that when you say one voting system is better than another you need to specify exactly how it is superior—according to what criteria. And you need to explain why those criteria are the most important.

In other words, one of the key steps in choosing a good voting system is ranking these criteria. You have to decide which of the political goals embodied in these criteria are the most crucial to you. This requires that you spend some time right now thinking about these political criteria. Your own priorities may not be at all obvious at first. There are many competing criteria here, and you were probably unaware of at least some of them before you read this chapter. So some effort to reflect on your priorities in voting system reform will be time well spent. The clearer you are about your political values and political goals, the easier it will be to find the system that best embodies them.

It is helpful to begin by first considering your priorities by yourself—uninfluenced by group pressure. But it is also very useful to discuss priorities with others. Having a discussion with even just one other person is helpful, but a larger group discussion is even better. Group discussions about how to rank these criteria can be an invaluable aid in clarifying group and individual priorities. The following two exercises are designed to facilitate this kind of group discussion. You can also do these exercises by yourself, though you probably won't get as much out of them as you would if you did them with others.

EXERCISE ONE

First, photocopy this chapter and hand it out to the participants ahead of time so that they have the opportunity to read it and think about these criteria. When you gather, have all participants write down on a piece of paper what they believe are the top five criteria that should be used in choosing a voting system. Go around the room and have everyone share his or her list. If you have a blackboard or a pad and easel, write down each person's list so that everyone can see them all. Then initiate a discussion about why people made their particular choices. You could ask each person why he or she believes his or her criteria are most important. Or you could ask them why they left some of the criteria off their list. The point is to encourage people to explain and defend their choices. The more people explore their justifications for their choices, the more useful the discussion will be.

If the discussion goes well, you will learn not only more about other people's priorities, but also more about your own. Consider, for example, the following hypothetical exchange that takes place between two discussion participants, Deborah and Brad:

"Why do you have fair party representation on your list?" Deborah asks.

"I just think it's important for all parties to be treated equally," replies Brad. "They all should get the seats they deserve. It's a basic matter of fairness. If a voting system favors some parties over others, then I begin to question how fair and democratic the process really is."

"OK. But is that the only reason you think this priority is important?"

"Well, I guess I also get upset when I vote for a third party—and a lot of other people do too—and that party doesn't win any seats. I feel like I've been ripped off. People who support major parties get representation, but I don't."

"Seems to me," says Deborah, "that what you are really upset about is wasting your vote. Maybe you should have made 'effective votes' one of your priorities."

"Maybe you are right. Now that I think about it, those two criteria are probably connected. Some parties don't get fair representation because their supporters' votes aren't effective—they are wasted. I guess effective votes are important to me too. Everyone should have the right to representation, and you can't be represented unless you have an effective vote."

"All right," says Deborah, "but let me ask you this. Why didn't you include ease of use on your list? I have it on mine."

"I guess I think that having a more complicated system is not too high a price to pay for one that finally achieves fair representation for everyone."

"So you think ease of use is unimportant?"

"No, I don't think it's unimportant, but I thinks it is less important than some other considerations—like ensuring that everyone is represented."

"But wouldn't it be a real problem if people had trouble using a new kind of ballot? They might spoil their ballot or simply give up and not vote at all. A new voting system wouldn't do us any good if people couldn't use it."

"Maybe, but I think people can learn to use new ballots. And if we had a good voter education program on how to use a new system, this could reduce a lot of the potential confusion. So for me, it's not a major consideration."

"Well, I am not as optimistic as you, so I am going to keep it as one of my priorities."

In the first part of this exchange, Brad learns more about what he really cares about in these criteria. At first he maintains that fair party representation is a high priority, and he grounds this in the basic principle of equal treatment. But as Deborah continues to press him for his reasons, he realizes that underlying that priority is another one: the importance of not wasting votes. He sees that this is actually one of his priorities as well. And this one he justifies by an appeal to another basic political principle: that everyone should have the right to representation.

In the second part of the exchange, about the ease of use criterion, neither Brad nor Deborah changes their mind, but they probably now have a better understanding of each other's position, the trade-offs they are willing to make, and the reasons underlying those choices. As this illustrates, the point of these discussions is not necessarily to generate agreement, but to deepen understanding.

Some groups examining voting system reform have used a variation of this exercise—one that requires an additional step and a bit more time. You begin by having the group first try to come up with some criteria on their own. Go around the room and ask each person to offer several criteria and explain why they are important. After this discussion, have people read the description of criteria from this book. People could then talk about whether they wanted to add any new criteria to their list of priorities and explain why. This variation of this exercise is particularly useful for getting people to think about their initial assumptions about how voting systems should be judged.

EXERCISE TWO

Another way to approach prioritizing these criteria is to think first about what political problems you would like to address. What you make the highest priority in voting system reform may depend greatly on what you think are the most serious political problems in your area. These problems will be functions of both the drawbacks of the particular system you are now using and the political context in which that system operates. For example, you may live in an area with a complex residential mix of different racial and ethnic groups, such as New York City. In your current voting system, some minorities may have little chance to elect representatives and may feel left out of the political system. In this situation, you might want to put a high priority on ensuring fair representation for all of these minorities. An area with a homogeneous racial makeup may be less concerned with this problem. Or you may live in a city in which different neighborhoods have their own particular problems. One neighborhood might be concerned about crime, and another more concerned with the quality of schools, but a city council elected by at-large voting might not be responsive to these different neighborhood needs. This situation might lead you to prioritize a voting system that assures council representation for all geographical areas in a city.

Prioritizing electoral problems is clearly a task that you could do by yourself, but, as with the previous exercise, more can be gained from doing it with a group of people. First, encourage everyone in your group to spend some time thinking individually about what they consider to be the problems, limitations, or drawbacks of their current voting system. Again it is helpful for them to read the criteria described in this chapter. There is a good chance that seeing these criteria will bring to mind problems that they wouldn't have been aware of before. It may not have occurred to them, for instance, that lack of sincere voting was a problem, or that low voter turnout and lack of female officials could be addressed by changing the voting system.

Participants should then write on a piece of paper the main problems that they would like to see addressed. Go around the room and have all participants describe the problems they identified and explain why they believe these problems are pressing ones. If possible, have someone list all the various problems that the group has identified on a blackboard or an easel.

Again the most useful part of this exercise is not simply listing the problems, but discussing them. Is there agreement on the problems with the current system? Why or why not? What is the evidence that these problems exist? Why are some problems considered more important than others?

An added benefit of establishing priorities by looking at voting system problems is that it also gets participants to think about the specific goals of voting system reform. If you become clear about the problems you want to address, then you also become clear about the goals you want to achieve, and you have a way of knowing when you have achieved those goals. For instance, if low voter turnout is a major problem, then you can try voting systems that promise to increase participation and you will be able to use turnout figures to help measure the success or failure of the reform.

In the end, these kinds of exercises should help you and/or your group think more clearly about the political priorities that you consider important to the issue of voting system reform. If you know what you want, you are much more likely to find it. Once you are clear about your priorities you will be ready to start considering the alternative systems—which we turn to in the next part of this book.

NOTES

1. G. Bingham Powell, "Voter Turnout in Comparative Perspective,"*American Political Science Review* 80, no. 1 (March 1986): 37.

2. John Adams, "Thoughts on Government" in *The Works of John Adams*, Vol. IV (Boston: Little, Brown and Co., 1852), p. 205.

3. See, for example, Wilma Rule, "Electoral Systems, Contextual Factors, and Women's Opportunity for Election to Parliament in Twenty-Three Democracies,"*Western Political Quarterly* 33: 477–98; and Pippa Norris, "Legislative Recruitment," in *Comparing Democracies: Elections and Voting in Global Perspective*, ed. Lawrence LeDuc et al. (Thousand Oaks, Calif.: Sage Publications, 1996), pp. 198–201.

CHAPTER 3

Plurality-Majority Voting Systems

The plurality-majority family of voting systems is undoubtedly the one most familiar to Americans. It includes the winner-take-all systems we most often use to elect officials to our local, state, and federal legislatures. We inherited this approach to voting from the British, and plurality-majority systems are used today primarily in Great Britain and its former colonies, including the United States, Canada, Australia, and India.

As shown in Figure 3.1, there are five voting systems in this family: single-member district plurality voting, two forms of single-member district majority voting, at-large voting, and combined at-large and single-member district voting. The single-member district plurality system is by far the most common one, and most of the others are simply variations on this system. It elects legislative officials one at a time in districts, and the winner is the candidate who gets the most votes, the plurality. The two majority systems—the two-round system and the instant runoff system—are nearly identical to plurality voting, sharing virtually all the same advantages and disadvantages. They differ only by requiring that the winning candidate win a majority, rather than a plurality, of the vote. At-large voting is also called *multimember district plurality voting*. As this phrase implies, this system differs from the others by electing several officials at once in larger districts, with the winners being the candidates with the most votes. Finally, there are combined systems that elect some members in single-member districts and some at-large. Like pure at-large systems, combined systems are used almost exclusively today in municipal elections.

HISTORY

Plurality-majority is the oldest family of voting systems. When European states were evolving into parliamentary democracies in the eighteenth and nineteenth centuries, almost all of them first used plurality-majority voting systems. Great Britain was one of the first countries to adopt democratic

Figure 3.1
Plurality-Majority Voting Systems

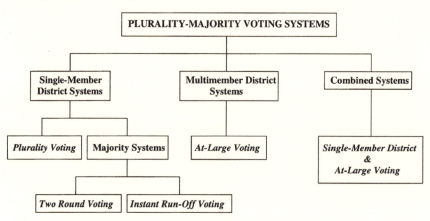

elections, and it embraced plurality voting from the very beginning. But it was not the single-member district version that we associate with Britain today. Until the late nineteenth century, almost all members of the British parliament were elected in two-member county or borough districts. Reforms in 1831 and in 1867 introduced some single-member districts and three-member districts, but two-member districts remained the rule. It was not until 1885 that legislation was passed to require single-member districts in virtually all British constituencies.

In most of continental Europe, democratic parliamentary elections began later than in Britain and developed along somewhat different lines. Most of these countries, including Austria, Germany, the Netherlands, and Italy, began with single-member district voting systems. But instead of using a plurality rule, they required a majority of votes to win office. Most of these systems incorporated the use of some kind of runoff system to ensure a majority winner. Typically, these systems continued into the twentieth century, when proportional representation voting systems replaced almost all of them.[1]

Since it began as a British colony, the United States naturally adopted the plurality form of voting used by its mother country. But as in Great Britain, there was no immediate commitment to the single-member district form of this system. At the founding, only five states chose to divide themselves into districts; the rest opted to elect all of their members of Congress in one statewide at-large district. This at-large approach continued in most of the smaller states until 1842, when Congress first passed a law requiring the use of single-member districts. The main purpose of the law was to prevent one party from routinely winning all seats from a state.

Single-member districts were not always the norm in state elections either. Three-quarters of the states used multimember districts to elect their legislatures during the nineteenth century, and a majority of these seats were still filled by this kind of voting system well into the middle of the twentieth century. So even though we have had a long tradition of plurality voting in this country, the actual form of the systems has been evolving over time, finally coalescing in the twentieth century into the single-member district system that is so common today.

OVERVIEW OF CHAPTER

In order to facilitate comparison, each of the chapters covering a family of systems is organized in the same way. First I acquaint you with the group of systems as a whole. Although some differences exist between the various plurality-majority voting systems, they do share many characteristics—a family resemblance, if you will. I identify the features they all have in common and describe the general political advantages and disadvantages that apply to this family collectively. Where there are disagreements about the political effects of these systems, I note them. From time to time, I also highlight some of these disagreements in "Spotlight on the Debate" sections. After considering these systems as a group, I turn to the individual systems. The workings of each system are described, then the advantages and disadvantages that are specific to that particular voting method are discussed. The emphasis in these sections is primarily on how each system compares to others in this family of voting systems.

COMMON FEATURES OF PLURALITY-MAJORITY SYSTEMS

Single-Member Districts

With the exception of at-large voting, all plurality-majority systems use single-member districts. The fact that members of legislatures are elected one at a time in small districts is much of what separates this family of voting systems from proportional and semiproportional systems, all of which use multimember districts.

Representation of Majorities Only

A second common characteristic is that they are all designed first and foremost to represent the majority (or plurality) of voters. Voters in the minority do not receive representation. In other words, these are winner-take-all systems. The British term for single-member plurality voting is *first-past-the-post*, a reference to horse racing. The analogy is apt: The first horse past the post wins the race and all the others are losers. In these voting systems, 100% of the representation goes to those who vote for the winner. Those who vote for the losers get no representation.

High Thresholds

The concept of a threshold—or what political scientists call a *threshold of exclusion*—is very important in the analysis of voting systems. The level of this threshold is much of what differentiates the families of voting systems from each other and it is responsible for many of the different political effects of these systems. So it is worth spending some time understanding what this threshold is.

Roughly speaking, the threshold represents the hurdle that parties must overcome in order to be sure of electing their candidates. More precisely, the threshold of exclusion is the smallest amount of the vote that a party or candidate must receive in order not to be excluded from winning office. Or to put it more positively, it is the minimum portion of the vote that must be won to ensure that a party wins at least one seat in a district. In plurality-majority systems, that threshold of exclusion is 50% + 1 vote. In a single-member district contest, for instance, a party must win over 50% of the vote in order to be *absolutely sure* that it wins the seat.

That doesn't mean that a party will always need 51% to win. If, for example, party A won 40% of the vote and parties B and C won 30% each, then A's candidate would win the seat. But 40% of the vote does not assure victory. Parties B and C might form an alliance around a single candidate that would then defeat party A's candidate. The only way that party A can be guaranteed the seat is to receive over 50% of the vote. Then it cannot be excluded from office, no matter what the other parties do.

Majority-plurality systems have the highest thresholds of all the families of voting systems. This high threshold is one of the main defining characteristics of this style of voting. In contrast, the thresholds in proportional and semiproportional systems are usually much lower. In some of these systems, parties must receive only 5% or 10% of the vote to be guaranteed winning at least one seat.

Emphasis on Geographical Representation

Again with the exception of at-large voting, all plurality-majority systems put a high priority on geographical representation. When plurality voting was first used in sixteenth-century England, there were no political parties, so elected officials were considered the representatives of their particular borough or county. Representation was geographical, not partisan or ideological. This is still a strong element in plurality-majority systems. One of their main purposes is to produce a legislature that ensures that all geographical areas are represented. Some more recent types of voting systems put a primary emphasis on the representation of parties. But in plurality-majority systems, elected officials are still thought to represent specific regions, not just their political parties.

GENERAL ADVANTAGES

Because these plurality-majority voting systems share so many basic characteristics, they also tend to produce many of the same results—the same political benefits and drawbacks. The general advantages of these systems are described next.

Simplicity

One of the most often cited advantages of these systems is their simplicity. Voters find them very easy to use; they simply cast their votes for their preferred candidates. In the single-member district plurality system, they put an X next to the name of their favorite candidate. This straightforward and familiar process results in very few spoiled or invalid ballots.

It is also easy for people to understand how votes are translated into seats: The most popular candidate in the district is elected. These systems require neither the complicated ballots nor the elaborate vote-counting methods that are seen in some other voting systems.

Geographical Representation

Single-member district systems are clearly the best in terms of ensuring geographical representation—because that is what they are designed to do. And since each representative is beholden to a specific geographical area, issues that are important to a particular neighborhood or region are sure to have a champion. This is not true of all voting systems. For example, Israel uses a party list voting system in which the entire country is one district. There are no local districts that elect representatives.

Close Constituency Ties

Single-member district systems usually use relatively small districts where candidates are able to get to know their constituents. Also, since it is clear which representative is obliged to serve which constituents, people readily know whom to contact about their concerns. Many voters consider these close ties important. (For more on this issue, see Spotlight on the Debate 3.5: Can One Person Represent a District?)

Voting for Individual Candidates

In plurality-majority systems, people vote for individual candidates, not parties. We in the United States tend to take this for granted in a voting system, but it is not true of all of them. In a few party list systems, for example, voters are able to cast votes only for an entire party slate, not for specific candidates. Being able to vote for individuals gives voters more direct control over exactly who is elected and gives them the power to get rid of their particular representative.

Critics like to point out, however, that many other voting systems also allow votes for individual candidates, including many proportional and semiproportional systems. So this is not an advantage unique to plurality-majority systems.

Reinforcement of Two-Party System

Plurality-majority voting encourages a two-party system. This tendency is well documented in the scholarly literature and it is easy to understand.[2] It is one of the effects of the high thresholds that are typical of these systems. A candidate must receive over 50% of the vote in order to be guaranteed victory. And even if a candidate can squeak by with only a plurality of the vote, he or she will usually have to garner at least 40%–45% of the vote to win. The large number of votes needed to win means that typically only candidates from the two major parties stand a realistic chance of being elected. Since it is so hard for minor party candidates to win under these rules, they often hesitate to run and many potential supporters are reluctant to waste their votes on them. One beneficial result of this is a ballot in which voters are given a simple and clear-cut choice between the two major party candidates.

Single-Party Legislative Majorities

One result of a two-party system is the likelihood that one party will win the majority of seats in the legislature. In contrast, proportional representation voting systems usually produce coalition governments, where several parties combine their seats to form a ruling majority. Several political advantages are associated with single-party majorities. For example, single-party majorities can pursue more coherent policy agendas—uncomplicated by political bargaining between coalition partners.

These majorities are also seen as readily accountable. Voters know whom to blame if they don't like what the government does; the party in power cannot pass the buck to other parties in a coalition. And if the ruling party loses the support of the public, it can be easily voted out of power. In contrast, in a coalition system, a party that loses favor with the public and loses seats in the legislature may still be able to become part of a new majority coalition. With single-party majorities, parties either rule or they do not—there is no in-between.

Stable and Efficient Government

Another commonly cited advantage of single-party legislative majorities is more stable and efficient government. In coalition governments, majorities might fall apart if a minor party pulls out. This doesn't usually happen with single-party governments. They tend to have durable majorities. In addition, these coherent single-party majorities are in a position to act efficiently and decisively to pass their policy agenda.

The experience of the United States and Great Britain, where single-member plurality systems have produced long-lasting, single-party governments, is often contrasted with that of Italy. When Italy used a pure proportional representation system, it suffered from fragile coalitions and unstable governments.

Critics, however, do not agree with this sanguine view of single-party majorities. For more on their views on this issue, see Spotlight on the Debate 3.1: How Stable Are Single-Party Majorities?

Spotlight on the Debate 3.1
How Stable Are Single-Party Majorities?

One of the key arguments in favor of plurality-majority voting is its tendency to produce single-party majorities in legislatures. It is argued that these majorities are more stable than multiparty coalitions and so this system creates more political stability and makes it much easier to pass policies efficiently.

Critics argue, however, that single-party majorities are often not monolithic and in fact are themselves coalitions of various political groups. Moreover, given the weak party discipline in the United States, these coalitions sometimes break down, thus making it more difficult to pass legislation. In the early 1990s, for instance, conservative Democrats in Congress would sometimes bolt the party to vote with Republicans to block Democratic legislation. Later, when the Republicans were in the majority, moderates in that party would sometimes ally themselves with the Democrats to impede implementation of parts of the Republican agenda. In this sense, all legislative majorities are fragile coalitions.

In addition, critics observe that plurality-majority voting and single-party majorities can create their own kind of political instability. Under these voting rules, small changes in voter sentiments can produce large shifts in legislative power and sudden changes in policy direction. If voter support for the party in power drops from 52% to 48%, it is thrown out of power and replaced by a completely new single-party majority. The new party may pursue a radically different set of policies even though voter opinion has changed very little—as was the case with the "Republican Revolution" pursued by the GOP when it took over the U.S. House of Representatives in 1994 with 52.4% of the vote.

These abrupt reversals of previous policies can be disruptive. People who have become used to one set of tax policies or environmental regulations may suddenly find themselves having to respond to a very different set of requirements. And when the previous party returns to power, another reversal in policy direction is likely. Proponents of proportional representation (PR) maintain that multiparty coalition governments can avoid this problem. In these systems, an election with moderate changes in voter opinion usually results in the modification of the ruling coalition, not a complete replacement of the parties in power—thus ensuring greater policy continuity. PR advocates note that some scholars have argued that policy continuity is a key to effective management of the economy and that PR and coalition governments are better able to provide this kind of steady policy-making.[3]

Broad-Based Appeals

Another result of plurality-majority voting is the tendency to produce so-called umbrella parties that must make broad-based appeals in order to get elected. Parties that need a majority or plurality to win must try to generate wide-based support. This is thought to have a moderating effect. Parties cannot hope to win seats by narrow appeals to special interests or to specific racial or religious groups.

Resistance to Extremism

The tendency of plurality-majority voting to reward broad-based appeals and to discourage minor parties means that extremist groups have little ability to get a toehold in the political system. The very high thresholds in these systems make it unlikely that such groups would receive the votes necessary to elect any representative to government. One possible exception would be if large numbers of extremists were concentrated within a small geographical area.

Critics acknowledge that the high thresholds of these systems do discourage extremist parties but argue that in the process they often "throw the baby out with the bathwater" by excluding all small parties, even legitimate ones.

GENERAL DISADVANTAGES

Wasted Votes

Since all plurality-majority voting systems are winner-take-all, they produce a large number of wasted votes—votes that elect no one to office. People who cast wasted votes are denied representation. In a typical election for the U.S. House of Representatives, over 25 million people cast wasted votes and leave the polls with no one to represent them in this body.

In a two-person race, up to 49% of the votes may be wasted. In a three-person contest where the winner might only garner 40% of the vote or less, a majority of the votes would be wasted. Majority systems may waste fewer votes than plurality systems, but up to 49% of the votes can still be wasted. People whose votes are routinely wasted may lose enthusiasm for the process.

Unfair Party Representation

Probably the most common criticism of plurality-majority voting is that it produces distortions in party representation. Numerous studies have documented that tendency.[4] As a rule, these systems are biased in favor of the largest party. Typically, the largest major party gets more seats than it deserves based on its level of voter support, and the smaller major party receives fewer seats than it deserves. The bias exists because the smaller party almost always wastes a lot of its supporters' votes.

These distortions are common and sometimes very substantial. In the 1996 elections for the U.S. House of Representatives in Massachusetts, the Democrats won 66% of the votes but received 100% (ten of ten) of the seats. The Republicans cast 33% of the vote, but they were all wasted and they received no representation. In that same year, in Oklahoma, Republicans won 61% of the vote and won six out of six seats. Such distortions tend to produce unrepresentative legislatures.

Violations of Majority Rule

Under plurality-majority rules, party representation can become so distorted that it produces an election result that violates the principle of majority rule. A party that receives only a minority of the vote can win a majority of the seats in the legislature. Political scientists call this a *manufactured majority*: a legislative majority that is artificially created by the voting system. This is contrasted with an *earned majority*, in which a party wins the majority of both the votes and the seats.

Manufactured majorities are most likely to occur when more than two parties are vying for office. If one party gets 40% of the vote and two others 30% apiece, then the largest party can win a majority of the seats even though a majority of the electorate voted against their candidates. In Great Britain, under single-member plurality rules, the Conservative party ruled with large parliamentary majorities for almost two decades, despite having never won more than 45% of the vote in any election. (For more on this issue, see Spotlight on the Debate 3.2: Are Manufactured Majorities a Serious Problem?)

An even more extreme violation of majority rule occurs when the party that comes in second in the polling wins more seats than the first-place party. This occurred in national elections in Great Britain in 1974, Canada in 1979, and New Zealand in 1978 and 1981, when the party receiving the most votes actually won fewer parliamentary seats than its main rival did. American examples include the 1996 elections for the House of Representatives in Wisconsin, where the Democratic party came in second with 47% of the vote but won 56% of the seats. That same year, in Washington state, it was the Republicans who took second place with 47% of the vote and won 67% (six of nine) of the House seats. However, defenders of plurality-majority voting point out that these results are actually quite rare—occurring in less than 10% of these elections—and so should not be considered a serious drawback.

Spotlight on the Debate 3.2
Are Manufactured Majorities a Serious Problem?

Proponents of plurality-majority voting maintain that manufactured majorities—whereby a party that wins less than 50% of the votes wins over 50% of the seats in the legislature—are not as large a problem as critics make them out to be. First, they argue that manufactured majorities are fair because they give the majority of seats to the most popular party. Second, they point out that manufactured majorities produce single-party rule in the legislature, and the political benefits of this arrangement far outweigh the fact that the seat allocation may not be exactly proportional. In their view, the purpose of elections is not simply to produce a representative legislature, but to produce a strong and effective government.

Critics counter that manufactured majorities are clearly unfair and unrepresentative. They violate the principle of majority rule and give power to a party that most people actually voted against. They give the illusion of a public mandate when none actually exists. This problem also undermines the ability of the public to hold a ruling party accountable and throw it out of power. A ruling party may lose the support of a majority of the voters and yet retain a majority of the seats in the legislature. For critics it is much more democratic to have legislatures ruled by coalitions of parties who actually represent the majority of voters than by a single party that does not.

Defenders of plurality-majority voting also argue that theirs is not the only voting system capable of producing manufactured majorities. Some proportional and semiproportional elections have also produced these results. But while it is true that manufactured majorities are indeed possible in many voting systems, in practice they are much more common in plurality-majority systems. One study of elections in fourteen countries with plurality-majority systems found that this situation occurred in 43.7% of the elections between 1945 and 1996.[5] In contrast, this problem occurred in only about 9% of the countries with proportional representation elections during that same period.

Nonrepresentation of Third Parties

Under plurality-majority rules, third parties are likely to receive no seats at all, even if they show substantial amounts of voter support. Minor parties find it extremely difficult to amass the plurality or majority of the vote necessary to win any representation. Critics see this as a disadvantage because it limits voter choices and produces legislatures that do not reflect these minority political views.

Nevertheless, some proponents of plurality-majority voting argue that discouraging minor parties is actually an advantage, not a disadvantage. It simplifies voters' choices by preventing the ballot from being flooded with a confusing array of parties. Also, as mentioned earlier, it lessens the chances of extremist parties' gaining representation.

Underrepresentation of Racial and Ethnic Minorities

Since plurality-majority systems were designed to represent majorities and pluralities, it is not a surprise that they usually do a poor job of representing racial and ethnic minorities. These minorities are often submerged in predominantly white districts and so are unable to elect their own candidates. In fact, it is the failures of these systems that have prompted much of the growing interest in alternative voting systems among some minority voting rights advocates.

Proponents, however, argue that minority representation can be enhanced by using the Voting Rights Act to encourage the creation of special districts where minorities are in the majority—so-called majority-minority districts. In practice, this strategy has worked to give some minorities a fairer chance to win representation under plurality rules. However, critics point out that this approach requires minorities to be segregated into specific geographical areas. If the minority population is widely dispersed through an area, then it may be impossible to create a district in which they are the majority. Moreover, these districts are under political and legal attack, and several Supreme Court decisions in the 1990s declared some of them unconstitutional. Without such districts, plurality-majority voting is unlikely to produce fair representation for these minorities.

Gerrymandering

Gerrymandering is the manipulation of voting district lines to give an advantage to a certain candidate or party. It is a built-in possibility in all single-member district systems. After every census, district lines must be redrawn to balance out populations, and this practice provides the opportunity for gerrymandering. The large number of wasted votes produced in single-member districts systems makes this problem possible. Gerrymandering seeks to arrange those wasted votes for political gain. In one approach, often called *cracking*, supporters of a particular party are split up among a number of districts so that they cannot form a majority in any of them and all of their votes are wasted. The other common approach is *packing*, whereby a district is drawn in which the voters of a particular party make up a huge majority of the voters, perhaps 70% to 80%. Votes in excess of what the party needs to win the seat are thus wasted.

The results of gerrymandering can sometimes be dramatic. An effective gerrymander can allow a party that comes in second in the vote to actually win the majority of seats in the legislature. One particularly blatant gerrymander in Texas allowed the Democrats to win 63% of the U.S. House seats in 1994, even though they won only 42% of the votes statewide. So with plurality-majority voting, which party wins the most seats and ultimately controls the legislature may depend not only on the total votes cast for the parties, but also on how district lines are drawn and how votes are distributed among those districts. (For more discussion of this issue, see Spotlight on the Debate 3.3: Is Gerrymandering a Serious Problem?)

Spotlight on the Debate 3.3
Is Gerrymandering a Serious Problem?

Critics of single-member plurality systems often focus on the evils of gerrymandering, believing it is one of the major disadvantages of this system. They argue that it allows the party that controls districting to protect its incumbents and effectively to steal seats from other parties. But some political commentators suggest that this problem is overblown. One scholar, for instance, has argued that parties are not always successful at gerrymandering. He suggests that voters can't always be accurately classified as to their party preferences and this makes it difficult to draw lines in a way that will always guarantee a certain partisan outcome.[6]

Some defenders of plurality voting argue that there are ways to minimize the problem of gerrymandering without changing voting systems. One favorite way is to try to take redistricting out of the hands of the politicians in state legislatures and give it to independent, nonpartisan commissions. These commissions attempt to draw district lines without taking into account the interests of parties or incumbents.

However, critics of plurality voting maintain that "independent" commissioners are very hard to find. Most of them have some party affiliations and therefore cannot be counted on to be completely neutral in their work. More importantly, they also argue that at best such commissions can only get rid of "intentional" gerrymandering, but that they cannot avoid "unintentional" gerrymandering.

Unintentional gerrymandering refers to the fact that no matter how district lines are drawn, they always help some political groups and hurt others. Even if districts were drawn completely at random, it is inevitable that one party or another world have a majority of the voters in each district. This means that the minority party in each district would likely be denied representation. So even if there is no gerrymandering by design, there will always be some gerrymandering by result. This situation led one scholar to conclude that "districting is gerrymandering."[7] In this view, drawing single-member districts inevitably produces some form of gerrymandering, and thus this problem can

Table 3.1
Average Voter Turnout in the 1990s

Country	Voting System	Average Turnout
Italy	Mixed Member PR	90.2%
Iceland	Party List PR	88.3%
Belgium	Party List PR	84.1%
Sweden	Party List PR	82.6%
Denmark	Party List PR	81.7%
Austria	Party List PR	79.6%
Spain	Party List PR	79.0%
Norway	Party List PR	75.7%
Netherlands	Party List PR	75.2%
Germany	Mixed Member PR	72.7%
United Kingdom	**Single-Member District Plurality**	**72.4%**
France	**Single-Member District Majority**	**60.6%**
Canada	**Single-Member District Plurality**	**60.1%**
United States	**Single-Member District Plurality**	**44.9%**

Source: International Institute for Democracy and Electoral Assistance, "Voter Turnout from
1990s," http://www.idea.int/voter_turnout/voter_turnout_pop9.html (November 27,
1999).

only be solved by switching to a multimember district voting system such as
proportional representation.

Safe Seats and Lack of Competition

Plurality-majority systems tend to produce large numbers of safe seats—
as one party has a significant majority of the voters in the district and
their candidates are easily and routinely elected. Some safe seats result
from a natural concentration of one party's voters, but many are the intentional products of the kind of gerrymandering described earlier. In either case, one party has an essential monopoly. So instead of a two-party
system, these districts become virtual one-party systems, because no other
parties stand a chance on election day. This stifles competition. In some
of these districts, the dominant party's candidates often run unopposed.
For example, in 41.2% of the races for state legislative seats in 1998,
one of the major parties in the district did not even bother to offer a candidate.[8]

Low Voter Turnout

Compared with other voting systems, plurality-majority systems often
suffer from low voter turnout. Experts note that countries that use single-
member district voting systems generally tend to cluster near the bottom
of the list of turnout rates (see Table 3.1). Some of the disadvantages

that have already been mentioned help to explain the negative effect on voter participation. Voters who know their vote will be wasted have little reason to show up at the polls. Likewise, voters who feel they are unable to cast a sincere vote may also stay away. And those who live in safe-seat districts may feel that the election results are preordained and not worth their effort.

Poor Political Integration

Many experts give plurality-majority systems mixed marks on political integration. On the one hand, the broad umbrella parties encouraged by plurality-majority voting do help to bring together various political factions. In this sense, they do encourage political negotiation and integration. But as seen earlier, this system may also exclude various political and racial minorities from our legislative bodies. This failure to represent diverse political viewpoints can alienate some groups from the political system. In the 1960s, for example, many African Americans lived in cities where the entire city council was white, and many felt it necessary to resort to demonstrations and boycotts to get their concerns heard.

Spotlight on the Debate 3.4
Is Plurality-Majority Voting as Good as It Gets?

After reading about all the alleged problems of plurality-majority systems, it is useful to note something interesting about the way advocates of these systems go about defending them against criticism. They use a very different strategy than defenders of proportional representation (PR). As you will see in the next chapter, PR advocates consistently deny that their system has any major drawbacks, and they constantly try to rebut criticisms. But many advocates of plurality-majority voting take a very different tack: They do not deny the existence of many of the problems that are cited by critics. They frankly admit that their system can produce wasted votes, inaccurate party representation, lower voter turnout, and safe seats—perhaps because there is a great deal of evidence of these problems.

But while they acknowledge that plurality-majority voting is not perfect, they argue that it is still the most desirable system—because all of the alternatives are much worse. Adopting a system like proportional representation, they contend, would create even more serious political problems than we have with plurality-majority voting. They primarily defend their system by attacking the alternatives and arguing that things could easily be much worse. In their view, plurality-majority voting is as good as it gets.

SINGLE-MEMBER DISTRICT PLURALITY VOTING

Single-member district plurality (SMDP) voting is the system most commonly used for legislative elections in the United States. It is the one most

Ballot 3.1
Single-Member District Plurality Voting

Official Ballot		
Municipal Elections		
DIRECTIONS TO VOTERS	**City Council Candidates**	
1. To Vote: Mark an "X" in the box next to your preferred candidate	**District One**	
	Stan Pike (Democrat)	
	Nina Kleinberg (Republican)	
2. To vote for a person whose name is not printed on the ballot, write the candidate's name on the extra line provided and put an "X" in the box next to the name.	Thomas Chou (Independent)	
	Edward Royce (Libertarian)	
	Write-In	

people think of when they think of the word *voting*. In Great Britain and Canada, this system is often called *first-past-the-post*.

How It Works

All the candidates appear on the ballot and the voters indicate their choice of one of them—by marking an X, pulling a voting lever, and so on (see Ballot 3.1). All the votes are then counted and the winner is the candidate with the most votes. In the results shown in Table 3.2, Pike is the winner with 43% of the vote. As this example illustrates, winners need not collect a majority of the votes, only more votes than their opponents do—a plurality of the votes.

Virtually all of the general advantages and disadvantages described earlier apply to SMDP voting, but it does produce a few political consequences that differ from those of other voting systems in this family.

Advantages Specific to This System

Some Minority Representation

One major advantage of single-member district voting over at-large voting in cities is that it may provide better representation for geographically concentrated racial and ethnic minorities. Although this system is not specifically designed to represent these minorities (and often fails to do so), it may if there is enough residential segregation so that the minorities can make up the majority in a district. Also, as seen earlier, as long as the minority population is not very dispersed, special "majority-minority" districts can be created deliberately to give them a fairer chance to elect their own representatives.

Table 3.2
Results of Plurality Election

Candidates & Parties	Vote Totals	% of the Vote
*Stan Pike (Democrat)	43,000	43%
Nina Kleinberg (Republican)	42,000	42%
Thomas Chou (Independent)	8,000	8%
Ed Royce (Libertarian)	7,000	7%
Total	100,000	100%

*Winning candidate.

Inexpensive and Easy to Administer

Because this is the current method of voting in most jurisdictions, election administrators feel very comfortable with the details of this process: designing the ballots, counting the votes, and so on. Also, the voting machines and other technologies associated with casting and counting ballots are already in place so there is no additional expense necessary to keep using this system.

Disadvantages Specific to This System

Violations of Majority Rule

One disadvantage of plurality voting is that it allows a candidate to win with less than a majority of the vote. If there are more than two candidates running in a district, the winning one often gets less than 50% of the vote. In the result shown in Table 3.2, Pike is the winner, but he has the support of only a minority of the voters, 43%. In other words, under plurality rules the winner can be someone the majority actually voted against. In this case, 57% of the voters voted against Pike. This outcome can seem unfair to some voters, who may question whether the winner has a valid mandate to rule. In this way, plurality rules may undermine the political legitimacy of some elected officials.

The drawback of plurality winners is particularly evident in primaries where there can be large fields of candidates vying for a nomination. In a 1998 race in Massachusetts to determine the Democratic nominee for an U.S. House seat, ten candidates ran and the winner attracted only 23% of the vote. Parties naturally want to put up the strongest candidate with the most widespread appeal, but it is difficult to find that person when the voting system allows a candidate to win with only a very small minority of the vote.

Sincere Voting Discouraged

In some situations, this system discourages sincere voting—voting for your most preferred candidate. This occurs when there are three or more candidates vying for office. Even if voters prefer minor party candidates, it makes little sense to vote for them because they have almost no chance of winning under plurality rules. The voters will most likely be wasting their vote, and they may even inadvertently help to elect their least liked candidate. In the preceding hypothetical election, supporters of the independent and Libertarian candidates are clearly wasting their votes. In this way, single-member plurality voting encourages supporters of third party and independent candidates to abandon their first choice and cast a strategic vote for the lesser of two evils of the major party candidates.

Spoiler Candidates

Plurality voting does not always work to the advantage of the major parties, and the problem of spoilers is a case in point. Spoilers are independent or third-party candidates who take away enough votes from one major party candidate to ensure the victory of another candidate who would not have won otherwise. In our hypothetical election, the Libertarian Royce may have been a spoiler by siphoning off some conservative voters who would have otherwise supported the Republican Kleinberg.

A real example of this problem occurred in a 1998 election for the U.S. House in New Mexico, where a Green party candidate won 10% of the vote. She took away votes from the Democratic candidate, who ended up with 43%. This threw the election to the Republican candidate with 46% of the vote, much to the chagrin of the Democrats. The political dissatisfaction surrounding this incident created some interest in New Mexico in voting systems that could prevent this problem, and a constitutional amendment to enact instant runoff voting for federal and state elections passed the state Senate before losing in the House.

Negative Campaigning

Critics maintain that plurality voting encourages negative campaigns between the two major party candidates. Since minor party candidates have little chance of winning, the two leading candidates can safely ignore them and concentrate on attacking their rivals. In what is essentially a two-person race, personal attacks become a good strategy. Mudslinging is an easy and effective way to turn voters away from your opponent. And even if those alienated voters don't come over to your side and simply decide not to vote, this also works to your advantage.

MAJORITY SYSTEMS: TWO-ROUND RUNOFF VOTING

Majority systems are designed to solve one of the obvious problems of plurality voting: the possibility of electing a candidate supported only by a minority of the electorate in the district. One of the most common versions of majority voting is the two-round system (TRS), also known as the *runoff system* and *second-ballot system*. It is seen as an incremental improvement on SMDP voting—a way of preserving all of the basic elements of the original system, while solving the problem of plurality winners. In nineteenth-century Europe, many countries that first adopted winner-take-all voting opted to use a majority system. Today, however, only two countries in Western Europe continue to use TRS, France and Monaco. Several developing countries that came under French influence also use this system, including Mali, Togo, Chad, Gabon, and Haiti.

The two-round system is also found in a number of jurisdictions in the United States, mostly on the local level and mostly in the South. Runoffs were first used at the beginning of the twentieth century when parties began to have primaries. These primaries often attracted more than two candidates and the resulting winner would sometimes garner much less than a majority of the vote. Today, runoffs are also used in some U.S. cities that have nonpartisan elections, again primarily because such contests are more likely to draw more than two candidates.

How It Works

In order to ensure that the winning candidate receives a majority of the vote, this system uses two rounds of voting and polling takes place on two separate days. Ballots are identical to those used in plurality voting (see Ballot 3.1), and voters mark them in the same way. In the first round, all candidates are listed on the ballot and voters indicate their preference of one of them. All these votes are then added up and if a candidate receives a majority of the vote (50% + 1 vote), that candidate is declared elected. If no one receives a majority, the field is cut down, usually to the top two candidates who received the highest number of votes, and a runoff election is held. In the case of the results seen in Table 3.1, Pike (43%) and Kleinberg (42%) would be the two candidates advancing to the runoff. The second election is typically held several weeks after the first. The winner is the candidate who gets the most votes, which is inevitably a majority. Table 3.3 illustrates the results of the runoff in our example. Most of the votes from supporters of the eliminated candidates went to Kleinberg, allowing her to win with 52% of the vote.

Table 3.3
Results of Runoff Election

Candidates & Parties	Vote Totals	% of the Vote
*Stan Pike (Democrat)	48,000	48%
Nina Kleinberg (Republican)	<u>52,000</u>	<u>52%</u>
Total	100,000	100%

*Winning candidate.

Because this majority system differs in only one major respect from single-member district plurality voting, they share almost all of the same general advantages and disadvantages. But this majority system also has a few unique characteristics.

Advantages Specific to This System

Majority Rule

The primary advantage of this system over plurality voting is that it ensures that the winning candidate enjoys the support of the majority of voters. This avoids the problem that the winning candidate in a district being opposed by the majority of the voters and thus lacking in political legitimacy.

However, several points should be kept in mind about this majority rule feature. First, this system only guarantees that a candidate gets a majority of the votes of people who turn out for the second election. As noted late in the discussion of the disadvantages, this number may be far less than voted in the first election. Second, this system guarantees majority rule on the district level, but that doesn't mean it also guarantees it at the legislative level. In fact, like all single-member district systems, two-round runoff voting can produce both manufactured majorities and minority rule in legislatures. As Table 3.4 illustrates, if the largest party wastes many of its votes because of excessively large majorities in some districts, it may easily win fewer seats than its rival. In example B, the Republicans gain only 44% of the vote and have fewer votes than the Democrats, but they win three of the five seats.

Table 3.4
Minority Rule in Two-Round Runoff Voting

	Example A Dem. Vote/Rep. Vote		Example B Dem. Vote/Rep. Vote	
Election Districts				
1	57,000/43,000		67,000/33,000	
2	51,000/49,000		69,000/31,000	
3	56,000/44,000		48,000/52,000	
4	61,000/39,000		47,000/53,000	
5	55,000/45,000		49,000/51,000	
Vote Totals	Dem. 280,000	Rep. 220,000	Dem. 280,000	Rep. 220,000
Seats Won	Dem. 5	Rep. 0	Dem. 2	Rep. 3

Note: Five districts with a total of 500,000 voters.

Elimination of Spoilers

Besides assuring majority district winners, this system addresses the spoiler problem caused by the presence of third-party and independent candidates in a plurality system. These candidates may still take away votes from a major party candidate in the first round of voting, but this will not allow another candidate to slip into office with a plurality of the vote.

More Sincere Votes

Supporters of third party and independent candidates are able to vote sincerely without fear that their vote will automatically be wasted. In our example, supporters of Chou the Independent and Royce the Libertarian candidate could vote for them in the first round. If these candidates did not make the runoff, then their supporters would still be able to vote for one of the other remaining candidates.

Small Increase in Effective Votes

Also, this system ensures that at least 51% of the vote will be effective, and that may sometimes be better than the results of plurality elections.

Nevertheless, even majority runoff systems end up wasting large portions—up to 49%—of the votes. In contrast, most proportional representation systems have less than 15% wasted votes.

Wider Range of Voter Choice

TRS tends to give voters a wider range of choices among candidates than may be found in many plurality contests. More independent and third-party candidates are likely to run because the wasted vote and spoiler problems are less severe. But although more such candidates might run, their chances of winning would still be relatively small in a system that eventually requires a majority of the vote to win. In many cases, while the first-round contests will initially be multiparty affairs, the second round of voting and the legislatures themselves could remain dominated by the two major parties. So although this system is friendlier to minor parties than plurality voting, it is not as friendly as proportional representation voting systems, which allow for the routine election of minor party candidates.

Interparty Alliances

This system not only encourages more parties to run candidates, but also encourages alliances of parties, especially in the second round of voting. Experience with this system in France has shown that parties that make the runoff need to increase their support to win, so they often try to make deals with parties that have been eliminated. This necessity encourages co-operation between parties. It also helps minor parties to gain some political influence even if they are unable to elect their own candidates to office. The winning major party candidates realize that part of their support is from the supporters of minor parties, and this gives these parties some leverage in trying to influence the behavior of these officials.

Disadvantages Specific to This System

More Expensive

Since this system often requires the government to pay for two separate elections, it is more expensive than one-round election systems such as plurality voting and instant runoff voting. It usually costs at least one to two dollars per resident to administer an election, so the costs of a second election can be considerable.[9] In San Francisco, runoff elections for their Board of Supervisors seats often cost hundreds of thousands of dollars. Increased expenses are incurred not only by government but also by the runoff candidates. They have often spent nearly all of their campaign funds in the first round, and so they are then forced to find additional funds for another (albeit brief) campaign.

Lower Turnout in Second Round

Because it offers voters more choices and less chance of wasting their vote, this system may encourage higher levels of voter turnout in the first round of voting. Unfortunately, it is also plagued by low voter turnout in the second and decisive round of voting. Often voter participation drops off dramatically from that of the first round. This drop-off is probably due to several factors, including voter fatigue and absence of the excitement that surrounds the general election. Supporters of candidates who do not make the runoff may also be less likely to vote a second time. Since voter turnout is already low in American elections, any further drop in turnout inevitably raises more questions about whom the winner actually represents. If turnout for the runoff falls from 50% to 30%, and the winner only garners a bit more than half of that, that person has the explicit support of only about 20% of the eligible voters.

Fewer Sincere Votes

There are also a few situations in which this system discourages people from casting sincere votes for minor party and independent candidates. For example, let's say that your preferred candidate on the ballot is Royce, a Libertarian. But polls indicate that Royce is likely to finish last and has virtually no chance of making the runoff. A vote for Royce could then take a vote away from your next preferred candidate—say, Kleinberg, the Republican—and thus hurt Kleinberg's chances of making it to the runoff. In this case, it would make sense to abandon your first choice and vote for your second choice. But although this situation could occasionally occur, most political scientists don't consider this possibility a very serious drawback, and it is clear that the two-ballot runoff system doesn't discourage sincere votes for minor party candidates in nearly the same way that plurality voting does.

Some Negative Campaigning

This system has a mixed impact on the quality of campaigns. In the first round of voting, candidates might be less likely to engage in negative personal attacks because they do not want to offend the other candidates' supporters, who might eventually become their supporters, in a runoff. However, in the second round of voting, in a head-to-head runoff, the incentive to engage in negative campaigning would return because the previous political drawbacks have disappeared.

Elimination of Possible Winners

Finally, this system could eliminate a candidate who might turn out to be the winner. This problem is most likely if the second and third-place candidates are relatively close, and the third is arbitrarily eliminated. Assume, for example, that in the first round of voting Pike received 34% of the vote, Chou 28%, Kleinberg 27%, and Royce 11%. This system would eliminate Kleinberg and Royce, even though it is conceivable that Kleinberg might beat Pike in a runoff.

Advocates of TRS acknowledge that this possibility exists. However, they point out that it could occur only in very special circumstances. Such a rare problem should not, they argue, be considered a serious drawback. They also point out that such candidates would have lost in plurality voting as well.

Spotlight on the Debate 3.5
Can One Person Represent a District?

In all single-member district systems, the elected official is considered to represent everyone in the district. He or she is "their" representative in the legislature and is there to fight for their interests. But critics argue that while officials like to claim to represent all the people in a district, they do not. Officials primarily represent the people who voted them into office. Conservative Republican voters will hardly feel represented by a liberal Democratic legislator who is voting against everything they hold dear. And some constituents may feel uncomfortable approaching a representative of a different political persuasion. Critics suggest that no one official can ever effectively represent all the different constituents in a single-member district, because constituents inevitably have opposing views on many important issues, such as abortion, taxes, and military spending.

Advocates of single-member districts respond that people in a geographical district often can be viewed as a whole—that they have shared interests in such issues as a clean environment, a healthy economy, and an efficient government. In these areas, the official can represent the interests of all of his or her constituents. In addition, representatives see it as their responsibility to be open to the concerns of all citizens, irrespective of the party to which they belong. Officials argue that they try to keep in touch with all elements of their district constituency and that they welcome communication with all their constituents.

MAJORITY SYSTEMS: INSTANT RUNOFF VOTING

Instant runoff voting is also known as *IRV* and *majority preferential voting*. In Australia, where this system is used to elect the lower house of parliament, it is called the *alternative vote*. Although primarily used abroad, IRV was invented in the 1870s by a professor at the Massachusetts Institute of Technology.

Like two-round voting, this system was developed to ensure that the winning candidate enjoys the support of the majority of the voters in the district. It was also thought to be an improvement over the two-round system because it does not require a separate election—it provides

Ballot 3.2
Instant Runoff Voting

Official Ballot	
Municipal Elections	
DIRECTIONS TO VOTERS	**City Council Candidates** **District One**
Do not use X marks. Mark your choices with NUMBERS only. Put the figure 1 opposite your first choice, the figure 2 opposite your second choice, the figure 3 opposite your third choice, and so on. You may make as many choices as you please. Do not put the same figure opposite more than one name.	Stan Pike (Democrat)
	Nina Kleinberg (Republican)
	Thomas Chou (Independent)
	Edward Royce (Libertarian)
	Write-In
	To Vote for a Write-In Candidate: Next to the name you have written in, put a number that represents your choice for that candidate.

an "instant" runoff. In this way, proponents of IRV claim that it has the advantages of the two-round system and avoids many of its disadvantages.

How It Works

In IRV voting, as in plurality voting, all candidates are listed on the ballot. But instead of voting for only one candidate, voters rank the candidates in the order of their preference. This ranking process is illustrated in Ballots 3.2 and 3.3. On Ballot 3.2, voters simply write a 1 next to their first choice, a 2 next to their second choice, and so on. Ballot 3.3 is an AccuVote ballot, which allows ballots to be scanned and tabulated by computer; it is similar to the standardized tests used in schools. On this ballot, voters fill in numbered boxes to indicate their ranking of the candidates.

The counting of the ballots is also different from that in plurality voting. First, all the number-one preferences of the voters are counted. If a candidate receives over 50% of the first-choice votes, he or she is declared elected. If no candidate receives a majority, then the candidate with the fewest votes is eliminated. The ballots of supporters of this defeated candidate are then transferred to whichever of the remaining candidates they marked as their number-two choice. (It is as if you told the supporters of the last-place candidate, "Your candidate cannot possibly win, so which of the remaining candidates would you like your vote to go to?") After this transfer, the votes are recounted to see whether any candidate now has a majority of the vote. The process of eliminating the lowest candidate and

Ballot 3.3
Instant Runoff Voting (Scannable Version)

Official Ballot **Municipal Elections**		
INSTRUCTIONS TO VOTERS **Mark Your Choices by Filling in the Numbered Boxes Only** Fill in the number one ⒈ box next to your first choice; fill in the number two ⒉ box next to your second choice; fill in the number three ⒊ box next to your third choice; and so on. You may fill in as many choices as you please. Fill in no more than one box per candidate. Fill in no more than one box per column.	**Candidates for City Council** **District One**	*Only one vote per candidate* Only one vote per column
	Stan Pike (Democrat)	⒈ ⒉ ⒊ ⒋
	Nina Kleinberg (Republican)	⒈ ⒉ ⒊ ⒋
	Thomas Chou (Independent)	⒈ ⒉ ⒊ ⒋
	Edward Royce (Libertarian)	⒈ ⒉ ⒊ ⒋
	Write-In	⒈ ⒉ ⒊ ⒋
	To Vote for a Write-In Candidate: Next to the name you have written in, mark a numbered box to indicate your choice of number for that candidate. Do Not Use Red To Mark Ballot	

transferring his or her votes continues until one candidate receives a majority of the continuing votes and wins the election.

This transfer process is illustrated in Table 3.5. In this hypothetical election, no candidate receives over 50% of the vote in the first round. So the lowest candidate—Royce—is eliminated and his ballots are transferred to their second choices. Of Royce's supporters, 1,000 gave Chou as their second choice, and 6,000 indicated Kleinberg as their second choice. The new totals show that no one yet has a majority, so Chou is eliminated. Of Chou's votes, 4,000 are transferred to Kleinberg and 5,000 are given to Pike. (If some of Chou's ballots had listed Royce as the second choice, they would have been transferred to their third choice, since Royce had been eliminated.) After this latest transfer it is clear that Kleinberg now has over 50% of the vote and she is declared the winner. As this example illustrates, this system essentially operates as a series of runoff elections, with progressively fewer candidates each time, until one candidate gets a majority of the vote.

Advantages Specific to This System

Majority Rule

Like the two-round system, IRV helps eliminate the problem of winners' garnering only a plurality of the vote. The transfer process usually assures

Table 3.5
Transfer Process in Instant Runoff Voting

	First Count	Second Count		Third Count	
Candidates & Parties	Original First Choice Votes	Transfer of Royce's Votes	New Totals	Transfer of Chou's Votes	New Totals
Stan Pike (Dem.)	43,000	+ 0	43,000	+ 5,000	48,000
*Nina Kleinberg (Rep.)	42,000	+ 6,000	48,000	+ 4,000	52,000
Thomas Chou (Ind.)	8,000	+ 1,000	9,000	-------	-------
Edward Royce (Libert.)	7,000	-------	-------	-------	-------

*Winning candidate.

that the winning candidate will have the support of the majority of the voters, thereby increasing the political legitimacy of elected officials. Again, however, there is no guarantee that other violations of majority rule at the legislative level, such as manufactured majorities, will not occur.

Elimination of Spoilers

Under IRV rules, third-party or independent candidates cannot inadvertently (or intentionally) throw the election to one of the major party candidates, as can happen in plurality voting. These candidates may take some votes away from a major party candidate in the first count, but this will not allow another candidate to slip into office with a plurality of the vote. And in subsequent counts these votes are likely to be transferred to the most preferred major party candidate.

More Sincere Votes

Unlike plurality voting, IRV does not discourage sincere votes for third-party and independent candidates. Supporters of such candidates need not fear that their votes will automatically be wasted. In the race shown in the ballots, supporters of the independent Chou can vote sincerely for their candidate, secure in the knowledge that if Chou cannot win, their vote will be transferred to their next preferred candidate.

Small Increase in Effective Votes

Like the two-round system, IRV ensures that at least 51% of the vote will be effective, and that result may sometimes be better than the result of a plurality election. Nevertheless, as a winner-take-all system, IRV still ends up wasting large portions—up to 49%—of the votes. Again, this contrasts with proportional representation systems, in which often as few as 10% to 15% of the votes are wasted.

Wider Range of Voter Choice

IRV tends to give voters a wider range of choices among candidates than may be found in many plurality elections. More independent and third-party candidates are likely to run because the wasted vote and spoiler problems are less severe. But while more such candidates might run, their chance of winning would still be relatively small in a system that eventually requires a majority of the vote to win.

Cheaper Than Second Ballot

IRV is also designed to overcome several of the disadvantages of two-round runoffs. For example, IRV avoids the higher expenses associated with having a second election—so there is a significant cost savings for both governments and candidates.

No Drop in Turnout

IRV also prevents the drop in voter turnout that plagues two-round elections. In fact, IRV tends to encourage higher turnout. This system gives voters more choices and allows them to vote sincerely for the candidates they most prefer, and this serves as an incentive to go to the polls, especially for minor party supporters.

Less Negative Campaigning

Some experts maintain that IRV may have the added benefit of discouraging negative campaigns and mud slinging. In this system, candidates can benefit from being the second choice of voters. Often these transfer votes can prove to be the margin of victory. But if candidates viciously attack their opponents, they risk alienating these possible supporters. In the example, it would not be a good strategy for Kleinberg, the Republican candidate, to sling mud at Royce, the Libertarian candidate, since it is likely that Kleinberg might otherwise receive many of Royce's transfer votes. So under IRV, it pays for candidates to spend less time on negative campaigning and more on discussions of their own policies and values.

More Political Cooperation

Some political scientists believe that IRV may be beneficial in situations in which there are deep political, religious, or racial divisions.[10] It has been promoted in such countries as Northern Ireland and Fiji, which have suffered from such long-standing divisions. This characteristic of IRV is due to its tendency to encourage candidates to seek not only the votes of their supporters, but also the second preferences of others. IRV requires that a winning candidate have a broad appeal in order to gain the majority of votes needed to win. So instead of focusing on the narrow issues attractive to only one group of voters, candidates could be moved to make broader, more centrist appeals that would attract the maximum number of first and second-preference votes. In Australia, for instance, major parties have sometimes waged campaigns explicitly designed to increase their attractiveness to supporters of particular minor parties. In this sense, IRV may foster more cooperative and less divisive politics.

Disadvantages Specific to This System

Just as most of the advantages of instant runoff voting are attributable to its unique process of transferring votes, most of its specific disadvantages are associated with this unique procedure as well.

Unfamiliar to Voters

IRV would be a new and different system in most American jurisdictions, and voters would have to become familiar with this method of casting ballots. Some spoiled ballots would probably be inevitable when this new system was first used. However, most experts agree that American voters are unlikely to have much trouble learning the process of ranking candidates on the ballot. Other Western countries that use this system have not encountered voter confusion. In any case, a voter education effort would certainly be necessary to ensure a smooth transition to such a system.

Administrative Complexity and Expense

Election administrators would have to adapt to this new system and learn to master the process of transferring the ballots. In addition, if the ballots were counted by hand, then the transfer process could take some time. For a statewide election, it might take several days to collect all the ballots and to accomplish the transfer process manually. This process would take longer than a plurality vote, but it would still be shorter than a second (runoff) election. It would be similar to the time it takes to conduct a recount in a very close election.

The delay caused by hand counting could be eliminated with the use of voting machines. Computer-readable ballots or touch screen voting machines would enable the transfer process to take place very quickly. However, an expense would often have to be incurred to purchase the voting technology that could handle IRV.

Guarantee of Majority of Continuing Votes Only

Some critics point out that instant runoff voting only guarantees that the winner will receive a majority of the "continuing" votes, not a majority of the votes that were originally cast. IRV votes can become eliminated or "exhausted" if voters fail to mark enough preferences or if their only remaining preference is for a candidate who has already been eliminated. For example, if 1,000 of the voters who originally supported the independent candidate, Chou, did not mark any number-two preferences, then their ballots could not be transferred when Chou was eliminated. This would mean that a winning candidate would only have to garner a majority of the 99,000 continuing votes, not a majority of the original 100,000 votes that were cast.

Advocates of IRV maintain that this is hardly a major problem, and that even when it occurs, the winner still has more voter support than most nonmajority winners produced by plurality voting. They also argue that this possibility can be minimized by voter education campaigns that stress the importance of marking as many preferences as possible on the ballot. Australia has taken a somewhat different approach in its IRV elections: It requires voters to rank *all* the candidates running for office. This does help to minimize "exhausted ballots," but some reformers consider this too drastic a solution for what might only be an occasional problem.

Lack of Monotonicity

Some mathematically inclined critics of IRV point out that it can be *nonmonotonic*: In some circumstances more first-place votes may hurt, rather than help, a candidate's chances of being elected. This complicated paradox involves a situation in which a candidate's receiving more votes can change the order in which other candidates are eliminated, with the result that their votes are transferred in ways that ultimately help a rival of the first candidate.[11]

While it is clear that nonmonotonicity can theoretically occur in an IRV election, most experts believe that the conditions required for this paradox to occur are so special that it would be an extremely rare occurrence. One statistical study found that if IRV-like elections were held throughout the United Kingdom, a nonmonotonic result would occur less than once a century.[12]

MULTIMEMBER DISTRICT PLURALITY OR AT-LARGE VOTING

This system is unique among plurality-majority systems in that it uses multimember districts instead of single-member districts. For that reason political scientists often refer to it as *multimember district plurality* voting. Internationally it is often called *block voting*. As noted earlier, many representatives to state legislatures and even the U.S. Congress were at one time elected in multimember districts—often small two- or three-seat districts. Ten states still use some of these districts for state legislative elections.

Today, however, multimember district plurality voting is used primarily in local elections, primarily municipal elections, where it is called *at-large voting*. Typically an entire town or city is considered to be one large district, and all candidates for office run together against each other. Since it is mainly used in local elections, I generally use the term *at-large* to describe this system, and the examples I use in this section assume that it is being used in a municipal context.

At-large voting first began to be used in U.S. cities around the beginning of the twentieth century. Many Progressive reformers advocated it as a way to undermine the power of the political machines that dominated politics in many urban areas. Most of those cities used single-member districts to elect their city councilors. These districts, or wards, were where the parties raised campaign funds, mobilized voters, and distributed patronage. Reformers saw these wards as the centers of political corruption and the base from which various ethnic groups and other special interests wielded their political power. Having city councilors elected by the entire city in at-large elections was seen as a way to reduce the power of these neighborhood leaders and to ensure that city councilors represented the interests of the city as a whole, not special local interests. Reformers were less concerned with producing more fair representation for the various interests in the city than with producing what they thought was more enlightened representation—representation that would promote the common public interest.

How It Works

In at-large voting, two or more candidates are elected at one time in large multimember districts. Voters have the same number of votes as the number of seats to be filled. The candidates with the highest numbers of votes (a plurality) win. Ballot 3.4 would be used in a city election in which the members of a five-person city council would be chosen. All candidates for the five seats are on the ballot, and voters cast five votes for the candidates they prefer. Table 3.6 illustrates how the votes might be distributed and the winners chosen.

There are several variations of at-large voting. In one of them, which is used in Seattle and several other cities, the at-large seats are numbered and specific candidates vie for these individual seats. So candidates A and B would vie for seat one, candidates C and D for seat two, and so on. All the voters in the city cast one vote for their preferred candidates in each of these races, and the candidate with the plurality wins. In another variation, some cities use the numbered seats but also have a residency requirement. Candidates for a particular seat must live in a certain area or district of the city. This ensures that all neighborhoods have some representation. Again all the voters in the city are able to vote for each of the seats.

At first glance, at-large voting seems to be very different from the other

Ballot 3.4
At-Large Voting

Official Ballot	
Municipal Elections	
Instructions to Voters	**City Council Candidates**
1. To Vote: Mark on "X" in the box next to the candidate's name. 2. Vote for no more than FIVE candidates. 3. To vote for a person whose name is not printed on the ballot, write the candidate's name on one of the extra lines provided and put an "X" in the box next to the name.	Joan Cocks (Democrat) ▯ Steve Ellenburg (Democrat) ▯ Vincent Ferraro (Republican) ▯ Stephen Jones (Democrat) ▯ Penny Gill (Republican) ▯ Jean Grossholtz (Republican) ▯ Kavita Khory (Republican) ▯ Christopher Pyle (Democrat) ▯ Preston Smith (Democrat) ▯ Walter Stewart (Republican) ▯ *Write In* ▯ *Write In* ▯ *Write In* ▯

forms of plurality-majority voting. But this is an illusion. Even though races take place in multimember districts and voters have multiple votes, this remains in essence a plurality voting system. You could view it as a series of single-member district plurality elections put together. This can best be seen in the variations that use numbered seats. So despite its appearances, at-large voting is definitely a member of the plurality-majority family of systems. And since it is designed primarily to ensure representation for the majority, it shares almost all the same advantages and disadvantages of the other systems that take this approach. It does, however, have a few unique political attributes that should be noted.

Advantages Specific to This System

Citywide Representation

The advantage most often cited by advocates is the election of candidates that have citywide support among the voters. At-large representatives may thus be more likely to advocate what is good for the city as a whole. In contrast, district representatives may tend to vote for programs that benefit

Table 3.6
Results of At-Large Election

Candidates & Parties	Vote Totals
*Jean Grossholtz (Republican)	65,000
*Walter Stewart (Republican)	62,000
*Kavita Khory (Republican)	60,000
*Vincent Ferraro (Republican)	57,000
*Penny Gill (Republican)	51,000
Christopher Pyle (Democrat)	50,000
Preston Smith (Democrat)	42,000
Joan Cocks (Democrat)	40,000
Steve Ellenburg (Democrat)	37,000
Stephen Jones (Democrat)	36,000
Total	500,000

*Winning candidates.
Note: One hundred thousand voters casting five votes each.

their area but that may not be in the best interest of the entire community. District representatives might also fight against a program that puts a burden on their neighborhood but that benefits the city as a whole. For example, they might vehemently oppose locating a homeless shelter in their neighborhood, while an at-large councilor would realize that having such a facility was necessary for dealing with this problem.

No Gerrymandering

This is the only form of plurality-majority voting to escape the problem of gerrymandering. If there are no separate districts in a city, then gerrymandering is not a possibility. This eliminates the possibility of drawing district lines to benefit incumbents or the dominant party. All the political hassles involved in redistricting—the partisan battles and the expensive court suits—are also avoided.

Disadvantages Specific to This System

Poor Geographical Representation

Because there are no separate districts in standard at-large city elections, they do not ensure geographical representation, and some people consider this feature a drawback. Experts have found that it is common for many or most of the city councilors elected at-large to live in one area of the city—typically a middle-class white area.[13] As a result, some neighborhoods may find that they have no one on the city council working to ensure that their particular problems are addressed. Some critics argue that geographical representation is particularly important at the city level, where governance is less about ideology and more about delivering services equitably.

At-large proponents respond that this system can be modified to produce some geographical representation. As noted earlier, one variation of at-large voting has numbered seats that correspond to specific neighborhoods in the city, and candidates for those seats may be required to be residents of those areas. This arrangement, however, creates some ambiguity about whom the winning candidates actually represent. This is because these officials are not elected solely by the voters in these neighborhoods, but by voters citywide. So a candidate preferred by most voters in a neighborhood may be defeated by one preferred by a citywide majority.

Worst Representation of Parties

All plurality-majority systems are poor at ensuring fair representation for political parties, but at-large voting is the worst. It exaggerates the tendency to give the largest party more seats than it deserves based on its proportion of the vote. It is easy to see how this could be the case. In the election results in Table 3.6, the city is 60% Republican and 40% Democratic. If the voters largely stick to their parties, as they usually do, the same Republican majority can "sweep" all the seats and elect all five members of the city council. In our example, there is some crossing of party lines in the vote, but the Republicans are still able to win every seat. Even if the Democrats are a majority in some areas of the city, they are outvoted citywide by the more numerous Republicans. The result: Each Republican voter is represented many times, and each Democrat has no representation at all.

Worst Representation of Racial and Ethnic Minorities

Studies have shown that at-large voting also exaggerates the tendency of plurality-majority systems to underrepresent racial and ethnic minorities.[14] As seen earlier, single-member district systems present at least the possibility of minority representation through the creation of special majority-minority districts. This is not possible in at-large systems. As a result, these systems are the worst at providing racial and ethnic minorities with a fair chance of electing their own representatives. It is quite easy for a white majority, voting cohesively, to elect an all-white city council. It is revealing that after the Voting Rights Act was passed in the 1960s, many areas of the South switched from single-member district to at-large elections in an effort to make it more difficult for African Americans to get elected.[15] It is this high potential for racial bias that has caused this system to be increasingly challenged in the courts as being in violation of the Voting Rights Act and its amendments.

More Expensive Campaigns

Candidates must run citywide campaigns, which can be more expensive than campaigns in one district. Typically candidates must spend more on media advertisements to cover this wider area, and they must also develop an extensive campaign organization that will court voters in all areas of the city. Some studies suggest that this situation disadvantages third-party, independent, and minority candidates who may not have ready access to large amounts of campaign funds.[16]

Self-Defeating Votes

At-large voting can discourage voters from supporting all the candidates they want to see on the council. Voters usually cast their first vote for their most preferred candidate, but then they may realize that any additional votes they cast for other candidates may give those candidates enough votes to defeat their favorite. In the election example, for instance, the favorite candidate of a female Democratic voter might be Pyle, but she might also want to vote for some of the women on the ballot. But a vote for Gill could easily help her win the last seat instead of Pyle.

Proponents of at-large voting argue that this problem can be prevented if voters cast only a single vote for their most preferred candidate—a practice called *bullet voting*. But as critics point out, casting only one vote means that you will have less impact on who gets elected to the council than those who cast all of their votes. This is the political dilemma in which racial minorities often find themselves. They must give up all of their other votes if they are to have any hope at all of electing their first choice candidate.

COMBINED AT-LARGE AND DISTRICT SYSTEM

Combined systems are those in which some representatives are elected at-large and others elected from single-member districts. These voting systems are found almost exclusively in cities. Historically, they have gained popularity as support has declined for at-large systems, and today they are very common. As noted earlier, at-large voting has been under increasing political and legal attack since the 1960s for its inability to represent racial and ethnic minorities adequately and its neglect of neighborhood representation. This has led to the search for alternatives. This search has usually not been very wide-ranging and has not included the proportional and semiproportional voting systems to be examined later. Typically the only alternative considered has been single-member district plurality voting. Some reformers, however, have not wanted to abandon the advantages of

Ballot 3.5
Combined At-Large and Single-Member District Voting

Official Ballot
Municipal Elections

Instructions to Voters	Councilor At Large *Vote for Not More Than Three*	
	Douglas Campbell (Democrat)	
1. To Vote: Mark on "X" in the box next to the candidate's name.	Susan Rosen (Republican)	
	Richard Ramirez (Democrat)	
	Edward Royce (Republican)	
	Amy Zeldes (Republican)	
2. To vote for a person whose name is not printed on the ballot, write the candidate's name on one of the extra lines provided and put an "X" in the box next to the name.	Cynthia Daniels (Democrat)	
	Write In	
	Write In	
	Write In	
	Councilor from District One *Vote for One*	
	Alberto Sandoval (Democrat)	
	Magdalena Gomez (Independent)	
	Write In	

---

the at-large system completely, so a combined system—one that incorporates the advantages of both systems—has been seen as a good compromise.

How It Works

There are usually two parts to the ballot: one for the at-large contests and one for the district race (see Ballot 3.5). The winners are decided by the plurality rules discussed earlier for at-large and single-member district elections. The number and mix of the seats in a combined system can vary considerably. Typically, a city might have ten district seats and five at-large, or five district seats and ten at-large.

Advantages Specific to This System

Advocates argue that combined systems incorporate the best features of district and at-large representation. Having district representatives allows for geographical representation. And evidence suggests that these systems produce better representation for racial and ethnic groups than pure at-large systems.[17] In addition, the at-large representatives can bring a citywide perspective to policy issues and therefore encourage a more wide-ranging political debate.

Disadvantages Specific to This System

Critics argue that these systems combine the worst of both district and at-large representation. For example, the districting element encourages gerrymandering and carries with it all the political battles and court suits often associated with redistricting. Also, these systems may fail to represent racial and ethnic minorities. If a minority is dispersed throughout a city, as Asian Americans are in some areas of the country, then they may be unable to win a district. And yet they may also be too few in number to win an at-large seat. Finally, these combined systems have most of the political shortcomings that characterize plurality-majority voting systems in general: overpresenting the largest parties, discouraging minor parties, wasting large numbers of votes, and so on.

CONCLUSION

The first time through, the details of all these systems and their various advantages and disadvantages can be a bit overwhelming and confusing. But several thoughts may help to keep it all in perspective. First, remember that most of these systems are simply variations on our basic winner-take-all, single-member district plurality voting. Second, try not to be distracted by all the differences between the various members of this voting family. These differences are minor compared to what these systems have in common, and minor compared to their differences from the proportional and semiproportional systems to be discussed later. The most significant choice you will be faced with is not between different types of plurality-majority systems, but between this voting system family and the others.

NOTES

1. For more on how winner-take-all systems evolved into proportional representation systems, see Andrew McLaren Carstairs, *A Short History of Electoral Systems in Western Europe* (London: George Allen and Unwin, 1980), especially chapter one.

2. See for example, Maurice Duverger, *Political Parties: Their Organization and Activity in the Modern State* (New York: Wiley, 1954); Anthony Downs, *An Economic Theory of Democracy* (New York: Harper-Collins, 1957); and Arend Lijphart, *Democracies: Patterns of Majoritarian and Consensus Government in Twenty-One Countries* (New Haven, Conn.: Yale University Press 1984).

3. Arend Lijphart, *Patterns of Democracy: Government Forms and Performance in Thirty-Six Countries* (New Haven, Conn.: Yale University Press, 1999), p. 259–260.

4. Douglas Rae, *The Political Consequences of Electoral Laws* (New Haven, Conn.: Yale University Press, 1971).

5. Lijphart, *Patterns of Democracy*, p. 166.

6. Mark Rush, *Does Redistricting Make a Difference? Partisan Representation and Electoral Behavior* (Baltimore: Johns Hopkins University Press, 1993).

7. Robert G. Dixon, *Democratic Representation: Reapportionment in Law and Politics* (London: Oxford University Press, 1968), p. 462.

8. Richard Winger, "Dems, Reps Failed to Nominate in 1998," *Ballot Access News* 14, no. 11 (February 1999): 3.

9. Robert Richie, Caleb Kleppner, and Terril Bouricius, "Instant Run-Offs: A Cheaper, Faster, Better Way to Conduct Elections," *National Civic Review* 89, no. 1 (Spring, 2000): 95–110.

10. Andrew Reynolds and Ben Reilly, *The International IDEA Handbook of Electoral Design* (Stockholm: Institute for Democracy and Electoral Assistance, 1997), pp. 38–39.

11. For a more lengthy description of this paradox, see David M. Farrell, *Comparing Electoral Systems* (New York, Prentice-Hall, 1997), pp. 134–136.

12. Crispin Allard, "Lack of Monotonicity—Revisited," *Representation* 33 (1995): 49.

13. J. D. William Boyd, "Local Electoral Systems: Is There a Best Way?" *National Civic Review* (March 1976): 138.

14. Albert Karnig and Susan Welch, "Electoral Structure and Black Representation on City Councils," *Social Science Quarterly* 63 (March 1982): 99–114.

15. Chandler Davidson, "Minority Vote Dilution: An Overview," in *Minority Vote Dilution*, ed. Chandler Davidson (Washington, D.C.: Howard University Press, 1984), p. 11.

16. Albert Karnig and Susan Welch, *Black Representation and Urban Policy* (Chicago: The University of Chicago Press, 1980), p. 148.

17. Susan A. MacManus, "Mixed Election Systems: The Newest Reform Structure," in *Local Government Election Practices*, ed. Roger L. Kemp (Jefferson, N.C.: McFarland and Company, 1999), p. 45.

CHAPTER 4

Proportional Representation Voting Systems

Proportional representation voting is the main rival to plurality-majority voting. In fact, among advanced Western democracies, proportional representation (PR) has become the predominant system. For instance, twenty-one of the twenty-eight countries in Western Europe use proportional representation, including Austria, Belgium, Cyprus, Denmark, Finland, Germany, Greece, Ireland, Luxembourg, Malta, the Netherlands, Norway, Portugal, Spain, Sweden, and Switzerland.

Proportional representation is not one voting system, but several. It is best to think of it as a basic principle that several different kinds of voting systems embody. The principle is simple: The number of seats a political party or group wins in a legislature should be proportional to the amount of its support among voters. So if a political party wins 30% of the vote, it should receive about 30% of the seats. As you will see, election designers have devised a variety of ways to achieve that goal. But all of them are versions of the three basic kinds of PR that you will be examining here: the party list system, the mixed-member system, and the single transferable vote, also known as choice voting.

HISTORY

Proportional representation systems were first developed in nineteenth-century Europe to remedy what were seen as defects in the reigning voting systems. Britain was using a plurality system, and many of the other European countries had adopted various forms of majority voting. As shown in the previous chapter, these majority runoff systems were invented to solve some of the problems of plurality voting—in particular, its tendency to elect candidates supported only by a minority of the voters. But it eventually became clear that both plurality and majority systems routinely produced unfair distortions in the representation of parties in the national legislatures, and this realization led to the next stage in the evolution of voting systems: the development of proportional representation systems. The late nineteenth century was a time when suffrage was being extended to most of the public and mass political parties were developing in these countries. It is no coincidence that as the importance and prevalence of mass parties grew, so too did the interest in having a voting system that gave these parties their fair share of seats—and that is precisely what PR promised to do.

The agitation for a change to proportional representation voting first occurred in Belgium and Switzerland. Both of these countries had deep ethnic and religious divisions among their populations, and citizens were interested in ensuring fair political representation for these various communities—something that plurality-majority systems could not guarantee. Belgium was the first country to adopt a list form of PR in 1899. Next were Finland in 1906 and Sweden in 1907. The switch to proportional representation quickly gained momentum after that, and by 1920 most countries in continental Europe had adopted this form of voting.

Throughout the twentieth century the trend in Western democracies continued to be away from plurality-majority and toward PR voting systems. In the 1990s over two-thirds of the emerging democracies in Eastern Europe and the former Soviet Union adopted proportional or semiproportional forms of voting. After a national referendum in the early 1990s, New Zealand switched from their traditional single-member district plurality system to mixed-member proportional representation. More recently, the newly formed parliaments of Scotland and Wales also used mixed-member PR for their first elections.

OVERVIEW OF CHAPTER

This examination of proportional representation voting systems is organized is the same way as the previous chapter. I first describe the general principles of proportional representation voting and the features that these systems have in common. Then I turn to an examination of the general political advantages and disadvantages that these systems share and that differentiate them from other voting systems. I again note where there are disagreements about these political effects. Descriptions of how each of the basic versions of proportional representation works follow. These descriptions include the advantages and disadvantages that are specific to each of these systems.

COMMON FEATURES OF PR SYSTEMS

List systems, mixed-member proportional representation, and choice voting all differ in the way ballots are structured, votes are cast, and seats

Figure 4.1
Fifty Single-Seat Districts

1	1	1	1	1
1	1	1	1	1
1	1	1	1	1
1	1	1	1	1
1	1	1	1	1
1	1	1	1	1
1	1	1	1	1
1	1	1	1	1
1	1	1	1	1
1	1	1	1	1

allocated. Nevertheless, these all are forms of PR and have a number of common characteristics.

Multimember Districts

First, all proportional representation systems use multimember districts. Instead of electing one member of the legislature in each local district, PR uses larger districts where several members are elected at once. Figures 4.1, 4.2, and 4.3 illustrate districting maps for a hypothetical fifty-person state senate. Figure 4.1 shows fifty single-seat districts, which are common in plurality-majority systems. Figure 4.2 depicts ten 5-seat PR districts, and Figure 4.3 shows five 10-seat PR districts.

In practice, the number of members elected in a district can vary considerably. Ireland uses small three-to five-person districts, while in the Netherlands the entire country is one district in which all 150 members of their parliament, the Tweede Kamer, are elected. Also, even within a particular country, the size of districts may vary. Belgium, for instance, uses districts that range in size from five to forty-eight seats. The districts with fewer seats tend to be in the more sparsely populated rural areas; the high-seat districts are in the urban areas.

Not Winner-Take-All

As you saw in the last chapter, all single-member district systems are winner-take-all. When only one candidate is elected, one party inevitably gets all of the representation. In contrast, multimember PR districts allow many parties to win seats in a district. This means that more voters have

Figure 4.2
Ten 5-Seat PR Districts

5 seats	5 seats
5 seats	5 seats
5 seats	5 seats
5 seats	5 seats
5 seats	5 seats

representation. In PR districts, 80%–90% of voters win representation compared to the 40%–60% typical of winner-take-all voting systems.

Proportional Allocation of Seats

Which candidates win the seats in these multimember districts is determined by the proportion of the votes a party or political group receives. In many ways, this is the central defining characteristic of these systems; it is why they are called proportional representation. Assume, for instance, that we have a ten-member PR district. If the Democrats win 50% of the vote, they receive five of those ten seats. With 30% of the vote, the Republicans get three seats. And if a third party receives the other 20% of the vote, it gets the remaining two seats.

Some PR systems are a bit more proportional than others. Often this is a function of the number of seats at stake in the multimember districts. As a rule, the results in small three-to-four-seat districts tend to be less proportional than in large districts with ten, twenty, or more seats.

Emphasis on Partisan Political Identity

Underlying this emphasis on party representation is an assumption about citizens' political identities. Proportional representation systems assume that most people tend to identify their political orientation according to parties and political ideologies—not geography. As you saw in the previous chapter, plurality-majority systems emphasize geographical representation over party representation. The reverse tends to occur in PR systems. Proponents argue that in the early days of democracy, people often were born, lived, and died in the same small geographical region. But in today's mobile

Figure 4.3
Five 10-Seat PR Districts

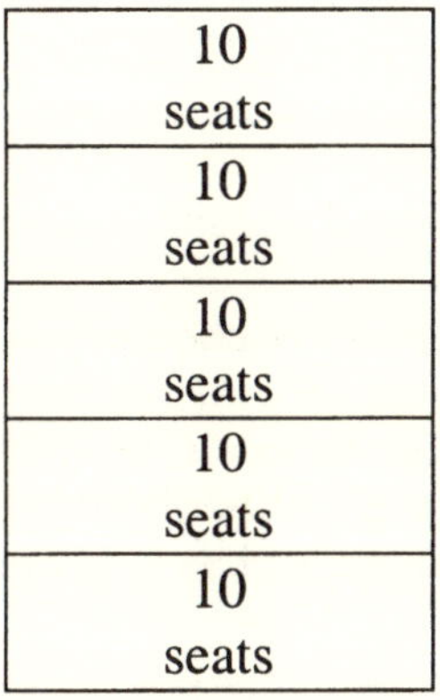

10 seats
10 seats
10 seats
10 seats
10 seats

society, geographical considerations play a much smaller role in people's political identity. Most voters tend to think of themselves primarily as liberals, conservatives, moderates, Democrats, Republicans, Greens, or feminists—rather than New Yorkers or Floridians. Proportional representation is primarily designed to ensure that voters are fairly represented along these partisan and ideological lines.

Low Thresholds

Another common feature of these systems is their low thresholds of exclusion: the minimum portion of the vote a party must have to be sure of winning a seat in the legislature. As indicated earlier, plurality-majority systems have a threshold of 50% + 1, the highest among voting systems. In proportional representation systems, a political group may be sure of winning representation even if it only gets 5% or 10% of the vote. The level of this threshold can vary considerably from one PR system to the next. In list forms of proportional representation, it is usually less than 5% and in a few instances may be around 1%. When PR has been used in the United States the thresholds have typically been around 10%. These thresholds can be adjusted up or down to produce various political effects. For example, Israel adjusted its threshold upward in 1992 in order to make it more difficult for very small parties to win seats.

GENERAL ADVANTAGES

Fair Representation of Parties

Since one of the main purposes of proportional representation voting systems is to ensure fair and accurate representation for parties, it is not surprising that they are good at achieving this political goal. No system can be perfectly proportional, but PR is much better than plurality-majority voting at giving parties the proportion of seats they deserve based on their voting strength. If a party wins 40% of the vote, it will receive around 40% of the seats—not 20% or 60%, as can happen in plurality-majority systems.

The contrast between PR and plurality-majority voting is well illustrated by the case of New York City. It used a form of PR—choice voting— between 1937 and 1947 for the election of its city council. In the first PR election, the Democrats won 47% of the vote and 50% of the seats—a typically proportional result. However, in 1949, after PR was abandoned and single-member district plurality elections reinstated, the Democrats won 52.6% of the vote and received 96% (24 out of 25) of the city council seats.

Fewer Wasted Votes and More Effective Votes

Because only a small percentage of votes is necessary to elect a candidate in proportional representation systems, far fewer votes are wasted and more help to elect candidates. In plurality-majority voting, a party that wins 30% of the vote in a district wins no representation, while in a multimember PR district, that party would win 30% of the seats.

As a result of PR rules, more voters win representation in legislative bodies. For example, in 1994, in our plurality elections for the U.S. House of Representatives, only about 59% of those who cast votes actually helped elect someone to that body. That same year, in elections for Germany's national parliament, over 80% of the voters cast effective votes. In the 1999 PR election in New Zealand, over 93% of the voters won representation. PR proponents argue that people should have not only the right to vote, but the right to representation as well. They assert that without the ability to cast an effective vote, the right to vote means little.

Friendlier to Minor Parties

Because of their low thresholds, proportional representation systems nurture minor parties. A small party that receives only 5% or 10% of the vote would be completely shut out in a plurality-majority system, but in most PR systems it would easily elect some members to the legislature. Thus PR rules create an electoral system in which minor parties are much more viable.

Sincere Voting Encouraged

Since minor parties are more likely to elect candidates in this system, it allows voters to cast sincere ballots for these candidates. In plurality-majority systems, voting for minor party candidates often makes little sense—even if they are your first choice. You will likely be wasting your vote; worse, you might help to elect the major party candidate you like the least. In proportional representation systems, minor party candidates stand a better chance of being elected so citizens can vote sincerely for the candidates they most prefer, instead of having to choose between the "lesser of two evils."

Elimination of Spoilers

Spoiler candidates are a common problem in single-member plurality voting systems. They are independent or minor party candidates who take away enough votes from one major party candidate to ensure the victory of another candidate who would not have won otherwise. In PR systems, votes for minor party candidates usually result in their election and do not aid inadvertently any major party candidates.

Multiparty System Allowed

Another effect of making minor parties more viable is that it allows for the emergence of multiparty systems. So it is not surprising that most countries that use PR voting also have multiparty systems in which combinations of larger and smaller parties vie for office and win seats in the legislatures. Proponents of PR believe that multiparty systems offer voters more choices and produce legislatures that are more representative of the varieties of political views among the public.

Critics of proportional representation argue that adopting this system would force a multiparty system on an American public that may have no desire for one and create political divisions where they did not exist before. (See Spotlight on the Debate 4.1: Does PR Produce Too Many Parties?) Defenders point out, however, that although PR rules allow for the development of a multiparty system, they do not inevitably produce one. In their view, PR voting does not mandate any particular kind of party system; it simply produces the kind of system that reflects the political divisions that already exist among the voters. If the public largely falls into two political camps, PR will produce a two-party system. For example, when choice voting was used in the relatively politically homogeneous city of Cincinnati, the result was a two-party system, while its use in a more politically diverse city, New York, produced a multiparty system in which four or five different parties won seats.

Spotlight on the Debate 4.1
Does PR Produce Too Many Parties?

Some critics argue that proportional representation results in an overproliferation of political parties. The existence of too many parties confuses voters and makes it more difficult to form stable ruling coalitions in legislatures. One example of this problem occurred in the 1988 elections in Israel, in which fifteen parties ended up in their parliament, the Knesset. The Netherlands has also at times had over a dozen parties in parliament. Would we want that kind of chaotic situation in the United States?

Defenders argue that although PR systems do tend to produce multiparty systems, they needn't result in an excessive number of parties clogging up the political system. They point out that only the most extreme forms of PR—such as that used in Israel and the Netherlands—tend to produce handfuls of parties. These countries have among the lowest thresholds of any PR systems—around 1%—so that it is very easy for microparties to win seats in these legislatures. A higher threshold would cut down on the number of parties winning seats. It has been estimated that if the threshold had been 5% instead of 1% in the 1988 Israeli elections, virtually none of the very small parties would have won seats. Most countries using more moderate forms of PR, like Germany, have around a 4%–5% threshold, which typically puts four or five parties into the legislature.

One of the advantages of proportional representation, according to proponents, is that a country can set the threshold level to create the kind of party system that it desires. For instance, when South Africa adopted PR, its leaders wanted to create an inclusive legislature that maximized the number of parties winning representation, so they chose a very low threshold of 0.25%. Many other countries have chosen higher thresholds to ensure that the number of parties is kept at a reasonable level. Most proposals for proportional representation in the United States have called for relatively high thresholds, often 10% or more.

Better Representation of Racial and Ethnic Minorities

Proponents of proportional representation argue that one of its main advantages is that it could finally resolve the problem of how to give racial and ethnic minorities a fair chance to elect their own representatives. They maintain that this problem is very difficult to solve if we keep single-member districts. Whites dominate most single-member districts, and it is very rare for a minority to win office in them. It is possible to create special districts in which minorities are the majority. But these require that minorities be segregated in certain geographical areas. More importantly, the Supreme Court has ruled that some of these "majority-minority" districts are unconstitutional, thus throwing into question their legal viability.

The advantage of using multimember PR districts is that they allow all racial groups—both whites and minorities—to win their fair share of representation. Assume, for instance, that we had a five-member district in which African Americans made up 22% of the voters. If all of them supported an African-American candidate, that person could win one of the five seats. In this way, PR voting allows for the fair representation of minorities without the creation of special districts.

Table 4.1
The Representation of Women in Twelve Western Democracies

Country	Voting System	Percentage of Women Elected to Lower House
Sweden	Party List PR	42.7% (1998)
Denmark	Party List PR	37.4% (1998)
Finland	Party List PR	37.0% (1999)
Norway	Party List PR	36.4% (1997)
Netherlands	Party List PR	36.0% (1998)
Germany	Mixed Member PR	30.9% (1998)
Belgium	Party List PR	23.5% (1999)
Canada	**Single-Member District Plurality**	**20.6% (1997)**
United Kingdom	**Single-Member District Plurality**	**18.4% (1997)**
United States	**Single-Member District Plurality**	**13.3% (1998)**
Ireland	Single-Transferable Vote PR	12.0% (1997)
France	**Single-Member District Majority**	**10.9% (1997)**

Source: Inter-Parliamentary Union, "Women in National Parliaments," 1999. http://www.
ipu.org/wmn-e/classif.htm (December 30, 1999).

Proportional representation systems are particularly appropriate in areas where the minority population is not geographically concentrated, but dispersed. This is often the case with Latinos in the Southwest and Asians in the Midwest. Dispersed minority populations make it impossible to fashion majority-minority districts. In PR voting, however, minorities may band together—irrespective or where they live in the multimember district—to elect their own representative.

Typically when proportional representation voting is used in areas with substantial minority populations, minorities are included in the slate of candidates nominated by one or both of the major parties in order to broaden their voter appeal. This is what happened in Cincinnati, where choice voting was used between 1926 and 1957. Both major parties began to nominate African Americans as part of their slates, and they were routinely elected to office for the first time. Studies have shown that in Cincinnati and other places where proportional representation have been used in the United States, it has produced fairer representation for racial and ethnic minorities.[1]

Better Representation of Women

Advocates of proportional representation maintain that it can result in fairer representation for women. They point out that the United States continues to lag far behind many other Western democracies in the number of women elected to our national legislature. As shown in Table 4.1, the percentage of women elected to the U.S. House of Representatives continues to hover around 13%, while in many other countries that figure for their lower houses is 20%, 30%, even 40%. Many factors affect the number of women elected in a country, including cultural attitudes toward the role of women in society and politics. But there is widespread agreement among scholars that voting methods are another key factor that affects the level of female representation in a political system.[2] And as Table 4.1 illustrates, countries using PR voting tend to elect more women than those using single-member plurality-majority systems.

Experts note that the clearest demonstration of the effect of voting systems on women's representation can be seen in countries like Germany and New Zealand that use the mixed-member form of proportional representation. Under this system, half of the members of the parliament are elected in single-member plurality districts and the other half chosen by party list proportional representation (this system is discussed further later). In the 1994 German election, the percentage of women elected in the single-member districts was 13%—about the same as in the United States—while the percentage elected from the party list PR contests was 39%. In New Zealand in 1999, those numbers were 24% for single-member district contests and 40% for party list PR.

What explains this effect? Scholars have found that many more women tend to be nominated in countries using PR voting, and the more women are nominated, the more they win office.[3] Instead of nominating one person per district, a slate of candidates is nominated in these multimember PR districts. In a five-member district, for example, each party nominates five candidates. If a party includes two women on their slate, and the party wins three seats, there is a good chance that at least one woman will be elected. If a party were to put only men on their slate, that would immediately be noticed. The party would be inviting charges of sexism and would risk alienating the feminist vote. So with PR voting there is some inherent pressure on the parties to nominate more women for office.

Another factor contributing to larger numbers of female representatives in PR countries is the use of quotas by some political parties. In Sweden, for example, several parties require that no less than 40% of the candidates on their slates be women. Some reformers have advocated similar quotas for United States parties, but this approach is not very practical in single-member district systems where candidates are nominated one at a time. Quotas work best in multimember district PR systems when candidates are nominated in slates.

Wider Range of Voter Choice

Because proportional representation encourages a multiparty system, it gives voters more choices at the polls than they would have in a two-party system. Minor party candidates become viable and realistic choices for voters because they stand a good chance of being elected. Most PR systems also give voters the opportunity to choose between different candidates of the same party. This enables them to choose someone who represents their wing of the party.

More Competitive Districts

One of the problems of single-member plurality voting is the proliferation of "safe seats"—districts where one party has such a large majority that other parties have virtually no chance of winning the seat. PR advocates argue that every multimember district is competitive because even parties in the minority are able to elect candidates. And if small parties increase their vote, they are able to take away seats from the larger parties. Also, it is not unusual for incumbents in safe seats to run uncontested. In 41.2% of the races for state legislative seats in 1998, one of the major parties in the district did not even bother to offer a candidate.[4] In multimember PR districts, there is never an uncontested election.

Critics point out that although it is true that many parties can win seats in multimember districts, "safe seats" do exist in this system. If, for instance, a large party consistently wins three or four seats in a ten-member district, at least the top two seats are "safe"—meaning that it is almost impossible for the party to lose them. The officials occupying those two seats are essentially immune to political competition, except from within their own parties.

More Representative Legislatures

Because of many of the factors already cited, the legislatures produced by proportional representation voting tend to be much more representative than those produced by plurality-majority voting. They are more representative ideologically because they include a wider variety of parties with more diverse ideological and policy perspectives. And they are more representative in terms of race and gender.

More Citizen Access to Representatives

PR proponents argue that these systems can improve constituency-representative relationships by encouraging greater access. They maintain that a significant number of voters in single-member districts are reluctant to approach an elected official of a different party, who they feel will not be sympathetic to their concerns. But in multimember districts, voters typically have access to representatives from several parties, and this makes it easier to find a sympathetic ear. Voters are thus more likely to seek help from those officials and to lobby them more actively concerning policy matters.

Virtually No Gerrymandering

By using large multimember districts, proportional representation reduces the importance of geographical lines and the incentive to gerrymander. Gerrymandering relies on the drawing of district lines so that particular parties waste their votes. For example, in a single-member plurality system, a district might be drawn where the Republicans have only 30% of the vote, all of which would be wasted on their losing candidate. But in a multimember PR district, a party that had only 30% of the vote would not be wasting its votes: It would win about 30% of the seats in the district. Since PR gives representation to minorities in districts, it becomes very difficult to create districts that deny fair representation to any significant political group.

However, critics point out that proportional representation does not completely eliminate the possibility of gerrymandering. Experience with choice voting in Ireland has shown that if the number of seats in a district is very small—with only three or four members elected—then some gerrymandering can take place. A three-member district has a threshold of 25%; that means that a party must get at least 25% of the vote to win a seat. So districts could be drawn where a particular party was supported by only 20% or less of the voters and those votes would be wasted. Noting this possibility, some political scientists have urged voting system designers to create PR districts with a minimum of five or six seats, which would virtually eliminate opportunities for gerrymandering.[5]

More Candor in Campaigns

Some proportional representation proponents argue that it can have a number of beneficial effects on campaigns. One claim is that PR voting allows candidates to be more honest with voters. In single-member plurality contests, candidates must woo large numbers of voters to win. If they widely publicize their stands on controversial issues such as gay rights or abortion, they risk alienating some of the potential supporters they need for victory. So the tendency is to concentrate on promoting a pleasing personal image rather than discussing difficult issues.

As proponents point out, under PR voting rules, candidates do not need to please most of the people most of the time to be elected. So being honest with the public might be less of a handicap. Candidates and parties could be candid about their stands on issues—even alienate many voters with their views—and still get elected.

More Policy Specifics in Multiparty Campaigns

Two-party systems make it easier for parties and candidates to be vague about their policy stands. They only need to give enough information to distinguish themselves from their single opponent. For example, in regard to the environment, Democratic candidates need say nothing more specific than that they support environmental protection more than their Republican opponents. But in multiparty contests, parties must give enough information to distinguish themselves from both parties on their Left and parties on their Right. So Democratic candidates would have to explain exactly how they differed from Republicans on the one hand, and Greens on the other hand. This would probably require them to become much more specific about exactly which environmental protection policies they supported and why. Do they support reductions in greenhouse gases? Which ones? By how much? On what timetable?

Less Negative Campaigns

The presence of multiple parties in elections might also serve to discourage overly negative campaigns. In two-party contests, fiercely negative campaigns can be very effective. For example, if a Republican candidate uses negative ads to disillusion the supporters of the Democratic candidate, those voters are likely either to switch to the Republican or simply not to vote—either of which works to the advantage of the Republican. But if there is a third-party candidate in the contest—let's say a centrist Reform party candidate—then smearing your opponent may not work as well. Even if the negative campaign alienates supporters from the Democrat, it may just drive them into the Reform candidate's camp, not the Republican's. So there may be less incentive to engage in this kind of campaign.

Greater Likelihood of Majority Rule

One of the central complaints about plurality-majority systems is the possibility of a party's winning a majority of the seats in the legislature while winning only a minority of the vote. As you saw in the last chapter, these manufactured majorities can occur relatively frequently in plurality-majority voting. In Great Britain, the Conservative party enjoyed large parliamentary majorities for almost twenty years, despite never having received more than 45% of the popular vote.

Proportional representation advocates argue that these manufactured majorities are a violation of the basic democratic principle of majority rule: They allow rule by a party that most voters voted against. They maintain that PR systems are much better at assuring that these manufactured majorities do not occur. Though not impossible in PR systems, this problem is much less likely to occur. The ruling majorities tend to be multiparty coalitions that do represent the majority of voters. One study found that manufactured majorities were relatively rare in PR elections, occurring only about 9% of the time. In contrast, 43.7% of the elections in countries using plurality-majority systems produced manufactured majorities.[6]

More Political Satisfaction

Proponents of proportional representation maintain that it increases public satisfaction with the political system. They point to surveys done in eighteen countries in 1995 and 1996 that asked citizens how satisfied they were with "the way democracy works" in their country. Countries with majoritarian political systems were compared to those with "consensus" political systems that are characterized by proportional representation, multiparty systems, coalition cabinets, strong bicameralism, and other several other features. The results showed that citizens in consensus systems were significantly more satisfied with the performance of democracy in their countries than those who lived in nations with majoritarian systems.[7] PR advocates argue that this finding is not surprising, considering that many more citizens are able to gain representation in these PR countries and the legislatures more accurately represent the variety of political opinions present among the public.

Higher Voter Turnout

As a rule, voter turnout is higher in countries that use proportional representation than in plurality-majority countries, as illustrated in Table 3.1 in the previous chapter. It is not unusual to see participation rates as high as 75% or even 85% in PR countries, in contrast to the 35%–50% rates typical in the United States. Many political factors affect turnout rates (such as registration methods and weekend voting) and voting systems only account for part of this difference. Nevertheless, political scientists have estimated that use of PR voting could increase turnout in the United States by 9%–12%—which would mean millions of more voters at the polls in national elections.[8]

The explanation for this higher turnout in PR systems may be found in many of the advantages already mentioned. Since multiparty systems offer voters more choices, they make it easier for voters to find a candidate or party they are really excited about. Also, with PR the votes that people cast are much more likely to be effective ones. Finally, under PR rules, all parties have a decent chance of winning seats in every district. And it makes a big difference whether a party gets 20% or 40% of the vote, because more votes means more seats. So there is more incentive to vote and parties try to mobilize their votes in all districts, not just a few.

Most critics of proportional representation do not dispute that it seems to have a positive effect on turnout, but a few question whether high turnout is necessarily a sign of a healthy democracy. They observe that we can find high voter turnout in countries like Indonesia and Albania, whose democratic credentials are highly suspect, and that some leading democracies such as the United States have low voter participation.[9]

Political Moderation

In plurality-majority systems, single-party majorities can lead to wide swings in policies, as a party of the Left alternates in power with a party of the Right. For example, in Great Britain during the 1970s, some observers complained about a lack of policy consistency caused by alternating Conservative and Labour party governments that often reversed the policies of their predecessors. According to PR proponents, multiparty majority coalitions tend to produce more moderate governments. Typically, coalitions include a centrist party so that they are of the center-Left or center-Right variety and thus tend to pursue a more middle-of-the-road policy agenda. In Great Britain, if Labour and Conservatives had been forced to rule in coalition with the centrist Liberal Democrats, they would have had to pursue more moderate policies.

GENERAL DISADVANTAGES

Unstable Coalitions and Legislative Gridlock

Probably the most common criticism of proportional representation is that as it increases the representativeness of government it also increases its instability. This accusation is based on the tendency of PR elections to produce multiparty legislatures. The more parties elected, the more likely it is that one party will not win the majority of seats and that the legislature will have to be ruled by a coalition of major and minor parties. Critics maintain that these multiparty coalitions may be quite fragile, breaking apart as a result of squabbles between the parties over policy issues. They often cite Italy, which was plagued for decades by coalitions that were continually falling apart and re-forming, as the classic case of this problem.

Proportional representation proponents have several responses to this criticism. First, they admit that multiparty majorities are somewhat more likely to break up than single-party majorities, but they argue that the instability of these coalitions has been greatly exaggerated by critics of PR.

They note that multiparty coalitions are usually quite stable, and that scholars have found no widespread or systematic evidence of persistent instability in countries that use proportional representation voting.[10] They maintain that if this problem were common, you would expect to see it in most countries that use proportional representation. But the record of PR use in dozens of European countries over many decades shows only a few instances—Italy is one of them—in which instability has been a serious problem. The vast majority of PR countries have enjoyed stable and efficient governments. Even though there have been several parties in these legislatures, in practice the parties have tended to form into two broad coalitions of the Left and the Right—and thus operate much like a two-party legislature. And once ruling coalitions are formed, there is a great deal of incentive to keep them together. These coalitions have usually lasted many years, and in some cases, decades. PR proponents point to a study that found that several PR countries have had governments that are actually as stable as, or more stable than, that of Great Britain, which has been ruled primarily by single-party majorities.[11]

Second, PR proponents argue that even if legislative coalitions were not perfectly stable in the United States, this would not be as large a problem here as it would be in a European country. Most European democracies are parliamentary systems in which the breakup of a legislative coalition often requires a reshuffling of the cabinet, or even the resignation of the prime minister and new elections. But this would not be the case in the United States, and so the problem of unstable coalitions is much less of a concern here.

Critics of PR maintain that there still is a concern because the presence of multiple parties and the potential for unstable coalitions would make it more difficult to pass bills in Congress. Having so many different parties increases the danger of creating legislative gridlock. But PR proponents note that gridlock has not been a common problem in the multiparty legislatures found in PR countries. They observe that the ruling coalitions in many of these European democracies have been so strong and disciplined that these parliaments passed legislation much more quickly and efficiently than our own Congress.

Finally, some proponents of PR maintain that even if there were some shifting of coalition partners in multiparty legislatures, this would be simply be business as usual in American politics. In Congress, for example, conservative Democrats sometimes break away from their party to join the Republicans to form a majority to pass a piece of legislation, and at other times moderate Republicans form coalitions with the Democrats. Thus the presence in PR legislatures of shifting coalitions around policy issues would not be all that different from the situation found in legislatures today.

Overly Stable Coalitions

Some critics maintain that the multiparty coalitions created by proportional representation may be too stable—that they are so persistent that it becomes difficult to throw a party out of power. One of the advantages of two-party systems and single-party majorities is that if the public becomes dissatisfied with the ruling party, they can easily throw them out of power by switching votes to the rival party. In PR systems, a party may lose favor with the public but continue in power as part of a coalition of parties. For example, voter support for the largest party in a ruling coalition may fall from 48% in one election to 38% in the next. Yet that party could easily remain as part of the ruling coalition along with another party that received 20% of the vote. Germany is sometimes cited as an example of an over-stable system. There the larger Christian Democrats and the smaller Free Democrats formed a ruling coalition that lasted almost two decades, from 1982 to 1998.

Critics of PR argue that one of the main purposes of democratic elections is to be able to "throw the bums out"—to make a clean break with a government that displeases the voters. PR voting can make that more difficult. As one critic observed, "What is really important is not to select a new government but to be able to oust an existing one."[12]

Advocates of PR reply, however, that it is not necessarily easy to "throw the bums out" in plurality-majority systems. The problem of manufactured majorities means that even when an electoral majority votes against it, the current government may continue in office. As one scholar has noted, in eight of the fourteen national elections in Great Britain between 1950 and 2000, the reigning party remained in power even after a majority of voters cast ballots against it.[13]

Too Much Power to Small Parties

In a multiparty system, a small party can be in a position to determine the composition of the ruling coalition. For example, if one large party wins 42% of the seats and another 38%, and a small party wins 20%, that gives the small party the balance of power and puts it in the position of "king-maker." It can decide which larger party it joins to form a legislative majority. Thus it can be a small party, not the voters, that really decides who wins the election. This is especially a problem when a small party bypasses the party that received the most votes to form a ruling coalition with the party that came in second place. Critics argue that it is arbitrary and undemocratic to exclude the most popular party from government.

Defenders of proportional representation acknowledge the potential for this problem to occur. But they argue that this possibility can be minimized if parties are pressured to announce before the election who their likely coalition partners will be, as already happens in some countries. They also note that it is rare for a small party to bypass the party with the most voter support when looking for a coalition partner: It happens only about 12% of the time. The smaller party almost always forms a coalition with the most popular large party, and in this sense it is following, not frustrating, the public will.

Too Many Concessions to Small Parties

A related concern about small parties is that they are able to exercise undo power in the ruling coalitions. Critics fear that these small parties can use their leverage to wring concessions from their larger coalition partners, perhaps causing the adoption of radical policies not supported by most voters. In Israel, for example, small ultrareligious parties have sometimes won support for some of their policy proposals by threatening to pull out of the ruling coalition.

Proportional representation proponents argue that in most cases there is nothing wrong with smaller parties' having some influence over the coalition's agenda. Indeed, that is part of the point of power-sharing coalitions—they pursue a mixture of policies that represent the interests of voters who supported those parties. In addition, the record of PR use in European democracies provides very few examples of small parties' acting as "the tail that wags the dog."

Spotlight on the Debate 4.2
Would Proportional Representation Balkanize American Politics?

Many critics of proportional representation are concerned that it will increase political conflict—that the proliferation of different political parties would balkanize American politics, further fragmenting our society into warring political factions. Given the serious political, racial, religious, and economic divisions that already exist in our society, what we need is a political system that brings us together, not one that splits us apart. Whereas our two large umbrella parties do bring different political factions together to negotiate and compromise, a multiparty PR system would divide people into smaller parties and further entrench our political divisions.

PR proponents argue that multiparty systems also encourage dialogue and negotiation; they simply do it at a different point in the election process. In a two-party system, negotiations usually take place *before* the elections. During party conventions and primaries, the various groups in umbrella parties try to settle their differences and build an electoral coalition. In a multiparty PR system, the political bargaining takes place in the legislature *after* the election. After the various political groups elect their representatives, then they engage in negotiation and coalition building. A study of PR use in five Ohio cities found "no systematic evidence of greater dissension on PR-elected councils compared to councils elected by other methods."[14] The multiparty legislative coalitions typical of PR systems may actually require parties to be more co-operative and less adversarial in their relationships.

Proponents also note that overseas PR voting is often seen as the best system for societies with deep and even violent political divisions. Two countries, Northern Ireland and South Africa, have chosen to use PR voting, in part because the fair representation of all factions in the legislatures is seen as an essential element in promoting increased political stability and integration.

More Expensive Campaigns

The larger size of districts used in proportional representation may increase the costs of campaigns. Consider elections for a city council. With single-member district voting, the candidates' campaigns only have to cover one district. But if all the candidates ran in one large citywide PR district, they would have to reach many more voters in their campaigns.

PR proponents respond by observing that because candidates can be elected with a smaller percentage of the vote—say, 10% or 20%—their campaigns don't have to try to reach all the voters. They can target their campaigns toward their likely supporters and this strategy may keep costs lower.

Poor Geographical Representation

Critics often argue that the much larger multimember districts used in proportional representation produce poor geographical representation. In Israel and the Netherlands, for instance, the entire country is one district and legislators are elected from national lists. In this situation, it is possible that some local areas may not end up with a representative to fight for their regional interests.

PR proponents admit that this problem can occur at times but maintain that it is largely limited to one form of PR: the particular party list system used in Israel and the Netherlands. Most other countries that have party list voting use regional lists in order to assure that representatives come from all geographical areas of the nation. Other forms of PR use different approaches to solving this problem. The mixed-member form of PR elects half of the legislature from small local districts in order to ensure good geographical representation. Choice voting typically uses relatively small multimember districts to achieve the same goal. Also, this system enables voters to cast votes for candidates from their local areas if geographical representation is an important concern.

Weak Constituency-Representative Ties

Critics also are concerned that the larger districts used in PR will undermine the intimate relationship that exists between constituents and representatives in small single-member districts. PR districts are so large that access and communication could become a problem.

As noted in the earlier discussion of the advantages of PR, defenders argue that multimember districts actually encourage more communication between constituents and representatives. Because local voters have access to representatives from several parties, they are more likely to find an official that will give them a sympathetic hearing.

Less Resistance to Extremism

Because proportional representation makes it easier for small parties to get elected, it also makes it easier for extremist parties to run candidates and elect some of them to office. Critics of PR argue that this situation serves to encourage these parties and give them the opportunity to spread their ideology and recruit more followers. (For a more extended treatment of this charge and the responses to it, see Spotlight on the Debate 4.3: Does PR Encourage Extremism?)

Spotlight on the Debate 4.3
Does Proportional Representation Encourage Extremism?

A common accusation against proportional representation is that it encourages extremism. Critics charge that extremist parties of the Left and Right can find a friendly environment in PR voting. As evidence of this, they often cite the rise of the Nazi party in Germany. The proportional representation system used in Weimar Germany allowed the small Nazi party to get a toehold in the political system, and it eventually used that to increase its popularity and take power. Would we want something similar to happen in the United States?

Proportional representation proponents argue that using the rise of the Nazis to condemn PR is simplistic and misleading. They point out that the rapid growth of the Nazi party in the 1930s is widely acknowledged to have been due to a complex combination of factors, primary among them the economic depression of that time and the association of the Weimar Republic with Germany's defeat in World War I. Given these conditions, the appeal of the Nazi party was strong and its power would have grown irrespective of what voting method was used.[15] Adding support to this interpretation of the German situation is the fact that many other European countries during the time were also using PR voting systems and did not produce fascist governments.

However, critics maintain that it cannot be denied that the low thresholds of proportional representation make it easier for small extremist parties to get elected, and that one of the advantages of plurality-majority voting is that its high threshold makes it more difficult for extremists to win office.

Proponents usually grant this point, but they also argue that this worry about extremism is greatly exaggerated. First, they charge that critics are ignoring a great deal of systematic evidence. The overall record of PR use in

Western democracies shows that extremism has not been a problem. Most European countries have been using PR during the last fifty years and have not been plagued by extremist parties. This is largely because the threshold levels in most of these countries have been set high enough—as in the 5% level in Germany—to make it difficult for these very small parties to win any seats.

Secondly, they argue that even if an extremist group elected a few members to a legislature, it would not be a political disaster—it might even have some benefits. Extending political representation to these groups can have a moderating and co-opting effect. If these groups feel that they have some voice in the political system, their sense of political alienation could decrease, making them less likely to employ violence or other undesirable means to attract attention to their views. A recent study of voting systems in other countries found that the use of proportional representation has discouraged discontented ethnic groups from "engaging in extreme forms of resistance to the status quo."[16]

Greater Administrative Expense and Complexity

Finally, some critics charge that adopting proportional representation in the United States would make administering elections much more difficult and expensive. Election officials would have to learn new vote-counting methods and seat allocation formulas. And in some cases, expensive new voting machines would have to be purchased to accommodate the new voting techniques.

Defenders respond that election administrators in countries that use PR have had no problems mastering the vote-counting and seat allocation processes. So that should not be a problem in the United States. Moreover, most PR systems can be used with existing voting machines; the single transferable vote is the possible exception.

PARTY LIST VOTING

The origins of party list proportional representation can be traced to the mid-nineteenth century. Its invention is usually associated with several people: Victor d'Hondt of Belgium, Eduard Hagenbach-Bischoff of Switzerland, and A. Sainte-Lagüe of France. Political momentum for this system began to develop after a conference of electoral reform activists in Antwerp in 1885 chose d'Hondt's party list system as the best voting method. By the 1920s almost all European democracies were using some version of the party list vote. Today party list systems are by far the most common form of proportional representation. Over 80% of the PR systems used worldwide are some form of party list voting. It remains the system used in most European democracies and in many newly democratized countries, including South Africa.

Ballot 4.1
Closed Party List Voting

Official Ballot
Election for the United States House of Representatives
District One

Voting Instructions
1. You only have ONE vote.
2. Place an X in the box UNDER the party for whom you wish to vote.

Democratic	Republican	Reform	Green	Independent Candidate
☐	☐	☐	☐	☐
1. Benjamin Foster	1. Wendy Berg	1. Steven Wong	1. Tom Wartenberg	1. Robert Moll
2. Sam Rosen-Amy	2. Steve Grolnic	2. Deborah Gorlin	2. Juan Hernandez	
3. Colin Volz	3. Sarah McClurg	3. Brad Crenshaw	3. Beata Panagopoules	
4. Benjamin Pike	4. Gerald Epstein	4. Daniel Czitrom	4. Alice Morey	
5. Megan Gentzler	5. Fran Deutsch	5. Meryl Fingrutd	5. Sarah Pringle	

How It Works

Legislators are elected in large, multimember districts. Each party puts
up a list or slate of candidates equal to the number of seats in the district.
Independent candidates may also run, and they are listed separately on the
ballot as if they were their own party (see Ballot 4.1). On the ballot, voters
indicate their preference for a particular party and the parties then receive
seats in proportion to their share of the vote. So in a five-member district,
if the Democrats win 40% of the vote, they would win two of the five
seats. The two winning Democratic candidates would be chosen according
to their position on the list.

There are two broad types of list system: closed list and open list. In a
closed list system—the original form of party list voting—the party fixes
the order in which the candidates are listed and elected, and the voter
simply casts a vote for the party as a whole. This is shown in Ballot 4.1,
which illustrates an election for the House of Representatives in a five-seat
district. Voters are not able to indicate their preference for any candidates
on the list but must accept the list in the order presented by the party.
Winning candidates are selected in the exact order they appear on the original list. So in the example here, if the Democrats won two seats, the first
two candidates on the preordered list—Foster and Rosen-Amy—would be
elected.

Most European democracies now use the open list form of party list
voting. This approach allows voters to express a preference for particular
candidates, not just parties. It is designed to give voters some say over the

Ballot 4.2
Open Party List Voting

Official Ballot
Election for the United States House of Representatives
District One

Voting Instructions
1. You only have ONE vote.
2. Place an X in the box next to the candidate for whom you wish to vote.
3. Your vote counts both for your candidate and your party.

Democratic	Republican	Reform	Green	Independent Candidate
Benjamin Pike	Fran Deutsch	Steven Wong	Tom Wartenberg	Robert Moll
Sam Rosen-Amy	Steve Grolnic	Deborah Gorlin	Juan Hernandez	
Megan Gentzler	Wendy Berg	Brad Crenshaw	Beata Panagopoules	
Ben Foster	Gerald Epstein	Daniel Czitrom	Alice Morey	
Colin Volz	Sarah McClurg	Meryl Fingrutd	Sarah Pringle	

order of the list and thus which candidates get elected. One version of this is illustrated in Ballot 4.2. Voters are presented with unordered or random lists of candidates chosen in party primaries. Voters cannot vote for a party directly but must cast a vote for an individual candidate. This vote counts for the specific candidate as well as for the party. So the order of the final list completely depends on the number of votes won by each candidate on the list. The most popular candidates rise to the top of the list and have a better chance of being elected. In our example, if the Democrats won two seats, and Volz and Gentzler received the highest number of individual votes, they would rise to the top of the list and be elected. This example is similar to the system used in Finland and widely considered to be the most open version of list voting. Some less open systems allow voters the additional option of simply voting for an entire list that has been preordered by the party; that means that votes for individual candidates have less impact on the final order.

There are other ways that list systems may vary, besides being open or closed. For example, some list systems elect candidates from regional district lists (Finland), national lists (Netherlands), or both regional and national lists (South Africa). Also, a variety of different formulas exist for accomplishing the actual allocation of seats to the parties. Some of these may give a slight advantage to either large or small parties, and they are described in Appendix A. But let's take a look at one of them right now, so that you may get an idea of how they work.

One of the simplest seat allocation formulas is the *largest remainder formula*. In this approach, the first step is to calculate a quota, which is determined by taking the total number of valid votes in the district and dividing this by the number of seats. In the example in Table 4.2, 100,000

Table 4.2
Seat Allocation Using Largest Remainder Formula

Parties	Votes	First Allocation Of Seats	Remaining Votes	Second Allocation of Seats	Final Seat Total	% of Vote to % of Seats
Republican	38,000	3	**8,000**	1	4	38% / 40%
Democratic	23,000	2	3,000	0	2	23% / 20%
Reform	21,000	2	1,000	0	2	21% / 20%
Green	12,000	1	2,000	0	1	12% / 10%
Moll	6,000	0	**6,000**	1	1	6% / 10%

votes were cast and 10 seats are to be filled: 100,000/10 = 10,000—which is the quota. The quota is then divided into the vote that each party receives and the party wins 1 seat for each whole number produced. So the Republican party received 38,000 votes, which is divided by 10,000 to produce 3 seats—with a remainder of 8,000. After this first allocation of seats is complete, the remainder numbers for the parties are compared and the parties with the largest remainders are allocated the remaining seats. In our example, two seats remain to be allocated and the Republicans and Moll, the independent candidate, have the largest remainders, so they get the seats. Ultimately all the parties end up with the number of seats that as closely as possible approximates their percentage of the vote.

Advantages Specific to this System

Highly Proportional

Party list proportional representation tends to be the best system for producing proportional results for political parties. Such systems are very accurate in giving parties the number of seats in the legislature that reflects their voting strength. In part this is because these systems tend to use districts with large numbers of seats. The more seats contested in a district, the easier it is to allocate them proportionately among the parties. For this reason, party list voting tends to be more proportional than choice voting, which typically uses much smaller districts. A few party list countries, for example, the Netherlands and Israel, take large districts to the extreme and have made the entire country into one large district from which all the members of the legislature are elected.

More Party-Oriented and Issue-Oriented Campaigns

Since this is a party-centered voting system, it has an effect on the style of election campaigns. In single-member district plurality elections, the emphasis on campaigns tends to be on the individual candidate, and the focus is often on their personal strengths and weaknesses. In party list systems, campaigns become more centered around the parties and their platforms. In European campaigns, for instance, candidates are more likely to say, "Vote for my party and its policies," than "Vote for me." For this reason the focus of the candidates and the press is more on the issues and the ways parties differ on them.

Greater Diversity of Candidates in Closed Lists

Closed list systems allow parties to include a diverse range of candidates on their slates, in terms of ethnicity, gender, or other factors. This ensures a diversity of representation even if that is not a concern of voters. For example, a party could balance its slate with men and women in alternate positions so that equal gender representation would be encouraged, despite any sexism among voters. In South African elections, race is obviously an issue, and so several parties, including the African National Congress, included black, white, coloured, and Indian candidates on their closed lists.

Increased Voter Power in Open Lists

Open lists tend to take power away from parties and give it to voters. Voters have more influence over who actually gets elected. Some argue that it allows voters to encourage more diverse representation when parties fail to provide leadership in this area. In some Scandinavian countries, for example, feminist voters have been able to vote for female candidates and help them to get elected even when it has not been a high priority for a particular party. But for this to work, the systems must be as open as possible—the ideal is the unordered list used in the Finnish system, in which the votes for individual candidates completely determine the final order of the list.

Disadvantages Specific to This System

Weak Constituent-Representative Ties

Because party list systems tend to have the largest districts, they also more actively undermine the traditional geographical link between constituents and their representatives—especially when compared to the mixed-member and single transferable vote versions of PR. This tendency is accentuated in the few small countries like Israel where the entire nation is one large district and there are no regional districts. In these systems there is not even a pretense of officials' representing particular geographical constituencies and the relationship between voters and individual representatives becomes more amorphous. This may be less of a problem in systems that use regional lists.

Too Much Power to Parties in Closed Lists

Advocates of open lists argue that closed lists give too much power to parties to determine which candidates are elected. Since voters have no say in the order of the list, parties are in a position to dictate who represents the voters.

Destructive Intraparty Rivalries in Open Lists

Critics of open lists argue that they pit candidates of the same party against each other in destructive ways. Instead of campaigning only against the other parties, candidates may also campaign against their rivals in their own parties. This process can undermine party unity and discipline and thus decrease the political effectiveness of the party.

MIXED-MEMBER PROPORTIONAL VOTING

Mixed-member proportional representation goes by a variety of other names, including *the additional member system, compensatory PR, the two-vote system,* and *the German system.* It is an attempt to combine a single-member district system with a proportional voting system. Half of the members of the legislature are elected in single-member district plurality contests. The other half are elected by a party list vote and added on to the district members so that each party has its appropriate share of seats in the legislature. Proponents claim that mixed-member proportional voting (MMP) is the best of both worlds: providing the geographical representation and close constituency ties of single-member plurality voting along with the fairness and diversity of representation associated with PR voting.

At first glance, MMP looks like a system dreamed up by a British election system designer living in Europe who wanted to combine the English tradition of single-member districts with the party list system used in his new home. And in fact, that is not far from the truth. At the end of World War II, the British occupied a portion of West Germany. During that time they introduced the Germans in their zone to the benefits of the British voting system. These British-imposed experiments with single-member districts had an influence when the German parties sat down in 1949 to design the electoral system for their new democracy. Some parties favored PR, others wanted the British system, and they eventually compromised by creating this hybrid voting mechanism.

For a long time West Germany was the only country using mixed-member proportional representation, but it has also been adopted in Bolivia and Venezuela. It is still one of the least used PR systems, but in recent years it has begun to garner a great deal of attention. In fact, it is now one of the "hottest" systems being considered by those involved in electoral

Ballot 4.3
Mixed-Member Proportional Representation Voting

Official Ballot
Election for the United States House of Representatives
District One

You Have 2 Votes

District Vote	Party Vote
This vote decides who will be elected to the House of Representatives from this district. Vote by putting an "X" in the box immediately before the candidate you choose. Vote for only one candidate.	This vote decides the share of seats that each of the parties listed below will have in the House of Representatives. Vote by putting an "X" in the box immediately before the party you choose. Vote for only one party.

⌐—— Vote Here	⌐—— Vote Here
Fred Smith Republican	Republican Party Kim, Dirks, Case, Packard, Deutsch
Damon Washington Democrat	Democratic Party Matteo, Myers, Lee, Bork, Gorr
Cheryl Houston New Party	The New Party Morkarski, Pine, Lebaro, Fletcher, Devino
Naomi Lintz US Taxpayers	US Taxpayers Daves, Chevalier, Brown, Noyes, Parker
John Henderson Independent	
Write In	

---

design. In part this growing attention is a result of MMP's unique claim to be a "compromise" between the two main rival systems. In the 1990s New Zealand abandoned its traditional single-member plurality system for MMP. Hungary also adopted this approach. Most recently, the newly formed parliaments of Scotland and Wales used it for their first elections.

How It Works

People cast votes on a double ballot (see Ballot 4.3). First, on the left part of the ballot, they vote for a district representative. This part of the ballot is a single-member district plurality contest to see which person will represent the district in the legislature. The person with the most votes wins.

Table 4.3
Voting Results and Seat Allocations in Mixed-Member Voting

Political Parties	Number of District Seats Won	Percentage of the National Party List Vote	Total Number of Seats Deserved by Party	Number of Seats Added from Party Lists
Democratic	28	40%	40	12
Republican	18	36%	36	18
U.S. Taxpayers	4	18%	18	14
New Party	0	6%	6	6
Totals	50	100%	100	50

Typically half of the seats in the legislature are filled in this way. So in a hypothetical 100-member state legislature, the winners of these district contests would occupy 50 of the seats.

On the right part of the ballot—the party list portion—voters indicate their choice among the parties, and the other half of the seats in the legislature are filled from regional lists of candidates chosen by these parties. The party lists are closed in the German version. These party list votes are counted on a national basis to determine the total portion of the 100-seat legislature that each party deserves. Candidates from each party's lists are then added to its district winners until that party achieves its appropriate share of seats. Table 4.3 illustrates how this process works for our hypothetical election. The Democrats won 40% of the party list votes in the 100-member state legislature, so they would be entitled to a total of 40 of the 100 seats. Since they already elected 28 of their candidates in district elections, the Democrats would then add 12 more from their regional party lists to come up to their quota of 40 seats.

In the German version two electoral thresholds are used, either of which a party must overcome to be allotted seats in the legislature. A party must either get 5% of the nationwide party list vote or win at least three district races to gain any seats in the legislature. In our hypothetical case, the New Party did not win any district seats, but they did win over 5% of the nationwide vote, so they deserve their share of legislative seats—which in this case would be six seats, all of which would be filled from the regional party lists.

It is possible, though not usual, in this system for a party to win more seats in the district contests than it deserves based on its portion of the party list vote. Let's say, for example, that the Democrats won forty-one of the district seats, but they received only 40% of the party list vote. In these cases, the parties are allowed to keep all the seats they won on the district level, and the size of the legislature is enlarged temporarily until the next election. In our case, the legislature would temporarily have 101 seats.

Many variations of the mixed-member system are possible. Another single-member district system, such as instant runoff voting, could be used instead of plurality voting for the district seats. The party lists could be open instead of closed. Party list members could be selected from a national list instead of regional lists. Different threshold levels could be used. You could also change the percentage of seats determined by each side of the ballot. Scholars have calculated that the top-off seats from the party list could be as little as 25% of the total seats in the legislature and you would still have enough of them to ensure that the parties would be represented proportionally in the legislature.

Advantages Specific to This System

Geographical Representation

Unlike party list proportional representation, MMP ensures local geographical representation. The use of many relatively small single-member districts means that all geographical areas will have at least one representative promoting their interests in the legislature.

Close Constituency Ties

Small geographical districts also encourage close ties between representatives and their constituents. Officials are able to get to know their constituents. And since it is clear which representative is obliged to serve which constituents, people readily know whom to contact about their concerns.

Better Expression of Political Views

Having two different votes allows voters to express more complicated political views. For example, voters may split their votes as a way of expressing their support for a particular coalition of parties. Supporters of the Greens would cast their party list vote for their own party to ensure that it wins some seats in the legislature. Then in the district contest, they might cast their other vote for the major party candidate who has the best chance to win and is closest to their political perspective—probably the Democratic candidate. In this way, they would effectively express their preference for a coalition of Greens and Democrats.

Disadvantages Specific to This System

Two Classes of Representatives

MMP creates two distinct classes of legislators: those who represent specific geographical constituencies and those who represent the parties. This means that some representatives will have close local ties and spend part of their time on constituency service, and others will not. In addition, most or all of the representatives of smaller parties will often be chosen from the party list portion of the ballot. Critics suggest that this lack of geographical ties could insulate these officials from public opinion and give them a lighter workload.

Advocates of MMP point out, however, that there is nothing to prevent party list representatives from opening one or more local offices and making themselves available to local constituents. This could create even more opportunities for close ties between constituents and officials. Advocates also point out that many American cities already have two kinds of city councilors—those elected in districts and those elected at large—and there are rarely any complaints about this arrangement.

Bias toward Large Parties in Districts

Use of single-member district plurality voting has some of the common disadvantages of that system. One of them is the tendency for the candidates of the larger parties to be favored in the district contests. These are the only candidates who stand a realistic chance of getting the plurality of votes necessary to win these seats.

Some Discouragement of Sincere Votes

Plurality voting in districts also discourages supporters of minor party candidates from casting sincere votes. They are usually forced to vote for the next-best major party candidate; otherwise they would be wasting their vote.

Violations of Majority Rule

As in any plurality voting system, the district representative in MMP may win with less than a majority of the vote. So an official whom most people voted against may represent a district. Hungary has avoided this problem by using a majority system for its district contests: two-round runoff voting.

Gerrymandering

Some critics of MMP point out that the retention of single-member districts means that gerrymandering can easily take place in this system. District lines can be manipulated to unfairly favor the candidates of a particular party. MMP defenders acknowledge this possibility but point out that gerrymandering in this system cannot give a party more than its fair share of seats in the legislature—as can often happen in pure single-member plurality systems. The PR component of this system guarantees that despite whoever wins on the district level, the parties will still get their fair share of seats on the national level. For this reason, gerrymandering is less of a concern in this system.

Spotlight on the Debate 4.4
Would PR Hurt the Democrats and Republicans?

Advocates of proportional representation often argue that adopting this system in the United States would be good for both minor and major parties, ensuring all of them fair and accurate representation. But many critics scoff at this contention and maintain that proportional representation would be bad for the Republican and Democratic parties. It would encourage the creation of minor parties that would try to steal supporters away from the major parties. And it would allow disgruntled factions within the major parties to split away and form their own parties. Right now that is unlikely because minor parties stand so little chance of electoral success. For all of these reasons, PR would work against the interests of these major parties.

Proportional representation proponents argue that this system would actually help many Republican and Democratic voters by assuring them of representation, which is often not the case in single-member plurality elections. Currently, Democrats living in predominantly Republican areas have little chance to win representation, and vice versa. Almost all the wasted votes cast in the United States are cast by supporters of the major parties—not supporters of minor parties.

In addition, proponents suggest that losing some voters to minor parties would not necessarily be a disaster for the major parties. For one thing, the defection of dissatisfied party members would cut down significantly on the internal conflicts that often plague these parties now. Perhaps more importantly, these defections might in a sense only be "temporary." Even if, for instance, a Christian Coalition party broke off from the Republican party, these parties would come together again in the legislature as natural allies, joining their conservative forces in legislative battles with the Left.

Nevertheless, critics respond, you cannot ignore the fact that adopting PR would tend to encourage a multiparty system. This would inevitably cut into the support for the Republican and Democratic parties and thus undermine their current dominant position in the political system.

SINGLE TRANSFERABLE VOTE OR CHOICE VOTING

This system of proportional representation is known by several names. Political scientists call it the *single transferable vote*. It is called the *Hare-Clark system* in Australia. In the United States, electoral reform activists have taken to calling it *choice voting*, a term I also use at times.

The single transferable vote (STV) was invented in the mid-nineteenth century by two men working completely independently of each other: Thomas Hare, an English lawyer; and Carl Andrae, a Danish politician and mathematician. In England, the philosopher John Stuart Mill picked up on Hare's system and worked to popularize it. Following in this intellectual tradition, choice voting continues to be the favorite voting system of many electoral scholars. Many believe that it is the approach that best maximizes voter choice, effective votes, constituency ties, and fair representation of parties.

Currently this system is used to elect parliaments in Ireland and Malta. In Australia it is used to elect the federal Senate, as well as the legislatures in several states there. It is also the PR system that was used in a number of cities in the United States during the twentieth century, including New York, Cincinnati, Cleveland, Toledo, and Boulder. It continues to be used today in Cambridge, Massachusetts, for elections to their city council and school board. (For a history of this system in the United States, see Appendix B.)

How It Works

The voting process is illustrated by Ballot 4.4. All candidates are listed in the same place on the ballot. Instead of voting for one person, voters rank each candidate in their order of preference. So if you like Campbell best, you mark the 1 after his name; if you like Gomez second best, you mark 2 by his name, and so on. You can rank as few or as many you want. This ballot illustrates the AccuVote system used in Cambridge, Massachusetts, to elect its city council and school board. Voters fill in the ranking numbers as they would for standardized tests taken in school, to allow for computerized vote counting and ballot transfers.

You may have noticed that the ranking process in the single transferable vote is identical to that used in the instant runoff voting system described in the previous chapter. Like IRV, choice voting involves some transfer of votes in the counting process, though it is a bit more complicated in this system. To understand how the transfer process works, it may be best to start out with a simple analogy. Imagine a school where a class is trying to elect a committee. Any student who wishes to run stands at the front of the class and the other students vote for their favorite candidates by standing beside them. Students standing almost alone next to their candidate will soon discover that this person has no chance of being elected and move to another candidate of their choice to help him or her get elected. Some of the students standing next to a very popular candidate may realize that this person has more than enough support to win and decide to go stand next to another student whom they would also like to see on the committee. In the end, after all of this shuffling around, most students will be standing

Ballot 4.4
Single Transferable Vote (Choice Vote)

<table>
<tr><td colspan="3" align="center">Official Ballot
Municipal Elections</td></tr>
<tr>
<td>INSTRUCTIONS TO VOTERS

Mark Your Choices by Filling in the Numbered Boxes Only

Fill in the number one [1] box next to your first choice; fill in the number two [2] box next to your second choice; fill in the number three [3] box next to your third choice, and so on. You may fill in as many choices as you please. Fill in no more than one box per candidate. Fill in no more than one box per column.</td>
<td>Candidates for City Council District One
(Three to be elected.)

Douglas Campbell   Dem.

Martha Dains   Rep.

Terry Graybeal   Reform

Robert Gomez   Dem.

Cynthia Daniels   Indep.

Robert Higgins   Rep.

Write In

Write In

Write In</td>
<td>Only one vote per candidate

Only one vote per column

[1] [2] [3] [4] [5] [6] [7] [8] [9]

[1] [2] [3] [4] [5] [6] [7] [8] [9]

[1] [2] [3] [4] [5] [6] [7] [8] [9]

[1] [2] [3] [4] [5] [6] [7] [8] [9]

[1] [2] [3] [4] [5] [6] [7] [8] [9]

[1] [2] [3] [4] [5] [6] [7] [8] [9]

[1] [2] [3] [4] [5] [6] [7] [8] [9]

[1] [2] [3] [4] [5] [6] [7] [8] [9]

[1] [2] [3] [4] [5] [6] [7] [8] [9]</td>
</tr>
</table>

next to candidates who will be elected, and that is the ultimate point of this process.

In the single transferable vote, votes are transferred around just as the students move from candidate to candidate in the analogy. The exact order of the transfer process is illustrated in Figure 4.4. An example of how the votes are actually transferred is shown in Table 4.4. For the sake of simplicity, assume that there is a three-seat district in which six people are running for office. The first step in the process is to establish the threshold: the minimum number of votes necessary to win a seat. The threshold usually consists of the total number of valid votes divided by 1 plus the number of seats to be filled, plus 1 vote. The formula looks like this: Threshold = (valid votes/1 + seats) + 1 vote. So in our 3-seat districts with 10,000 voters, a candidate would need 10,000/1 + 3 (which is 2,500) plus 1 more vote, for 2,501. (You may notice that given this formula, the more seats in a district, the lower the threshold and the easier it is to get elected. In a 9-seat district with 10,000 voters, for instance, the calculation is 10,000/1 + 9, plus 1 vote, for a threshold of 1,001—considerably lower than in a 3-seat district.)

Figure 4.4
Diagram of STV Vote Counting Procedures

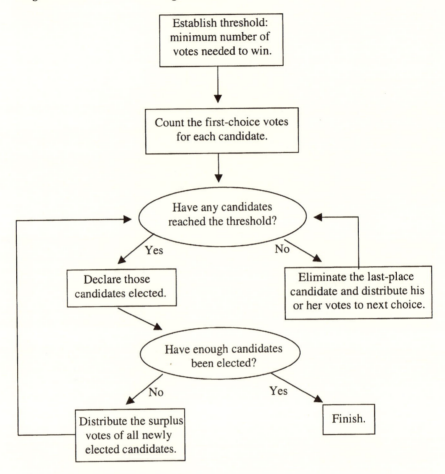

The second step is to count all the number-one choices to see whether any candidates have reached the threshold of 2,501. In this case, the Democrat Gomez has 2,900 votes and he is declared elected. But Gomez actually has 399 more votes than he needs to win. These votes are considered wasted if they stay with Gomez, so they are transferred to the second choices on the ballot. (There are several different ways to make this transfer, which are described in Appendix E.) In the second count, we see the effect of this transfer. The other Democratic candidate, Campbell, gets 300 of those second-choice votes, and the independent candidate, Daniels, gets the other 99. The vote totals are now recalculated to see whether anyone is now over the threshold. No one is, so the next transfer takes place. The candidate with the least chance to win is eliminated and his or her votes

Table 4.4
Counting of a Single Transferable Vote Election

Candidates	1st Count Number Of Votes	2nd Count Transfer of Gomez's votes and results	3rd Count Transfer of Higgins' votes and results	4th Count Transfer of Dains' votes and results	5th Count Transfer of Campbell's votes and results
Douglas Campbell (Dem.)	400	+300 700	700	700	--
Martha Dains* (Rep.)	2,300	2,300	+500 2,800	2,501	2,501
Terry Graybeal (Reform)	2,000	2,000	2,000	+200 2,200	+100 2,300
Robert Gomez* (Dem.)	2,900	2,501	2,501	2,501	2,501
Cynthia Daniels* (Ind.)	1,800	+99 1,899	+100 1,999	+99 2,098	+600 2,698
Robert Higgins (Rep.)	600	600	---	---	---

*Winning candidates.

are transferred to the voters' second choices. This candidate is Higgins, the Republican, and 500 of his votes are transferred to the other Republican candidate, Dains; the other 100 votes are given to Daniels. Again the votes are recounted to see whether anyone has reached the threshold. Dains has reached it with 2,800 votes, so she is declared elected. Once again her excess votes are redistributed to the voters' second choices—200 to Graybeal and 99 to Daniels. But still no one has reached the threshold, so again the lowest candidate is eliminated and those votes transferred. That candidate is Campbell, the Democrat, and 100 of his votes go to Graybeal, and 600 go to Daniels. This puts Daniels, the independent candidate, over the threshold with 2,698 votes, and she is the last one elected.

Even advocates admit that this transfer process is a bit complicated, so why does it exist? The transfer process was invented primarily to reduce the problem of wasted votes. As you saw in the last chapter, plurality-majority systems routinely waste large numbers of votes and this is why they are prone to such problems as party misrepresentation, minority rule, gerrymandering, and spoilers. The transfer process in STV is designed to ensure that the fewest votes are wasted and that the maximum number of people gets to elect a representative to office. It acknowledges that there are two kinds of wasted votes: votes for candidates who stand little chance of winning and votes in excess of what a winning candidate needs. Transferring these votes to the next-ranked choice makes it more likely that they will actually contribute to the election of a candidate.

Transferring votes also produces other effects. It eliminates spoilers and allows voters to cast their votes sincerely for the candidates they most prefer. If their first-choice candidate cannot win, then their vote will likely be transferred to someone who can win. Transferring votes also increases the accuracy of party representation. In choice voting, parties tend to win close to their fair share of representation, especially if voters tend to stick to one party in their ranking of preferences.

Advantages Specific to This System

Maximum Voter Choice

One of the central strengths of choice voting is that the ranking process maximizes voter choice. First, unlike in closed party list voting or single-member district voting, the voter can choose among several candidates of the same party. Voters are thus able to help elect members of the factions of parties that best represent their political views. So, for example, a Republican voter could choose to be represented by either a moderate or a conservative Republican. This puts more power in the hands of voters and less in the hands of the party.

Second, unlike some other voting systems, choice voting allows voters to cross party lines with their rankings. So a Democratic voter might rank a Democratic candidate first but then give her number-two ranking to a female Republican candidate she particularly likes.

Voting for Candidates, Not Parties

Under this system, citizens vote for and elect every single legislator. This means that no officials win office simply by being a part of a party list. STV advocates argue that this fact makes officials more directly accountable to the voters. They also maintain that many so-called open list versions of party list voting do not have much of an effect on the original order of the list determined by the party.

Usable in Nonpartisan Elections

Some local areas in the United States like to use nonpartisan elections where candidates appear on the ballot without any party designation. It would be impossible to use party list or MMP voting in this context because they require that candidates be listed by party. But the single transferable vote can be easily used in nonpartisan elections, since the candidates can be listed with or without their party affiliation.

All Representatives from Districts

As seen earlier, one of the criticisms of mixed-member proportional voting is that it creates two separate kinds of representatives: those who represent local constituencies and those who represent parties. Choice voting prevents this problem. All representatives are district representatives, so they are accountable to specific regions and groups of voters. All representatives also have the incentive to provide good constituency service.

Close Constituency Ties

A common criticism of PR is that its larger districts undermine the close relationship between constituents and their representatives. Advocates of choice voting argue that this form of PR usually uses relatively small districts, and that it actually works to improve constituency-representative relationships. Virtually all voters will have a representative whom they helped to elect and who will be sympathetic to their political concerns. In many cases, they will even have more than one representative from their party in their district, and there is an incentive for these officials to compete to provide constituency service.

Some critics have maintained that there may be too much incentive for constituency service in this system—that it creates an "excessive localism" in which rival representatives in a district may spend too much time trying to ensure that their local constituents will support them in the next election. They point to the case of Ireland, where parliamentary officials are sometimes accused of spending the bulk of their time servicing constituency needs to the neglect of the larger national issues that need attention.

Basis of Representation Determined by Voters

In single-member district voting, constituencies are defined by geography. People are represented on the basis of where they live. These plurality-majority systems assume that geographical representation is what is most important to voters, and they are designed to ensure that all voters have a representative from their local area. However, geographical representation is not privileged in the single transferable vote. Voters in various areas of a multimember district may group themselves together into "voluntary constituencies" based on their common political interests and be represented on that basis. For example, voters from different areas may band together to vote for a female candidate if they value that kind of representation. Widely dispersed racial or ethnic groups may follow a similar strategy. And if some voters do put a high priority on geographical representation, they can vote for a candidate from their local area. In this way, STV allows voters to be represented in the ways they think are most important. A similar effect can be achieved in completely open party list systems, such as the Finnish one, in which voters can only cast a vote for individual party candidates.

Less Negative Campaigning

Many proponents claim that choice voting discourages the kind of negative campaigning and mudslinging that have become common in single-member district contests. Candidates are discouraged from this type of behavior by the fact that they may benefit from being the second choices of voters. If they engage in vicious personal attacks against their opponents, they risk alienating these possible supporters. So while candidates do criticize their opponents, they also highlight areas of agreement. And parties tend to emphasize their similarities as well as their differences, again in order to attract those second-choice votes.

Elimination of Primaries

Choice voting can eliminate the need for primaries. In a city council election, for example, all the candidates could run in the general election. The ones with the least support would be eliminated in the ballot transfer process, much as they would have been in a primary. Voters who support the least popular candidates would not have to worry about wasting their vote. More importantly, all the expense, administrative burden, and low turnout associated with primary elections could be avoided.

Spotlight on the Debate 4.5
Do Coalition Governments Have More Legitimate Mandates?

PR proponents argue that large coalition governments have more support among voters and thus more legitimate political mandates. They observe that some of the single-party governments produced by plurality-majority voting are manufactured majorities supported by only a minority of the voters. For example, the Republicans won control of the U.S. House in 1996 and 1998, but both times only received 48.9% of the vote nationwide. It is difficult for these governments to claim a majority mandate to pursue their policy agenda when most people voted against them. Moreover, even governments that do enjoy majority voter support are often based on a very slim majority—perhaps only 52% or 53% of the vote—as was the case with Democratically controlled U.S. House in the early 1990s.

In contrast, proportional representation rarely produces manufactured majorities. The ruling multiparty coalition almost always represents the majority of voters. And those legislative majorities often tend to be larger than in plurality-majority voting. For instance, it is not unusual for a coalition of several parties to represent 55% or 60% of voters, or even more. PR proponents argue that these larger majorities have a much broader and more legitimate mandate to pursue their policies—that their policies will represent more of the public and thus have more support and legitimacy.

Critics of proportional representation argue that it is wrong to assume that coalition governments have the support of voters. Voters cast votes for specific parties, not coalitions. So if a ruling coalition is made up of a party with 40% of the vote and 20% of the vote, it is not supported by 60% of the electorate: it is supported by 0% since no one actually voted for those two parties together. Moreover, parties in coalitions often have to compromise on some of their platform promises, which can leave some parties supporters feeling betrayed.

PR proponents respond that in several PR systems, voters can cast votes that indicate their preference for certain coalitions. In mixed-member systems, voters can divide their two votes to indicate the coalition partners they favor; in choice voting, voters can also cross party lines in ranking their candidates. In addition, voters are often aware before the election of what the likely coalition will be, especially if parties are pressured to commit themselves to specific coalition partners before the vote.

Disadvantages Specific to This System

Complexity of the Count

Critics make much of the complex process of counting votes and making transfers. They argue that few voters can understand all the intricacies of this esoteric process. If voters cannot understand how the seats are allocated, then this may lead to mistaken voting strategies. Also, this lack of understanding can lessen the legitimacy of this voting system.

Choice voting advocates have several responses to this criticism. They acknowledge that the transfer process can be complicated but suggest that most voters can easily understand the basic principles at work. For example, it is not difficult to grasp that if your vote is unlikely to help your first-choice candidate get elected, it will be transferred to help your second choice.

In addition, advocates argue that the voting process in STV is very simple and that it may not be necessary for voters to understand all the mathematical details of the transfers in order to vote effectively and understand the outcomes. To use an analogy: People may not fully understand how all the electronic components in their radios work, but they are nevertheless able to use them effectively to find the kind of music they like.

Heightening of Intraparty Competition

Because voters can choose between various candidates in each party, the competition between these candidates increases. This can add fuel to the internal divisions in parties and foster destructive rivalries between candidates who are supposed to be working together toward the same political goals. In the United States we often see a similar kind of behavior in party primaries, as the rival candidates spend much of their time tearing each other down. With STV, these internal battles could occur in the general election as well. This explains why voters like the freedom to choose among several party candidates, but party officials often do not.

Gerrymandering

Choice voting is sometimes prone to gerrymandering. Critics usually point to the Republic of Ireland, where considerable evidence of this practice exists. Political scientists have noted that this problem is related to the fact that Irish districts tend to be relatively small, with many having only three or four seats being contested. In a three-seat district, any party with less than 25% of the vote will be unable to elect anyone. So district lines can be manipulated to create small pockets of voters who will waste their votes. However, scholars have also pointed out that larger choice voting districts, with five or more seats, would not be prone to this problem.[17]

Too Many Choices on Ballot

With a five-member district and three parties vying for office, you could easily have ten or fifteen candidates on a STV ballot. Critics suggest that many voters might find it difficult to become familiar with all of these candidates, and so they would be unable to make an informed choice. The ballot choices are usually simpler in party list or MMP systems. Defenders of STV respond that voters can use the system effectively without having to know all the details on every candidate. For example, conservative Republicans would not need a lot of information about candidates from a Green party or a socialist party in order to know that they don't want to rank them highly.

Somewhat Less Proportional Results

STV may produce somewhat less proportional results than the other PR systems. But the nature of choice voting makes this problem difficult to assess. Other PR systems include a party list vote, and it can easily be compared to the percentage of seats won by the party. But in choice voting, votes are cast for individuals, not parties. And voters may cast their first and second choices for candidates from different parties. All of this makes measuring the proportionality of this system more complicated and less reliable.

All that said, some political scientists have rated choice voting as somewhat less proportional than party list and MMP.[18] This may be due to the fact that choice voting usually takes place in relatively small districts. As a rule, the fewer seats in a multimember district, the less proportional the results. Nevertheless, choice voting clearly produces more proportional results than either plurality-majority or semiproportional systems.

Lack of Monotonicity

Ranking systems like instant runoff voting and STV are sometimes criticized for being *nonmonotonic*, meaning that in some circumstances having more first-place votes may hurt, rather than help, a candidate's chance of being elected. This complicated paradox involves a situation in which a candidate's receiving more votes can change the order in which other candidates are eliminated, causing their votes to be transferred in ways that ultimately help a rival of the first candidate.[19]

It is undisputed that nonmonotonicity can theoretically occur in a single transferable vote election, but most experts believe that the conditions needed for this paradox to occur are so special that it would be an extremely rare occurrence. One statistical study found that if STV elections were to be held throughout the United Kingdom, a nonmonotonic result would occur less than once a century.[20]

NOTES

1. See, for example, Kathleen L. Barber, *Proportional Representation and Election Reform in Ohio* (Columbus: Ohio State University Press, 1995), pp. 299–303.

2. See Wilma Rule and Joseph Zimmerman, *U.S. Electoral Systems: Their Impact on Minorities and Women* (Westport, Conn.: Greenwood Press, 1992); and Pippa Norris, "Women's Legislative Participation in Western Europe," *West European Politics* 8 (1995): 90–101.

3. Ibid.

4. Richard Winger, "Dems, Reps Failed to Nominate in 1998," *Ballot Access News* 14, no. 11 (February 1999): 3.

5. Arend Lijphart and Bernard Grofman, *Choosing an Electoral System: Issues and Alternatives* (New York: Praeger, 1984), p. 7.

6. Arend Lijphart, *Patterns of Democracy: Government Forms and Performance in Thirty-Six Countries* (New Haven, Conn.: Yale University Press, 1999), p. 166.

7. Lijphart, *Patterns of Democracy*, p. 286.

8. Arend Lijphart, "Unequal Participation: Democracy's Unresolved Dilemma," *American Political Science Review* 11, no. 1 (March 1997): 7; and Mark N. Franklin, "Electoral Participation" in *Comparing Democracies: Elections and Voting in Global Perspective*, ed. Lawrence LeDuc, Richard Niemi, and Pippa Norris (Thousand Oaks, Calif.: Sage, 1996), p. 226.

9. Michael Pinto-Duschinsky, "Britain's Removal Van Democracy," *The Times*, September 25, 1997.

10. For example, Vernon Bogdanor of Oxford University has concluded: "There is no evidence whatsoever that proportional representation is likely to lead to instability." *What Is Proportional Representation?* (Oxford: Martin Robertson, 1984), p. 147.

11. These countries include Iceland, Ireland, Austria, Netherlands, and Luxembourg. See David M. Farrell, *Comparing Electoral Systems* (New York: Prentice-Hall, 1997), pp. 155.

12. Pinto-Duschinsky, "Britain's Removal Van Democracy."

13. Arend Lijphart, "First-Past-the-Post, PR, Michael Pinto-Duschinsky, and the Empirical Evidence," *Representation* 36, no. 2: 134.

14. Barber, *Proportional Representation and Electoral Reform in Ohio*, p. 305.

15. Bogdanor, *What is Proportional Representation?* p. 147.

16. Frank S. Cohen, "Proportional versus Majoritarian Ethnic Conflict Management in Democracies," *Comparative Political Studies* 30, no. 5 (October 1997): 626.

17. Lijphart and Grofman, *Choosing an Electoral System*, p. 7.

18. Farrell, *Comparing Electoral Systems*, pp. 144–45.

19. For a more lengthy description of this paradox, see Farrell, *Comparing Electoral Systems*, pp. 134–36.

20. Crispin Allard, "Lack of Monotonicity—Revisited," *Representation* 33 (1995): 49.

CHAPTER 5

Semiproportional Voting Systems

In the debate about voting methods, the main alternatives are usually plurality-majority systems and proportional representation systems. These are the most prevalent and popular systems. But there is also a third family of voting systems: semiproportional systems. Around the world, these systems are less well known and much less commonly used. And although semiproportional systems are also relatively rare in the United States, they currently are used more often here than proportional systems, so they do merit some attention.

As the term *semiproportional* implies, these systems occupy a space somewhere between plurality-majority systems and proportional representation systems. For that reason, you might also call them *semiplurality* systems. They have some of the characteristics of both systems, and their political results often fall between those of PR elections and those of plurality elections. In particular, they tend to produce more proportional representation of political parties than plurality-majority voting, but less proportionality than full PR systems such as choice voting and mixed-member proportional voting (see Figure 5.1). Distortions in representation may be more muted than in plurality-majority systems. The largest party might still get more seats than it deserves based on its proportion of the vote, but less than it would have received under plurality-majority rules. The basic intents of these systems is to prevent the same majority of voters from dominating every seat and to allow for some minority representation—though as you will see, this is far from guaranteed.

Proponents of semiproportional systems like to think of them as a practical compromise between plurality and PR systems. They eliminate some of the problems of plurality voting, and they produce more proportional results. However, these systems are often attacked from two different sides. On the one hand, champions of plurality-majority systems see them as overly complicated and largely unnecessary reforms that lean too far backward to try to accommodate political minorities. On the other hand, ad-

Figure 5.1
Proportionality of Voting Systems

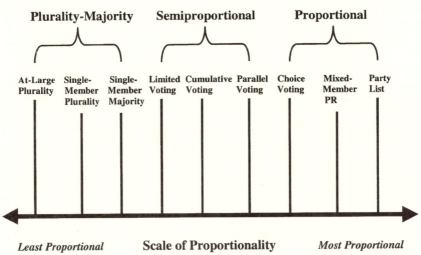

vocates of PR consider semiproportional voting a crude and unreliable version of proportional representation—one that pales in comparison. In their view, why settle for halfway measures when you can have the real thing?

In this chapter, you will become familiar with three different forms of semiproportional voting: cumulative voting, limited voting, and parallel voting. Limited and cumulative voting are variations of the at-large voting system that you saw in the chapter on plurality-majority systems. Like at-large voting, these two systems use multimember districts and voters have multiple votes. But some modifications are made that dampen the winner-take-all characteristics of at-large voting and that result in a more proportional allocation of seats among parties. Parallel voting approaches semiproportionality from the other direction. Instead of starting with a plurality system and making it more proportional, parallel voting starts with a proportional system—mixed-member proportional voting—and makes it less so. Like MMP, some legislators are elected from single-member districts and some from party lists. But unlike in MMP, no effort is made in parallel voting to ensure the proportional representation of parties, so the usual result is semiproportional.

HISTORY

The earliest forms of semiproportional representation were developed in the nineteenth century. By the mid-1800s, the drawbacks of plurality voting were becoming more obvious and less acceptable. As you saw in the chapter on plurality-majority systems, majority voting was invented as one way to solve some of the problems of plurality voting, especially the possibility of electing someone with only a minority of the vote in a district. But majority voting did not address several other common problems of plurality voting: the tendencies to misrepresent parties and to deny representation to political minorities. Under plurality rules, the largest party almost always received more seats than it deserved and the smaller parties fewer seats, and majority voting did nothing to change that. So reformers continued to search for new approaches. The limited vote and the cumulative vote were invented to try to produce more proportional results. They were the first, somewhat awkward, attempts to assure more fair and accurate representation for the mass political parties that were emerging at that time.

A few European countries experimented with these systems, but almost all eventually chose fully proportional systems, such as party list PR, as the alternative to plurality-majority voting. In large part this was because semiproportional systems were perceived as only semifair to parties. In addition, these systems were found to be inconsistent in their results, sometimes producing very unproportional results similar to those of plurality elections. Fully proportional systems were thought to be more fair and reliable.

Until recently it was relatively rare to see semiproportional systems in use either in the United States or abroad. No country uses the cumulative vote to elect their national legislature, and the limited vote is only used in Spain to elect its senate. However, these two systems have been used occasionally on the local level in this country. In the 1980s and 1990s, there was a resurgence of interest in the cumulative vote, primarily among those interested in finding new ways to ensure fair representation for racial and ethnic minorities. Several towns and counties have adopted cumulative voting in response to these voting rights concerns. Abroad, the 1990s saw a surge of interest in parallel voting. It was adopted by several emerging democracies in Eastern Europe and the former Soviet Union.

The relative scarcity of working examples of these systems has meant that there are fewer studies of them than of plurality-majority or PR systems. For this reason, we know less about the political impacts of these systems, and what we do know is somewhat more tentative. For instance, there have been few systematic studies of the impacts of these systems on voter turnout or women's representation. But there is still enough information available to get a relatively good idea of their general advantages and disadvantages.

COMMON FEATURES OF SEMIPROPORTIONAL SYSTEMS

The variety of the systems in this family makes it a bit difficult to generalize about their common properties. Cumulative voting and limited voting do share a number of characteristics because of their similarity to at-large voting. To use the family analogy, they are much like siblings. Parallel voting, with its roots in PR voting, is more like a distant cousin related by marriage. In any case, it is possible to identify a few basic features that are common to these systems.

Multimember Districts

All of these systems utilize multimember districts (parallel voting uses both single and multimember districts). It is this feature that allows for the representation of minorities in districts and that produces more proportional results than plurality-majority systems. The number of seats in these districts can vary tremendously within and among these systems. The cumulative vote has sometimes been used with small three-seat districts, while the parallel system often utilizes regional districts where dozens of seats are at stake.

Candidate-Centered Voting

In some PR systems, voters cast votes for parties. All semiproportional systems use candidate-centered voting procedures and they resemble plurality voting in this respect. Votes are cast for individual candidates and the winning candidates are the ones with the most votes (with the exception of the party-list portion of the parallel vote).

Lower Thresholds

As you might expect, semiproportional systems typically have a threshold of exclusion that is lower than that of plurality-majority systems and higher than that of PR systems. This threshold is the minimum portion of the vote necessary for a group to be assured of winning a seat. Or to put it another way, it is that part of the vote that will guarantee that a party will not be excluded from representation. In plurality-majority systems, this threshold is 50%—the highest among all systems. In PR systems, the threshold is more typically much lower—usually less than 5% in list PR systems. In semiproportional systems this threshold can vary greatly, but it often falls in the 20% to 40% range, and this is part of what accounts for their semiproportional results.

GENERAL ADVANTAGES

More Proportional Than Plurality-Majority Voting

The main appeal of semiproportional systems is that they produce more proportional representation of parties than plurality-majority voting. Under plurality-majority rules, the largest party usually gets more legislative seats than it deserves, and the second largest and smaller parties get fewer seats than they deserve. This tendency is somewhat dampened in semiproportional systems.

One study of the limited vote in elections for the Spanish Senate aptly illustrates its semiproportional effects. In one election, the largest party won 47% of the vote and 65% of the seats. But if that election had been held under single-member plurality rules instead, it is estimated that the largest party would have had 81.7% of the seats.[1] Thus the largest party still received more seats in than it deserved, but not as many as it would have with plurality-majority voting. In this way, semiproportional systems reduce distortions in representation, although not to the extent usually found in fully proportional systems.

Minor Parties and Multiparty Systems Encouraged

As you've seen, plurality-majority voting can be very hostile to minor parties. It is usually difficult for these parties to win any representation at all. But the lower thresholds found in some semiproportional systems— especially cumulative voting and parallel voting—make it possible for some minor parties to win a few seats. A party may need only 10%–20% of the vote, instead of 50%, to be assured of some representation.

Naturally, champions of the two-party system would see this characteristic of semiproportional systems as a disadvantage rather than an advantage.

Fairer to Racial Minorities Than Plurality-Majority Systems

Just as semiproportional systems may aid the political aspirations of minor parties, they can also be helpful to racial and ethnic minorities. The lower thresholds in these systems mean that these minorities stand a better chance of winning some representation than they would in a pure plurality-majority system. When cumulative voting and limited voting began to be used in the 1980s in some local elections in Alabama, African Americans in those jurisdictions were able for the first time since Reconstruction to elect some representatives to their school boards and city and county legislatures. And a case study of cumulative voting in Chilton County, Alabama, found not only that more African Americans have been elected to office, but also that "voting has become less racially polarized, the black community has received a fairer distribution of public services, and black residents have felt more included in local government."[2]

As with fully proportional systems, semiproportional systems are particularly appropriate in areas where the minority population is not concentrated, but dispersed. This is often the case with African Americans in the rural South, Latinos in the Southwest, and Asians in the Midwest.

Dispersed minority populations make it impossible to fashion majority-minority districts. But in semiproportional systems, minorities may band together—irrespective or where they live in the multimember district—to elect their own representative.

Fewer Wasted Votes Than in Plurality Systems

Because political minorities do stand a somewhat better chance of winning some representation in these systems, there are usually fewer wasted votes than in plurality-majority systems. More voters come away from the polling booth with someone to represent them.

GENERAL DISADVANTAGES

Less Proportional than PR

Although these systems do often produce more proportional representation of parties than plurality-majority systems, they usually fall short of the more accurate proportionality offered by full PR systems such as mixed-member PR or choice voting. The main problem here is that these systems are inconsistently proportional. Occasionally they produce a proportional allocation of seats among parties, but usually the results are only somewhat proportional, or even glaringly unproportional. At times the largest party might sweep all the seats in a district or minor parties might be denied representation entirely. It is even possible for the second-place party to win the most district seats. It is this inconsistency of results that accounts for the semiproportionality of these systems.

So in this sense, these systems offer only the *possibility* of more fairness for parties. They may be just as unfair to parties as plurality-majority voting. And as you will see, the proportionality of these systems can often hinge on such factors as the number of candidates from each party. If too many candidates from the same party run, the results may be very disproportional. How party supporters cast their votes for their candidates can also make a big difference in many of these systems. Too many or too few votes for particular candidates can result in a party's winning far fewer seats than it deserves.

This kind of unreliability and capriciousness in a voting system is disturbing to critics and one of the main reasons many of them see PR as a better alternative to plurality-majority systems. If fair representation is an important political goal of elections, why settle for a system that only partially or occasionally achieves that goal? Why not choose a fully proportional system that will ensure more fair representation for all parties?

Unreliable Representation of Minor Parties and Racial Minorities

Semiproportional systems can often give minor parties and racial minorities a better chance of winning representation than they would have under plurality voting rules. However, they do not match the extent or reliability of minority representation produced by full PR systems, and they may actually deny representation to these smaller political groups. The problem here takes two forms. First, thresholds in these systems are sometimes so high as to make it difficult for minorities to win any seats. With limited voting, for instance, the threshold may be 40% or higher. In practice, this usually means that only the two largest parties in a district can win representation. Small third parties are denied representation just as they would be in plurality-majority systems. Also, even when the thresholds are lower, say in the 20%–25% range, it is unlikely that fourth or fifth parties can win any representation, as might easily happen in full PR systems.

The second source of problems for minorities is the inconsistency of these systems mentioned earlier. A large racial minority may still not win any representation if it fails to nominate the optimal number of candidates or if its voters fail to allocate their votes among these candidates in the most strategic manner. For example, in a 1991 cumulative vote election in Peoria, Illinois, two liberal black candidates split much of the African-American vote and neither was elected. So these systems only offer the *possibility* of representation for political and racial minorities. They do not assure it in the same way that fully proportional systems do.

Manufactured Majorities

Just as semiproportional systems may be less than fair to small parties, they may be more than fair to the largest—giving them more seats than they deserve. This generosity can produce manufactured majorities when a party with less than a majority of the vote wins a majority of the seats. This has often been the case, for instance, in limited voting elections for the national senate in Spain. In one typical election, the Socialist party won only 47% of the vote, but 65% of the seats.[3] Critics of semiproportional voting see this as a violation of the principle of majority rule.

Fewer Single-Party Majorities

One of the most often cited advantages of plurality-majority voting is that it tends to produce single-party majorities in the legislature and eliminates the necessity of forming potentially unstable multiparty ruling coalitions. Some critics of semiproportional systems charge that their increased openness to political minorities may undermine the chance of creating these efficient single-party majorities.

However, defenders point out that there is little evidence of this effect and that many of these systems routinely produce single-party legislative majorities. As you just saw, the limited vote in Spain tends to produce single-party manufactured majorities. In addition, a study found that when the cumulative vote was used in Illinois between 1870 and 1955, the largest party failed to garner a majority of the seats in the Illinois House of Representatives on only two occasions: in 1875, when the Independents won forty-one seats, and in 1913, when the Progressives won twenty-six seats.[4] In fact this tendency of semiproportional systems to continue to produce single-party majorities is one reason they are criticized by advocates of PR systems, many of whom prefer the compromise style of politics encouraged by coalition governments.

More Wasted Votes Than PR

Critics maintain that semiproportional systems do not go far enough to minimize wasted votes. These systems do better than plurality-majority systems but usually fall short of full PR systems in this regard. It is easy for some candidates in semiproportional systems to get more votes than they need to get elected, and for others to get too few to be elected. These wasted votes are in fact the source of much of the disproportionality in these systems. When a party's supporters are forced to waste their votes, their party will win fewer seats than it deserves. Full PR systems are designed to minimize wasted votes and maximize effective votes, and this accounts for their higher level of proportionality.

Spotlight on the Debate 5.1
Are Alternative Voting Systems Constitutional?

One of the most common concerns about proportional representation and semiproportional voting systems is their constitutionality. Would constitutional amendments be necessary if we were to use these systems on the state or federal level? The constitutional situation on the federal level is straightforward. There is nothing in the federal Constitution that requires states to use single-member district plurality voting for the House of Representatives. Article I, Section 4, of the Constitution clearly gives to the states and to Congress itself the power to decide how House seats will be elected: "The Times, Places and Manner of holding Elections for Senators and Representatives, shall be prescribed in each State by the legislature thereof; but the Congress may at any time by Law make or alter such Regulations, except as to the Places of chusing Senators."

The only legal barrier to the use of alternative voting systems for U.S. House elections is congressional legislation passed in 1842 and 1967 that requires the use of single-member districts. The original intent of these bills was not to prevent the use of proportional or semiproportional systems, but to stop the use of plurality at-large elections. In the 1960s, some southern states were trying to switch to at-large elections to discourage the election of African Americans to the House, and Congress wished to prevent this political maneuver. In recent years, several bills have been introduced in Congress that would repeal this prior legislation and allow states to adopt proportional or semiproportional systems for U.S. House seats. (Since the Constitution stipulates that members of the Senate must be elected one at a time in the states, proportional and semiproportional systems could obviously not be used for these elections without a constitutional amendment that changed this arrangement.)

The situation in the individual states is much more varied. Some state constitutions, such as those in Connecticut, Kansas, and Michigan, require single-member district plurality elections for their state legislatures. In many others, including Mississippi, North Carolina, and Oregon, the constitution is silent as to the method of election to these bodies, and so proportional and semiproportional systems could be adopted without constitutional amendment. Also, in most states, local election options are not restricted by state constitutions.

THE CUMULATIVE VOTE

In the United States, cumulative voting (CV) is the most talked about form of semiproportional voting. However, if you were to look in foreign handbooks on voting systems, the cumulative vote is often not even mentioned as an alternative. That is because it is not currently used in any other country besides the United States. The first effort to adopt CV in this country was spearheaded in the nineteenth century by U.S. Senator Charles Buckalew of Illinois. In 1867 he introduced a bill in Congress that would have mandated cumulative voting for the U.S. House of Representatives. He argued that one of the main contributing factors to the recently fought Civil War was the winner-take-all voting that polarized the North and South. It allowed the extremists on both sides to be represented to the exclusion of more moderate political voices. In his words, plurality voting failed "to secure to the friends of peace and union a just measure of political power."[5] Though his bill failed to become law, Buckalew later played a more successful role in helping to persuade Illinois to adopt cumulative voting for its House of Representatives. It was used there between 1870 and 1980, and it allowed both Democrats and Republicans to elect representatives from each district. It is currently used in city council elections in Peoria, Illinois.

More recently, voting rights advocates have expressed growing interest in this form of voting. The Harvard law professor Lani Guinier and others have argued that cumulative voting could produce fair representation for racial minorities without resorting to the creation of the special majority-minority districts that the Supreme Court has been frowning on in recent years.[6] And in response to voting rights suits, several local areas have abandoned plurality-majority systems and adopted cumulative voting. Chilton County, Alabama, was one of the first, substituting CV for an at-large voting scheme that was charged with discrimination against black voters. CV is also currently used in Amarillo and several other cities and towns in Texas to elect either their local school boards or city councils. Again the aim is to allow for some representation of ethnic minorities—in this case, Latino voters.

Interestingly, the most common use of cumulative voting in the United States is not in the public sector, but in the private sector. It is used for the election of boards of directors in hundreds of corporations. In fact, six state constitutions mandate this form of voting for corporate boards, and many other states allow its use for this purpose. The aim is to allow minority stockholders to elect some representatives to these governing bodies. Proponents of cumulative voting are fond of pointing out that it can hardly be considered a "radical" alternative if it is used so often by the traditionally conservative U.S. business community.

How It Works

The cumulative vote is really just a variation of at-large voting or multimember district plurality voting. Candidates run in multimember districts. Voters have as many votes as there are seats. Voters cast their votes for individual candidates and the winners are the ones with the most votes. The major difference is that voters may "cumulate" or combine their votes on one or more candidates instead of having to cast one vote for each candidate. In other words, voters may distribute their votes among the candidates in any way they prefer. For example, in elections for the county commission in Chilton County, Alabama, voters have seven votes to use to elect the seven commissioners. Voters can cast all seven for one candidate, one vote for each of seven candidates, four for one and three for another, or any other combination they desire. When CV was used to elect the Illinois House, it was used in three-seat districts. Voters could cast one vote for each of three candidates, three votes for one candidate, or one and one half votes for two candidates. (Casting two votes for one candidate and one for another was disallowed.)

As illustrated in Ballot 5.1, the ballot for the cumulative vote resembles somewhat the one used for at-large voting. However, it has spaces for voters to cast multiple votes for each candidate. This example shows a computer-readable ballot for the election of three officeholders to a city council. Voters fill in a square for each vote that they want to give to a candidate—up to a total of three for all the candidates.

Computing the results in cumulative voting is straightforward: The can-

Ballot 5.1
Cumulative Voting

<table>
<tr>
<td colspan="3" align="center">Official Ballot
Municipal Elections</td>
</tr>
<tr>
<td>INSTRUCTIONS TO VOTERS</td>
<td align="center">Candidates for City Council District One
(Three to be elected.)</td>
<td align="center">You may cast no more than three (3) votes.</td>
</tr>
<tr>
<td rowspan="7">You may cast up to three (3) votes. Your may distribute your three votes in any way among the candidates: all three for one candidate, two for one and one for another, or one for each of three candidates.

Cast votes for candidates by filling in the numbered boxes next to their name. For example, to cast three votes for a candidate, fill in boxes 1, 2 and 3.</td>
<td>Enid Lakeman   Democrat</td>
<td>1 2 3</td>
</tr>
<tr>
<td>Thomas Gilpin   Republican</td>
<td>1 2 3</td>
</tr>
<tr>
<td>J.F.H. Wright   Democrat</td>
<td>1 2 3</td>
</tr>
<tr>
<td>Clarence Hoag   Democrat</td>
<td>1 2 3</td>
</tr>
<tr>
<td>John Humphreys   Republican</td>
<td>1 2 3</td>
</tr>
<tr>
<td>Write In</td>
<td>1 2 3</td>
</tr>
<tr>
<td>Write In</td>
<td>1 2 3</td>
</tr>
<tr>
<td></td>
<td>Write In</td>
<td>1 2 3</td>
</tr>
</table>

didates with most votes win. The results in Table 5.1 show the outcome of a three-seat district contest. The candidates with the three highest vote totals are declared the winners, in this case two Democrats and a Republican.

As this example illustrates, if a political minority puts all of its votes on one candidate (often called *plumping*), then it stands a good chance of winning that one seat. Its chances depend primarily on the size of the minority and the threshold of exclusion for that particular election. The threshold for cumulative voting is calculated by dividing one by the number of seats being elected in the district plus 1. So the formula is $1/(\text{seats} + 1)$. For a 3-seat district the threshold is $1/(3 + 1)$, or 1/4, or 25%. Since the Republicans have about 35% of the vote in this example, this means that as long as they put all of their votes on one candidate, they cannot be excluded from winning that one seat. The more seats in a district, the lower the threshold. A seven-seat district, for instance, has a threshold of $1/(7 + 1)$, or 1/8, or 12.5%. (As you will see, it is possible sometimes for a political minority to elect a candidate when they have less than the threshold, but

Table 5.1
Results of a Cumulative Vote Election

Democrats		Republicans	
Candidate	Votes	Candidate	Votes
Lakeman	35,000*	Gilpin	48,000*
Wright	30,000*		
Hoag	25,000		
	90,000		
Result	2 seats		1 seat

*Winning candidates.
Note: Thirty thousand Democrats and 16,000 Republicans with three votes each.

the point here is that representation is not guaranteed unless they have more than the threshold of exclusion.)

You will notice that the level of the threshold depends directly on the number of seats at stake in the district. The more seats, the lower the threshold. If the number of seats in a district is very low, the threshold can be too high for small political and racial minorities to overcome. For example, CV is now used to elect school district representatives in over two dozen cities in Texas. But in many cities the elections for those seats are staggered, with only two or three seats up for election at any one time. This means that the threshold of exclusion is either 33% or 25%. One study found that Latinos make up less than 20% of the voters in several cities, so even if they concentrate all of their votes on a single candidate, they are unable to elect anyone without the support of other ethnic groups.[7]

Advantages Specific to This System

Like other systems in this family, cumulative voting offers semiproportionality in party representation and often increases the chance of minority representation. When used in Illinois in three-seat districts, CV usually resulted in the larger party's winning two seats and the smaller party's winning one seat. So instead of having representation by only Republicans or only Democrats in entire regions of the state, each region had a mix of representatives. However, there are some additional advantages to this system as well.

Ease of Use

Proponents of CV believe that Americans would find this system easy to use. It is not all that different from the at-large elections that are already used in many cities in the United States. And while the process of combining votes on candidates is a new one, it is not a particularly difficult one to understand. This ease of use is considered a major advantage of this system compared to some PR voting systems.

Minority Representation without Race-Conscious Districting

Many proponents argue that one of the main advantages of this system is that it increases the chance for racial and ethnic minorities to win representation, without the creation of special majority-minority districts. Chilton County, Alabama, for instance, continued to use a countywide multimember district as it had in previous at-large elections but simply changed to electing local officials by the cumulative vote. This allowed African Americans for the first time to elect members to the previously all-white county commission and school board.

In this way, CV allows for fair representation of racial minorities without being subject to the charge that the state is creating safe districts for minorities or that it is assigning political identities on the basis of race. Thus CV prevents the political and legal hassles that usually accompany trying to create single-member districts in which minorities predominate. Like proportional representation, cumulative voting offers the promise of fair representation for all racial groups, with a minimum of political disputes.

More Options for Representation

Because CV uses larger multimember districts, the primary emphasis is not necessarily on geographical representation. In contrast, single-member district systems assume that geographical representation is what is most important to voters, and they are designed to ensure that all voters have a representative from their local area. However, geographical representation is not privileged in cumulative voting. Voters in any area of the district may group themselves together into voluntary constituencies based on their common political interests and be represented on that basis. For example, voters from different areas may band together to vote for a female candidate if they value that kind of representation. Widely dispersed racial or ethnic groups may follow a similar strategy. And if some voters do put a high priority on geographical representation, they can vote for a candidate from their local area.

In this respect, it is interesting to note that after cumulative voting was introduced in 1988 in Chilton County, Alabama, there was an increase not only in African Americans' election to governing bodies, but also in the election of women and Republicans—two groups rarely represented on previous bodies. Proponents of CV see this as evidence that it gives voters more options for determining how they will be represented.

Less Prone to Gerrymandering

CV shares an advantage with at-large and multimember district PR systems: It lessens the opportunity for gerrymandering. If it is used in cities or counties where all the candidates are elected in one large district, then obviously gerrymandering is not even an issue because no district lines are drawn. But even if CV is used in state legislative elections where separate multimember districts must be drawn up, gerrymandering is less of a problem than in single-member plurality districts. Gerrymandering only works if you can draw districts in which the political minorities cannot elect anyone. Since the multimember districts of CV are designed to allow for representation of political minorities, attempts to manipulate district lines are less effective. As one early study of CV use in Illinois concluded, "Where the system of minority representation prevails, gerrymandering is largely shorn of its viciousness."[8]

Self-Defeating Votes May Be Avoided

You saw in chapter three that one disadvantage of at-large voting (and also of the limited vote) is that if you use all of your votes, you may help to defeat your favorite candidate. Votes cast for other candidates may inadvertently give them enough votes to defeat your most preferred candidate. This can be avoided in cumulative voting by putting all your votes on your preferred candidate.

Usable in Nonpartisan Elections

Unlike parallel voting and most forms of proportional representation, cumulative voting can be used in nonpartisan elections. Voters cast ballots for individuals, not parties, and the ballots can either indicate the party affiliation of candidates or not.

Disadvantages Specific to This System

Majority Sweeps

As mentioned earlier, semiproportional systems can be very inconsistent in their allocation of seats and can at times produce very unproportional results. In some cases the cumulative vote can give all the seats in a district to the majority (a "sweep") and completely deny representation to the minority. Ironically, this is exactly what this system was designed to prevent. This problem is illustrated in Table 5.2. This election has the same number of Democratic and Republican voters as the election shown in Table 5.1. But in this case the results are very different. The Republicans decide to

Table 5.2
Majority Sweep in a Cumulative Vote Election

Democrats		Republicans	
Candidate	Votes	Candidate	Votes
Lakeman	35,000*	Gilpin	24,000
Wright	30,000*	Humphreys	24,000
Hoag	25,000*		48,000
	90,000		
Result	3 seats		No seats

*Winning candidates.

Note: Thirty thousand Democrats and 16,000 Republicans with three votes each.

nominate one more candidate in the hope of winning another seat. But as a result they are completely shut out and the Democrats sweep all the seats—a result similar to that of plurality voting. Adding another candidate cause the Republican vote to become so spread out that all of it is wasted and none of its candidates can win.

One actual example of this problem occurred in elections in the town of Centre, Alabama. In its first CV election in 1988, one black candidate was elected. But in the next election in 1992, a second black candidate divided the vote and both minority candidates lost. Such problems do not arise in such PR systems as party list voting because the number of nominated candidates has no effect on the allocation of seats.

Minority Rule

The inconsistency of the results in cumulative voting can also produce another problem: minority rule, illustrated in Table 5.3. In this case, the source of the disproportional results is the misallocation of votes among a party's candidates. The first Democratic candidate, Lakeman, is very popular and many of the Democratic voters give her several of their votes. As a result, many of the votes cast for her exceed the number she needs to win office and are therefore wasted—leaving too few votes to elect another Democratic candidate. This allows the Republican minority to win two of the three seats—a clear violation of the principle of majority rule.

Proponents of cumulative voting acknowledge that minority rule does sometimes occur but argue that it is relatively rare. A study that looked at the use of CV elections between 1920 and 1954 in Illinois found that the minority party won the majority of seats in a district forty-five times—

Table 5.3
Minority Rule in a Cumulative Vote Election

Democrats		Republicans	
Candidate	Votes	Candidate	Votes
Lakeman	60,000*	Gilpin	24,000*
Wright	15,000	Humphreys	24,000*
Hoag	15,000		48,000
	90,000		
Result	1 seat		2 seats

*Winning candidates.
Note: Thirty thousand Democrats and 16,000 Republicans with three votes each.

4.9% of the 918 district elections. Critics maintain that any violation of majority rule is a serious problem and can be eliminated entirely by the use of a fully proportional voting system.

Strict Party Control of Nominations and Votes Required

Proponents of cumulative voting argue that problems like majority sweep and minority rule can be minimized if parties exert effective control over candidate nominations and the distribution of their supporters' votes. For example, parties in cumulative elections in Chilton County, Alabama, pass out sample ballots that tell voters how many votes to give to each of the party's candidates—three for this candidate, four for this one, and so on. However, there is no guarantee that voters will actually follow these directions. They may not allocate their votes as party leaders desire; even worse, they may engage in split-ticket voting—giving some votes to a candidate of another party. In any case, this effort at strict, top-down control over the casting of votes can alienate voters, who may consider it an infringement of their freedom to cast their votes as they see fit.

Similar kinds of voter resentment can be caused by party attempts to strictly control nominations. If parties become too good at estimating their optimal number of candidates, voters may feel that this is limiting their choices. For example, one of the complaints about the three-seat CV districts in Illinois was that the largest major party would often nominate only two candidates, the smaller major party only one candidate, and all three would inevitably win. By limiting the choice of candidates in this way, the entire election became noncompetitive. It was a foregone conclusion who would be elected and this upset some voters. Illinois eventually tried to address this problem by requiring that each party nominate at least two candidates.

The other problem with these control strategies is that they may not work very well. Candidates of the same party vying for office may try to maximize their own votes at the expense of their colleagues, irrespective of what the party hierarchy wants. This is what has happened in Chilton County, Alabama, where candidates began to ask voters for all seven of their votes, despite the fact that parties wanted voters to spread out their support among all their candidates. In addition, party nomination strategies may run into problems if parties are unsure of their exact level of voter support. This makes it difficult to predict the optimal number of candidates to nominate.

Finally, even if the major parties could predict accurately the best number of candidates to nominate, they could always fall victim to spoilers. A minor party might nominate a candidate who takes away some votes from one of the major parties and causes that party to win fewer seats than it would otherwise. In this way, spoilers can upset the well-planned nomination strategies of the major parties.

In proportional representation voting systems, parties do not need to restrict nominations or orchestrate vote distributions among candidates. These systems are designed to provide proper representation for parties no matter how many candidates they nominate or how their supporters' votes are distributed. (For more details on this, see Spotlight on the Debate 5.2: Cumulative Voting versus Choice Voting.)

Spotlight on the Debate 5.2
Cumulative Voting versus Choice Voting

Comparing cumulative voting to choice voting may be helpful in illustrating some of the basic differences between semiproportional and proportional voting systems. As you have seen, cumulative voting (and limited voting) can produce inconsistent results, sometimes giving parties far more or far fewer seats than they deserve, particularly on the district level. In contrast, choice voting tends to more reliably allocate seats proportionately among the parties. But why is this the case? The answer lies in the vote transfer process used in choice voting. As you will recall, choice voting involves ranking your preferred candidates. When your most preferred candidate cannot possibly win, your vote is transferred to your next choice. Also, votes in excess of what is needed to win office are also transferred to voters' second choices. This transfer process drastically limits the number of wasted votes, and this in turn helps to eliminate such problems as majority sweep and minority rule.

Consider, for instance, the election in Table 5.3. There Democratic voters gave many more votes to Lakeman than she needed to win. These excess votes were wasted, and as a result the Democrats won fewer seats than they deserved. In choice voting, however, excess votes above the threshold needed to be elected would have been redistributed to the voters' next choice so that they could help some other candidate win office. In the case of the election in Table 5.3, most of those votes would probably have gone to the other Democratic candidates, thus helping at least one of them to win office and preventing minority rule.

Choice voting also eliminates the problem of nominating too many candidates. In the election in Table 5.2, the Republicans nominated too many candidates, which spread out the Republican vote so thinly that all of their votes were wasted and none of their candidates won. But if choice voting were used, the Republican candidate with the lowest votes would have been eliminated and his or her votes transferred to the voters' second choices. Most of these would have gone to the remaining Republican candidate, who would have won office.

Other proportional representation systems do not use this transfer process, but they also prevent the problems of misallocations of votes and overnomination that can plague cumulative voting. All PR systems minimize the number of wasted votes, and since virtually all of the misrepresentation that takes place in cumulative voting is due to wasted votes, PR systems usually successfully avoid this problem.

Less Geographical Representation

Many criticisms of CV come from advocates of PR systems. But this particular complaint is usually aired by defenders of single-member district plurality-majority systems. They argue that the de-emphasis on geographical representation that can occur in the larger multimember districts used in cumulative voting is not a advantage, as proponents claim, but a serious disadvantage. For example, this arrangement may make it more difficult for representatives to establish close ties with their constituents. Evidence of this was found in interviews with citizens in Chilton County, Alabama, where some of them said that they no longer felt as clear about who "their" representative was.[9]

However, proponents of CV offer the same counterarguments to this criticism discussed earlier in relation to the PR system. They maintain that geographical representation is not always the most important thing for voters, and if it is, they can always vote for candidates from their area. This appears to have happened in Chilton County, where candidates have continued to be elected from all areas of the county.[10]

Cumulative voting advocates also argue that providing representatives from different parties in each district actually improves constituent relationships because it makes it easier for more constituents to find a representative who is sensitive to their particular political concerns. For example, when Illinois used the cumulative vote, both Democratic and Republican voters had representatives in their districts with whom they could interact. Now districts have only a Democratic or a Republican representative, and whole sections of the state, for example, Chicago, basically have one-party representation.

Voter Confusion

Proponents of plurality-majority systems sometimes charge that cumulative voting is overly complicated. The process of combining votes on different candidates may be confusing to many voters. As noted earlier, proponents believe that cumulative voting is easy to use. In their view, it is merely a slight modification of at-large voting, so most voters would have little trouble understanding or using it. Most experts support this view. A study of cumulative voting systems that have been recently adopted in the United States found that 95% of the voters understood the proper way to cast a ballot, and only 13% found CV to be "more difficult to understand" than systems utilized in other local elections in which they had voted.[11]

THE LIMITED VOTE

The limited vote (LV) is another variation of at-large voting. One of the first uses of LV was in England in the mid-nineteenth century. At that time most members of parliament were elected in two-seat districts. One of the obvious problems with this approach was that the largest party often swept the election, winning both seats and preventing the minority party in the district from having any representation at all. To remedy this lack of minority representation, England created in 1867 several three-seat districts but only allowed voters two votes. This limitation on the vote made it much more difficult for the largest party to win all three seats, and in most cases the smaller party was able to win one. Although it was largely successful in assuring minority representation, this experiment with the limited vote was abandoned in 1885, when England switched to all single-member districts. Today this system is relatively uncommon, and only Spain uses it to elect its senate. Until recently, a version of LV known as the single-nontransferable vote was also used in Japan. (See Appendix C for more details on the Japanese system.) In the United States, several cities and towns, mostly in Connecticut and Pennsylvania, have used the limited vote for many years—again primarily to ensure some representation for political minorities. More recently, twenty-one towns in Alabama adopted limited voting to settle voting rights suits.

How It Works

The limited vote works almost exactly the same way as at-large or multimember district plurality voting. Candidates run in a multimember district. People have multiple votes and vote for individual candidates. The

Ballot 5.2
Limited Voting

Official Ballot	
Municipal Elections	
DIRECTIONS TO VOTERS	**City Council Candidates**
1. To Vote: Mark on "X" in the box next to the candidate's name. 2. Cast no more than **TWO** votes. 3. To vote for a person whose name is not printed on the ballot, write the candidate's name on one of the extra lines provided and put an "X" in the box next to the name.	Joan Cocks (Democrat)
	Stephen Ellenburg (Democrat)
	Vincent Ferraro (Republican)
	Kavita Khory (Republican)
	Christopher Pyle (Republican)
	Preston Smith (Democrat)
	Write In
	Write In

winners are the candidates with the most votes. The crucial difference is
that voters have fewer votes than the number of seats to be elected. In a
three-seat district, voters might have two votes, as in the example of England mentioned earlier. The elections for the Spanish Senate typically use
four-seat districts in which voters have three votes. The number of votes
can vary; the only restriction is that they must be fewer than the seats. For
example, in a seven-seat district, voters might have five votes, or three, or
even one, though the most usual arrangement is for them to have one or
two fewer votes than seats.

The limited vote ballot is virtually identical to those used in at-large or
multimember district plurality voting, as illustrated in Ballot 5.2. In this
example, voters are electing three members of the legislature and are given
two votes. Counting the ballots and determining the winner are very
straightforward. As shown in Table 5.4, the winners are the candidates
with the most votes, in this case, two Democrats and one Republican. (In
this example, Ellenburg and Smith actually tied with the same number of
votes, and Ellenburg won the final seat through a tie-breaking procedure.)

One variation of this system is to combine it with limited nominations
(LN), which restrict the number of candidates each party can nominate.
For example, in a four-seat district where voters have three votes, parties
are able to nominate only up to three candidates. This is a further attempt
to assure that the majority cannot win all the seats in the district. At-large
members of the city council in Philadelphia have been elected using this
combined LN/LV systems.

The threshold of exclusion can be very different for limited voting than
it is for cumulative voting. In CV, the threshold for a five-seat district is

Table 5.4
Results of a Limited Vote Election

Democrats		Republicans	
Candidate	Votes	Candidate	Votes
Cocks	30,000*	Ferraro	16,000*
Ellenburg	15,000*	Khory	8,000
Smith	15,000	Pyle	8,000
	60,000		32,000
Result	2 seats		1 seat

*Winning candidates.
Note: Three seats to be filled; two votes each for 30,000 Democrats and 16,000 Republicans.

16.7%—relatively low. But it could be much higher in a five-seat limited vote district. The threshold in limited voting is calculated by dividing the number of votes given to each voter by that same number plus the number of seats: votes/(votes + seats). So in a five-seat district where voters have four votes, the threshold is 4/(4 + 5) or 4/9, or 44.4%—dramatically higher than that for cumulative voting. The threshold for LV is not fixed; it changes as the ratio of votes to seats changes. As the number of seats rises or the number of votes lowers, the threshold goes down. As Table 5.5 illustrates, the threshold in a five-seat district declines as voters are given fewer votes. But it does not match the low level of the cumulative vote until voters are given only one vote for the five seats. This difference in threshold levels accounts for some of the dissimilar political results of these two systems.

Advantages Specific to This System

The limited vote shares all the general advantages of this family of voting systems, including the ability to produce a more proportional allocation of seats and to allow for some minority representation. But it has several additional advantages as well.

Easy to Use and Administer

Because this system so closely resembles at-large voting, most voters find it very easy to use. Unlike some PR systems that require a new ballot form and a new style of voting, the limited vote offers voters a very familiar approach to electing officials. Election administrators also appreciate the

Table 5.5
Variations in Threshold in Limited Voting

Number of Seats	Number of Votes	Threshold of Exclusion
5 seats	4 votes	44.4%
5 seats	3 votes	37.5%
5 seats	2 votes	28.6%
5 seats	1 vote	16.7%

ease and simplicity of this system. The counting procedures are straight-forward, and changing to LV usually would not require changes in voting machines. Advocates consider this characteristic one of the main advantages of this system.

Reinforcement of Two-Party System

When the threshold of exclusion in limited voting extends into the 30% to 40% range, it can help to reinforce the two-party system. With such a high threshold, usually only the two major parties can win representation. Few minor parties can overcome such a high barrier to representation. Spain, for instance, uses four-seat districts with three votes, and so the threshold is 3/(3 + 4) or 42.9%. The usual result is that the largest party wins three of the district seats and the second largest wins the other. Such an effect is celebrated by those who advocate a two-party system but is obviously considered a serious disadvantage by those who value multiparty democracy.

Usable in Nonpartisan Elections

Like the cumulative vote, limited voting can be used in nonpartisan elections.

Disadvantages Specific to This System

Majority Sweeps

Like the cumulative vote, the limited vote has inconsistencies in seat allocations than can create a number of political problems. One is the occurrence of majority sweeps, illustrated in Table 5.6. In this case, the Republicans nominated too many candidates and their vote is spread too thin for any of their candidates to be elected. So even though they have 35% of the vote, they win no representation—more like the result you would get in a single-member plurality election. Mistakes in nomination strategies can easily result in this kind of disproportional result.

Table 5.6
Majority Sweep in a Limited Vote Election

Democrats		Republicans	
Candidate	Votes	Candidate	Votes
Cocks	30,000*	Ferraro	11,000
Ellenburg	15,000*	Khory	11,000
Smith	15,000*	Pyle	10,000
	60,000		32,000
Result	3 seats		No seats

*Winning candidates.
Note: Three seats to be filled; two votes each for 30,000 Democrats and 16,000 Republicans.

Minority Rule

Again the problem here is identical to that in cumulative voting. As illustrated in Table 5.7, if the Democrats do not manage to distribute their votes in the most strategic manner among their candidates, they end up wasting a great number of their votes. This can allow the minority party to win two of the three seats in that district.

Supporters of limited voting argue that minority rule and majority sweeps are not the common outcome of these elections and so should not be considered a major problem. Supporters of proportional representation, however, maintain that it is foolish to risk these unproportional results, when an alternative is available that essentially eliminates that risk.

Strict Party Control of Nominations and Votes Required

As with the cumulative vote, defenders of the limited vote usually argue that the problems stemming from inconsistent results can be minimized if political parties exert effective control over nominations and the way their supporters cast their votes. For example, if a small party is careful to nominate only the same number of candidates as voters have votes, they guarantee that they do not spread their vote too thin.

However, what the proper nomination strategy is for the largest party is much less clear. In a four-seat district, the larger party may not be able to gauge its support accurately enough to decide whether to go for two, three, or four of the seats. The result, studies show, is that they tend to be conservative and to nominate fewer candidates than they should.[12] This practice restricts voter choice and sometimes results in the loss of potential seats.

Table 5.7
Minority Rule in a Limited Vote Election

Democrats		Republicans	
Candidate	Votes	Candidate	Votes
Cocks	30,000*	Ferraro	16,000*
Ellenburg	15,000	Khory	16,000*
Smith	15,000		32,000
	60,000		
Result	1 seat		2 seats

*Winning candidates.
Note: Three seats to be filled; two votes each for 30,000 Democrats and 16,000 Republicans.

Perhaps more importantly, critics point out that it is very difficult to deal with the problem of misallocation of votes by party supporters. The only reliable solution is for the party to give explicit instructions to voters in each precinct about how they should distribute their votes—instructing voters in one precinct to vote for candidates Cocks and Ellenburg, in another precinct to vote for candidates Ellenburg and Smith, and so on—so that their votes may be distributed evenly among all their candidates. This is in fact exactly what the parties did when England experimented with the limited vote. But this rigid management of the vote greatly restricted voters' choices, and resentment over this heavy-handed approach is much of what led to the abandonment of LV. But without this kind of vote management, misallocation of votes is always a possibility. As critics point out, this kind of control over voting and nominations is not necessary in proportional representation systems.

Self-Defeating Votes

As with at-large voting, if you choose to use all your votes in limited voting, there is a chance that this strategy can be self-defeating. If your most preferred candidate is Cocks, and you also cast votes for Ellenburg and Smith, your vote may help those other candidates defeat your favorite one.

Somewhat Prone to Gerrymandering

If limited voting is used in cities or counties where all the candidates are elected in one large district, then gerrymandering cannot be a problem because no district lines are drawn. But it may be a problem when multi-member LV districts are used to elect state legislatures. If the version of LV has a relatively high threshold, then it is more vulnerable to gerrymandering. For instance, when the threshold in LV reaches 40% or more, it is easy to draw districts in which the political minority has less than 40% of the vote and so is shut out of the representation. (See Spotlight on the Debate 5.3: Is Limited Voting Less Friendly to Minorities?). This is easier to do than in cumulative voting, which often has lower thresholds.

Spotlight on the Debate 5.3
Is Limited Voting Less Friendly to Minorities?

Some advocates of semiproportional voting prefer the cumulative vote because they see limited voting as less friendly to minor parties and racial minorities. They often point to the higher thresholds that are possible in this system. A 40% threshold of exclusion usually effectively excludes small parties and racial minorities from representation. In a version of the limited vote used in Japan, a single party was able to dominate the government for over forty-five years.[13]

However, LV proponents respond that this system can be made more open to small political minorities simply by changing the proportion of seats to votes. The higher the number of seats and the lower the number of votes, the lower the threshold becomes. Table 5.5 illustrates how different arrangements change the threshold level. As you can see, in a five-seat LV district, the threshold drops significantly as the number of votes is reduced. With one vote, the threshold becomes exactly as low as that of a five-seat cumulative vote district. Ariton, Alabama, uses a limited vote system in which there are five seats at stake and one vote. The resulting threshold of 16.7% has allowed a small black population of 23.5% to elect one member to the city council.

But cumulative voting advocates point out that while it is possible to make the limited vote more open to the election of candidates from small political minorities, this hasn't often happened in practice. In the past, the two major parties often have controlled the form that limited voting has taken in the United States, and they have chosen a high ratio of votes to seats in order to enhance their own political power and discourage minor parties. They have been willing to allow each other some representation in districts, but not third parties. So the fairness of LV to small political minorities depends highly on the political factors that determine the exact form it takes. For some, cumulative voting seems less vulnerable to this kind of political manipulation and this makes it a more desirable semiproportional system.

Less Geographical Representation

Like the cumulative vote, limited voting uses multimember districts; therefore, it also comes under attack for de-emphasizing the kind of geographical representation that takes place in single-member districts. The details of this accusation and the defenders' replies are identical to the ones in the discussion of cumulative voting.

THE PARALLEL VOTING SYSTEM

The system is also sometimes called a *combination system*, and *noncompensating mixed-member proportional voting*. These alternative names indicate that the origin of this system is very different from that of cumulative and limited voting. While the other two are variations of at-large voting, parallel voting is a variation of mixed-member proportional voting (MMP). This means that it follows very different procedures and as a result has some different advantages and disadvantages as well.

This system had a burst of popularity in the 1990s when the former Communist countries of Albania, Azerbaijan, Croatia, Georgia, Lithuania, and Russia adopted it. In those countries it was often portrayed as a "compromise" between PR and plurality voting systems, much as MMP is where it is used. Some other countries using parallel voting are Guatemala, Japan, and South Korea.

How It Works

The procedures of parallel voting are almost identical to those of mixed-member proportional voting. As in MMP, one-half of the legislature is elected in single-member districts and the other half is elected from party lists. There are two parts to the ballot and voters cast two votes, as shown in Ballot 5.3.

The main difference between parallel voting and MMP is that there is no effort to ensure proportional representation for parties. As you may recall from the description of MMP, the results of the single-member district votes are often very disproportional. As with all plurality-majority systems, the larger parties usually win more seats than they deserve in these district contests and the smaller ones usually win fewer seats or no seats at all. In MMP the candidates from the party list side of the vote are added on to the district winners so that each party ends up with the number of seats in the legislature that reflects its proportion of the party list vote (see Table 5.8). But this compensating process does not take place in parallel voting. The second half of the seats are simply divided proportionately among the parties and then added to the district winners without any attempt to ensure proportionality for parties, as shown in Table 5.9. The Democrats, for instance, are awarded twenty of the fifty party list seats, reflecting its 40% of the party list vote; this total is simply added to their thirty-four district seat winners to make a total of fifty-four seats. The fact that the party list seats are not used to correct the distortions of the district vote is the reason this system is called *parallel*. Two separate voting systems—the district vote and the party vote—exist in parallel, with no effort to integrate them to produce a proportional outcome for the parties.

A comparison of these two tables demonstrates how different the results

Ballot 5.3
Parallel Voting

Official Ballot	
Election For the House of Representatives	
You Have 2 Votes	
District Vote	**Party Vote**
This vote decides who will be elected to the House of Representatives from this district. Vote by putting an "X" in the box immediately before the candidate you choose. Vote for only one candidate.	This vote decides the share of the party list seats that each of the parties listed below will have in the House of Representatives. Vote by putting an "X" in the box immediately before the party you choose. Vote for only one party.
── **Vote Here**	── **Vote Here**
☐ Fred Smith Republican	☐ Republican Party Berg, Grolnic, McClurg, Epstein, Deutsch
☐ Damon Washington Democrat	☐ Democratic Party Foster, Rosen-Amy, Volz, Pike, Gentzler
☐ Naomi Lintz Reform	☐ Reform Party Fosom, Moll, Hernandez, Fingrutd, Czitrom
☐ Cheryl Houston Greens	☐ Greens Wong, Gorlin, Crenshaw, Gerstel, Zussman
☐ Edward Ruley Independent	☐
☐ *Write In*	☐

can be in parallel and MMP systems. Most notable are the distortions in the representation of parties that occur in the parallel system. With parallel voting, the Democrats received 54% of the seats, even though they received only 40% of the vote. And the Reform party won 18% of the vote but only 11% of the seats. The results are obviously less proportional than in the MMP system. On the other hand, the seat allocation is more proportional than it would have been in a plurality-majority system. In plurality voting it is unlikely that the Reform party or Greens would have won any seats at all. In parallel voting, they get at least a few seats, although fewer than they deserve. It is easy to see why this system is categorized as a semiproportional system.

This system takes a variety of somewhat different forms. For example, in Azerbaijan and Lithuania, the district representatives are elected by two-round runoffs instead of plurality voting. Also, while some parallel systems

Table 5.8
Voting Results and Seat Allocations in Mixed-Member Proportional Voting

Political Parties	Number of District Seats Won	Percentage of the National Party List Vote	Number of Seats Added from Party Lists	Total Number of Seats	% of Party List Vote vs. % of Total Seats
Democratic	34	40%	6	40	40% / 40%
Republican	14	36%	22	36	36% / 36%
Reform	2	18%	16	18	18% / 18%
Green	0	6%	6	6	6% / 6%
Totals	50	100%	50	100	100% / 100%

Table 5.9
Voting Results and Seat Allocations in Parallel Voting

Political Parties	Number of District Seats Won	Percentage of the National Party List Vote	Number of Seats Added from Party Lists	Total Number of Seats	% of Party List Vote vs. % of Total Seats
Democratic	34	40%	20	54	40% / 54%
Republican	14	36%	18	32	36% / 32%
Reform	2	18%	9	11	18% / 11%
Green	0	6%	3	3	6% / 3%
Totals	50	100%	50	100	100% / 100%

have a fifty/fifty division of seats elected by each side of the ballot, others do not. In Japan, for instance, 60% of the seats are elected in single-member districts and 40% from the party lists. As a rule, the larger percentage of the seats elected in single-member districts, the less proportional the allocation of seats among the parties.

At first glance, many Americans might think of parallel voting as a completely new and somewhat strange approach to voting. But in reality, it closely resembles a method of voting that is already in common use in this country. Many cities and towns now use a combined voting system, in which some seats are elected in single-member districts and others from an at-large election. Parallel voting is very similar, except that a list vote is substituted for the at-large vote.

Advantages Specific to This System

Somewhat Friendlier to Minor Parties

As you saw earlier, cumulative voting and particularly limited voting can be hostile to small minor parties, sometimes preventing them from having any representation at all. In contrast, the party list part of parallel voting usually allows for some representation of minor parties, but usually less than they deserve by virtue of their proportion of the vote. As you know by now, how much a system is open to small minor parties depends very much on its threshold of exclusion. Parallel systems tend to have a very low threshold on the party list side of the vote, compared to the other semiproportional systems. In Russia, for instance, the threshold is 5%. These lower thresholds make it somewhat easier for minor parties to win some representation in this form of semiproportional voting.

Larger Party System and Broader Debate

Because parallel voting is somewhat more favorable to minor parties, it is more likely to result in multiparty races and multiparty legislatures. This in turn is more likely to broaden political debate, as more diverse points of view are represented in campaign debates and policy discussions.

Of course, proponents of plurality elections and two-party systems are likely to see its multiparty propensities as a disadvantage of parallel voting, particularly if they result in coalition government. However, it should be noted that because it is only semiproportional and tends to favor the largest party (discussed later), parallel voting is somewhat more likely to produce single-party legislative majorities than is PR. This may lessen some criticisms of its multiparty tendencies.

Geographical Representation

The cumulative vote and the limited vote both use only multimember districts. In parallel voting, half the seats are located in small, single-member districts, thus allowing more direct geographical representation. Each local area is assured of representation, and there is also the possibility of closer ties between the representatives and their constituents.

Better Expression of Political Views

Having two different votes allows voters to express more complicated political views. For example, voters may split their votes as a way of expressing their support for a particular coalition of parties. Supporters of the Greens would cast their party list vote for their own party to ensure that it would win some seats in the legislature. Then in the district contest, they might cast their other vote for the major party candidate who had the best chance to win and was closest to their political perspective—probably the Democratic candidate. In this way, they would effectively express their preference for a coalition of Greens and Democrats.

Disadvantages Specific to This System

Like those of CV and LV, many of the disadvantages of parallel voting are related to its inconsistent proportionality. But the cause of this inconsistency is very different than in LV and CV, in which the problem is rooted in mistakes in nominations and the misallocation of party votes. In parallel voting, the inconsistencies are caused by the use of single-member plurality districts. The use of such districts means that the results of parallel voting can sometimes resemble the disproportional results of plurality voting.

Violations of Majority Rule

Parallel voting may violate the principle of majority rule in two different ways, both of which are due to the presence of plurality voting. First, on the district level, plurality voting may result in the election of a candidate who is not supported by the majority of the voters. This is especially likely if there are more than two candidates running. In a parallel vote election in 1995 in Russia, so many parties put up candidates in the single-member districts that some seats were won with as little as 20% of the total vote.

The other way that parallel voting can violate majority rule occurs when a party with less than a majority of the votes wins a majority of the seats in the legislature—a manufactured majority. As shown in Table 5.9, the Democrats won 54% of the legislative seats with only 40% of the vote. Of course, proponents of plurality-majority voting who prefer single-party majorities may consider these manufactured majorities a strength rather than a defect of parallel voting.

Bias toward Large Parties

As Table 5.9 illustrates, the distortions in representation in this system tend to favor larger parties and to punish smaller parties. As a rule, large parties tend to get more seats than they deserve in the single-member district contests, and there is no attempt to compensate for this bias. For example, in a 1996 parallel voting election in Japan, the largest party received only 32.8% of the party list vote but ended up with 48.2% of the total seats. In contrast, in a mixed-member proportional election in New Zealand that same year, the largest party received 34.1% of the vote and 36.7% of the total seats.

Although this bias is similar to the one in plurality-majority voting, it is not quite as strong. Instead of completely shutting out minor parties, it merely gives them fewer seats than they deserve. In the Japanese parallel election mentioned earlier, one small party won 13.1% of the list vote, but only 5.2% of the total seats, while in the New Zealand MMP elections, a similar minor party received 13.1% of the vote and 14.2% of the total seats.

Gerrymandering

Because it utilizes single-member districts, parallel voting encourages gerrymandering: the drawing of district lines to advantage a particular party. In MMP, any gerrymandering that takes place in the districts is relatively harmless, because the final proportion of any party seats in the legislature is determined by the party list vote and thus cannot be distorted by gerrymandering. But since the parallel system makes no effort to ensure proportionality, gerrymandering is unchecked and can easily create misrepresentation of parties in the legislature.

Two Types of Representatives

Like MMP, parallel voting creates two kinds of representatives: one representing districts, the other not. This means that some representatives will have close local ties and spend part of their time on constituency service, and others will not. In addition, smaller parties will often have most or all of their representatives coming from the party list portion of the ballot. Supporters of plurality-majority voting suggest that this lack of geographical ties could insulate some officials from public opinion and also favor them with a lighter workload.

Some Discouragement of Sincere Votes

Plurality voting in districts discourages supporters of minor party candidates from casting sincere votes. They are usually forced to vote for the next-best major party candidate; otherwise they would be wasting their vote. However, people can vote sincerely on the party list part of the ballot, because those votes for minor parties are likely to be effective in winning some representation.

More Difficult to Use and Administer

Unlike the cumulative vote and the limited vote, parallel voting is not based on the familiar at-large approach to voting. This has led some critics to be concerned that American voters would be unfamiliar with this kind of ballot and confused by the two-vote system. But proponents argue that this two-ballot system is not all that different from the combined at-large/single-member district systems already in use in many American cities. They maintain that with a bit of education, voters should be able to pick up this voting system rather quickly.

Election administrators would have to spend some time learning new methods and procedures, although the single-member district part of this voting system would be familiar enough. On the positive side, this voting method could probably be easily used on many current voting machines.

Spotlight on the Debate 5.4
PR versus Semi-PR: Is Feasibility the Issue?

Advocates of proportional representation and semiproportional representation usually share many of the same political values and goals. But they can differ over the desirability of semiproportional systems. On one level, the disagreement is similar to that classic debate over whether the glass is half-empty or half-full. Critics of semiproportional voting argue that the glass is half-empty, insisting that these systems are inferior in many ways to full PR systems and too unreliable in their results. Supporters, on the other hand, insist that the glass is half-full—that semiproportional systems are superior to plurality-majority systems in many ways.

But another major source of contention between advocates of PR and semi-PR systems is the issue of political feasibility: How easy it is for a particular system to be adopted in the United States? Many advocates of semi-PR systems acknowledge that they have some drawbacks when compared to full PR systems but insist that systems like the cumulative vote are much more politically feasible—that they have fewer political obstacles and a much greater chance of being adopted in the United States than PR.

They emphasize that the cumulative vote is not very different from at-large voting—a system with which many Americans are familiar and comfortable. In fact, cumulative voting has sometimes been called *modified at-large voting* to stress the similarities between the two. It is thought that it is much easier to get the support of politicians, election administrators, and citizens if the change you are asking for is not too drastic. The problem with full PR systems is that they can be seen as a radical change from the status quo, and this perception could put off people who might find this kind of change uncomfortable or confusing. Yes, PR may be a "better" system than semi-PR, but that is of little good if it cannot be adopted. There is an old political saying, "The perfect is the enemy of the good." Insisting on the "perfect" PR solution may result in political defeat, whereas promoting the merely "good" semi-PR system stands a much better chance of victory. Or to use a different political aphorism: "Half a loaf is better than none." It is better to have some voting system reform than to have none at all.

Naturally, PR proponents disagree with this view of voting system feasibility. First, they point out that semiproportional systems are not necessarily easier to sell and that these systems have often run into serious political opposition where they have been proposed. Second, they argue that if Americans are given the proper information about PR, many will find it an easily understandable and desirable voting system. They point to New Zealand as an example of the feasibility of PR in Western countries similar to the United States. In 1993, after many years of study and debate, New Zealand citizens participated in a referendum in which they voted to reject their traditional single-member district system and adopted a mixed-member proportional system for their national parliamentary elections.

In recent years, there have only been a few referendums on PR in the United States—one in Cincinnati and the other in San Francisco. In both cases, the pro-PR forces had little money for public education campaigns and eventually lost the vote. However, supporters point out that they were still able to attract the support of over 40% of the voters in both cities—an impressive outcome that indicates that many Americans can easily appreciate the appeal of this system. Since they believe that PR is a feasible political goal, some PR supporters believe it is a waste of time and effort to promote alternatives such as semiproportional systems that are clearly inferior. Why settle for half a loaf when you can have a whole one?

NOTES

1. Arend Lijphart, Rafael Lopez Pintor, and Yasunori Sone, "The Limited Vote and Single Nontransferable Vote: Lessons from the Japanese and Spanish Examples," in *Electoral Laws and Their Political Consequences*, ed. Bernard Grofman and Arend Lijphart (New York: Agathon Press, 1986), p. 167.

2. Richard H. Pildes and Kristen A. Donoghue, "Cumulative Voting in the United States," *The University of Chicago Legal Forum* (1995): 301.

3. Lijphart, Pintor, and Sone, *Electoral Laws*, p. 167.

4. George S. Blair, *Cumulative Voting: An Effective Electoral Device in Illinois Politics* (Urbana, Ill., University of Illinois Press, 1960), p. 69.

5. "Senator Charles Buckalew: A 19th Century Champion of Democracy," in *Voting and Democracy Report 1995* (Washington D.C.: Center for Voting and Democracy, 1995), p. 33.

6. Lani Guinier, *The Tyranny of the Majority: Fundamental Fairness in Representative Democracy* (New York: The Free Press, 1994), pp. 16, 152.

7. Robert Brischetto, "Cumulative Voting at Work in Texas," in *Voting and Democracy Report 1995* (Washington D.C.: Center for Voting and Democracy, 1995), p. 63.

8. Blaine F. Moore, "The History of Cumulative Voting and Minority Representation in Illinois, 1870–1919." *University of Illinois Studies in the Social Sciences* 8, no.2 (June 1919): 34.

9. Pildes and Donoghue, "Cumulative Voting," p. 301.

10. Pildes and Donoghue, "Cumulative Voting," p. 294.

11. Richard L. Cole, Delbert A. Taebel, and Richard L. Engstrom, "Alternatives to Single-Member Districts," *Western Political Quarterly* (March 1990): 191–99.

12. Lijphart, Pintor, and Sone, *Electoral Laws*, p. 161.

13. Andrew Reynolds and Ben Reilly, *The International IDEA Handbook of Electoral Design* (Stockholm: International Institute for Democracy and Electoral Assistance, 1997), p. 51.

CHAPTER 6

Voting Systems for Single-Office Elections

This chapter is somewhat of a detour. The three previous chapters dealt with various voting systems used for legislative elections. And most of the current debate both here and abroad concerns these kinds of elections. However, many of the most important elections in the United States have nothing to do with legislatures. This chapter addresses the various voting systems that can be used for executive and administrative positions—what political scientists call *single-office elections*. If your main concern is with reforming city council or state legislative elections—and not single-office elections—then you could safely skip this chapter and simply continue on to the final chapter.

Our most powerful elected officials are those who occupy single-office positions, such as mayors, city treasurers, state attorneys general, judges, governors, and presidents. These officials wield extensive and wide-ranging administrative powers. In addition, these offices are the only ones for which everyone votes and these officials are the only ones who can legitimately claim to act on behalf of all the voters in a jurisdiction. And yet for all the importance of these single-office elections, most of us rarely think twice about the voting system we employ to choose these officials. We routinely use the traditional American voting system—plurality voting—for these elections. It just seems to be common sense that the winner of these contests should be the candidate who gets the most votes. Many Americans would undoubtedly be surprised to learn that not everyone agrees that plurality voting is the best approach to single-office elections; in fact, many experts consider it flawed. They observe that plurality voting can violate the basic democratic principle of majority rule—that it can result in the election of a candidate who is not supported by the majority of the electorate. Because of this problem several alternatives to plurality voting have been developed and already are in use in several other democratic countries.

Unlike legislative elections, only a few alternatives exist for single-office elections. Obviously those voting systems that require multimember

Ballot 6.1
Single-Office Plurality Voting

Official Ballot **Municipal Elections**	
DIRECTIONS TO VOTERS	**Candidates for Mayor**
1. To Vote: Mark an "X" in the box next to your preferred candidate. 2. To vote for a person whose name is not printed on the ballot, write the candidate's name on the extra line provided and put an "X" in the box next to the name.	Martinez, Richard (Democrat) ☐ Baylor, Susan (Republican) ☐ Chou, Thomas (Independent) ☐ Steadman, Peter (Libertarian) ☐ *Write-In* ☐

districts, such as proportional and semiproportional systems, cannot be used to elect a single official. So we are left with various forms of winner-take-all voting: plurality voting, two-round runoff voting, and instant runoff voting. As in prior chapters, first the workings of each system are described, followed by an explanation of its major political advantages and disadvantages. Naturally, much of this chapter reviews topics previously discussed in chapter three; however, the analysis is not identical. Much of the analysis of these systems in the earlier chapter had to do with their political impacts on the legislature—such as the extent of geographical or party representation—and these issues are not relevant in this chapter.

PLURALITY VOTING

The plurality voting system is used for most single-office elections in the United States, including races for mayor and governor. Besides being used commonly in the United States, this system is also used to elect the presidents of Mexico, the Philippines, South Korea, and Venezuela.

How It Works

The plurality voting system is so familiar to Americans, it hardly needs to be described. All the candidates appear on the ballot and the voters indicate their choice of one by marking an X, pulling a voting lever, and so on (see Ballot 6.1). All the votes are then counted and the winner is the candidate with the most votes. In the results shown in Table 6.1, Martinez is the winner with 43% of the vote. As this example illustrates, winners need not collect a majority of the votes, only more votes than their opponents—a plurality of the votes.

Table 6.1
Results of a Plurality Election

Candidates & Parties	Vote Totals	% of the Vote
Martinez, Richard (Democrat)	43,000	43%
Baylor, Susan (Republican)	40,000	40%
Chou, Thomas (Independent)	9,000	9%
Steadman, Peter (Libertarian)	8,000	8%
Total	100,000	100%

*Winning candidate.

Advantages

Simplicity

Virtually all experts agree that one main advantage of plurality voting is that it is a simple and elegant way to choose a winner. It follows the basic principle that the winner should be the person who gets more votes than any of the other candidates. It is also an easy and familiar system for American voters—all they have to do is indicate their preferred candidate.

Potential for Majority Winner

When only two candidates vie for office, as is often the case in our two-party system, this system produces a winner who has the support of the majority of the electorate.

Convenient to Administer

Plurality voting is also convenient for election officials to administer. The alternatives discussed later require either an additional election or a change in the ballots and the way they are counted. Continuing to use plurality voting means no changes in traditional administrative procedures or in voting machine technology.

Short Ballot and Clear-Cut Choices

Plurality voting also tends to create simple and short ballots—uncluttered by a large number of candidates vying for each office. It often discourages third-party and independent candidates from running for office, because they have little chance of winning under plurality rules. Only rarely can they get the plurality of votes needed to win, and this hurdle is often enough to deter them from entering the race. Thus in this system, voters usually end up with a clear and simple choice between the two major-party candidates.

However, critics of plurality voting maintain that American voters are not confused when more than two candidates run. Given adequate information, voters can easily make an informed choice among three, four, or five candidates for office. They also argue that the discouragement of third-party and independent candidates limits voters' choices and thus is actually a disadvantage of this system—a point that is discussed later.

Disadvantages

Violations of Majority Rule

The main charge against plurality voting is that at times it violates the most basic principle of democracy: majority rule. This problem occurs when more than two candidates vie for office. For example, in the results listed in Table 6.1, the candidates split up the votes in such a way that the winning candidate, Martinez, did not get a majority—only 43%. This means that although Martinez won, he had the support of only a minority of the voters.

In other words, under plurality rules the winner can be someone the majority actually voted against. In 1996, for example, governors elected in three states (Connecticut, Hawaii, and Maine) all received less than 37% of the vote. Almost two-thirds of the voters wanted someone else to be governor in those states. Critics of plurality voting argue that this lack of majority support undermines the political legitimacy of such officials. (For more on this point, see Spotlight on the Debate 6.1: Is It Important to Have a Majority Winner?)

This drawback of plurality voting is particularly evident in primaries, in which there can be large fields of candidates vying for a nomination. In a 1998 race in Massachusetts to determine the Democratic nominee for a U.S. House seat, ten candidates ran and the winner attracted only 23% of the vote. Parties naturally want to put up the strongest candidate with the most widespread appeal, but they are not sure to find that person when the voting system allows a candidate to win with only a very small minority of the vote. Also, if there are several centrist candidates who split the mainstream party vote, a candidate who represents an extreme faction of the party could win the nomination. In any case, it is difficult for someone to claim to represent a party when most of its supporters voted for someone else.

More Wasted Votes

All single-office voting systems waste a large number of votes—votes that elect no one to office. However, plurality voting can produce more wasted votes than majority voting systems. When three or more candidates vie for office, the wasted votes can easily surpass 50%.

Sincere Votes Discouraged

Plurality voting can also discourage citizens from casting sincere votes for the candidates they truly support. This problem primarily affects supporters of third-party and independent candidates—candidates who would have a tough time attracting the plurality of votes necessary to win in this system. These voters are often faced with a dilemma: If they vote for their preferred candidate, their vote will likely be wasted. Worse, voting for a minor-party candidate could throw the election to the voter's least favorite candidate. For example, in the 1992 presidential election, conservatives who cast their votes for Ross Perot took their votes away from George Bush and helped Bill Clinton win. In this way, casting a sincere vote can be self-defeating—it can actually hurt your political interests. Given this situation, minor-party supporters often are forced to abandon their true political ideals and vote for the lesser of two evils of the major-party candidates—or they decide not to vote at all. In 1992, nearly one-third of those who expressed a first preference for Perot ended up voting for one of the major-party candidates.

Reduced Range of Voter Choice

As noted, plurality voting can discourage minor-party and independent candidates from running. But although this does make for a simpler two-candidate ballot, it also reduces the competitiveness of elections and the range of political choices offered to voters.

Spoiler Candidates

Plurality voting does not always work to the advantage of the two major parties. When third-party candidates do run, they can act as spoilers in this system, taking crucial votes away from the major-party candidate who would have otherwise been the winner in a two-way race. In the results shown in Table 6.1, the Libertarian candidate may have acted as a spoiler by taking some conservative votes away from the Republican candidate, thus helping the Democrat to win.

In 1997, a spoiler played a key role in a special election to fill a U.S. House seat in New Mexico. The Democrats lost a seat that had traditionally been theirs because a popular Green party candidate, Carol Miller, won 17% of the vote and threw the election to the Republican candidate, who won with only 42% of the vote. The Democrats were naturally upset about these results and even some of the Greens were not happy with the outcome. This dissatisfaction created some interest in New Mexico in voting systems that could prevent this problem, and a constitutional amendment to enact instant runoff voting for federal and state elections passed the state senate before losing in the house.

Negative Campaigning

Critics maintain that plurality voting encourages negative campaigns by the two major-party candidates. Since minor-party candidates stand little chance of winning, the two leading candidates can safely ignore them and concentrate on attacking their rivals. In what is essentially a two-person race, personal attacks become a good strategy. Mudslinging is an easy and effective way to turn voters away from your opponent. And even if those alienated voters don't come over to your side and simply decide not to vote, this tendency also works to your advantage.

Spotlight on the Debate 6.1
Is It Important to Have a Majority Winner?

Proponents of plurality voting often argue that it should not matter whether the winner of the election gets a majority of the vote. The point of elections is to find the most popular candidate, and plurality voting does just that. As long as the victor receives more votes than any of the challengers, he or she is the legitimate winner. Besides, if the winner gets very close to half the votes, say over 47% or 48%, why quibble over the fact that it is not a formal majority?

Critics respond that minority winners may often receive substantially less than 50% of the vote, especially in crowded primaries. Furthermore, they argue, when a winning candidate fails to get a majority of the vote, this result raises some serious political questions. The first question involves legitimacy. Can a winning candidate be considered the legitimate representative of the voters if most of them voted for other candidates? When politicians occupy very powerful political positions such as mayor, governor, or president, they should have the maximum consent of the governed. A frequent complaint about the recent winners of presidential elections is that while they are supposed to lead the American people, they often receive the support of less than half the voters.

A related question concerns mandates. Most winning candidates claim a mandate to rule—a public endorsement of a certain set of public policies advocated by the candidate. But is there a valid mandate if the winner does not have the support of the majority of the voters? Consider the hypothetical election results described in Table 6.1. If Martinez is a liberal Democrat and independent Chou is a middle-of-the-road candidate, then it can be said that most voters cast their ballots for candidates who are more conservative than Martinez. Does Martinez really have a valid public mandate to pursue a liberal policy agenda? For critics, such questions raise serious doubts about the desirability of nonmajority winners' occupying important political offices.

TWO-ROUND RUNOFF VOTING

The two-round runoff system, also known as the *second ballot system*, has been in use in Western democracies since the nineteenth century. It was

Table 6.2
Results of the Second-Round Runoff

Candidates & Parties	Vote Totals	% of the Vote
Martinez, Richard (Democrat)	49,000	49%
*Baylor, Susan (Republican)	51,000	51%
Total	100,000	100%

*Winning candidate.

one of the first attempts to remedy the main problem of plurality voting: the possibility of the winner's receiving less than a majority of the votes. Currently it is used in many local elections in the United States and in some state legislative and federal races, mainly in primaries. Abroad, versions of it are used to elect presidents in such countries as Austria, Brazil, Bulgaria, Chile, Colombia, Finland, Poland, Portugal, and Russia.

How It Works

The main purpose of the runoff system is to ensure that the winning candidate receives a majority of the vote. In order to do this it uses two rounds of voting, with polling on two separate days. Ballots are identical to those used in plurality voting (see Ballot 6.1), and voters mark them in the same way. In the first round, all candidates are listed on the ballot and voters indicate their preference for one of them. All these votes are then added up, and if a candidate receives a majority of the vote (50% + 1 vote), that candidate is declared elected. If no one receives a majority, the field is cut down to the two candidates who received the highest number of votes, and a second election is held, usually several weeks later. The winner is the candidate who gets the most votes, and since there are only two candidates, the winning candidate inevitably receives a majority of the votes. (Some jurisdictions require only 40% of the vote to avoid a runoff, an arrangement that obviously does not ensure that a winner has majority support.)

For example, if the result of the first round of voting in the general election were that shown in Table 6.1, then the two top vote getters, Martinez and Baylor, would move on to the second round of balloting. The supporters of the eliminated candidates would then have an opportunity to switch their votes to one of the two remaining contenders. Table 6.2 shows the results of that second ballot, in which Baylor receives the majority of the vote and is declared the winner. Notice that even though Baylor took second place in the first round of voting, and so would have lost under plurality voting rules, she picks up enough votes in the second round to become the winning candidate in this system of voting.

Advantages

Majority Rule

The main advantage of this voting system is that it prevents plurality wins and ensures that the winning candidate enjoys the support of the majority of the voters who turn out to vote in the second round. Advocates argue that this increases the political legitimacy of elected officials and gives them a genuine mandate to govern.

Easy to Use and Administer

Like plurality voting, this system is easily understood by voters. It is also easy to administer and requires no changes in voting machines or counting procedures.

Elimination of Spoilers

Besides assuring majority winners, this system addresses the spoiler problem caused by the presence of minor-party or independent candidates. These candidates cannot take votes away from one major-party candidate and allow the other major-party candidate to win with a plurality of the vote. In the preceding example, the two major-party candidates made it to the runoff, where the results showed which of them was most preferred by the majority of the voters.

More Sincere Votes

This voting system allows supporters of minor parties to vote for their preferred candidates in the first round of balloting without fearing that they will waste their votes or throw the election to the least desirable major-party candidate. If their candidate cannot win and is eliminated, then they can switch their vote to another preferred candidate in the second round of balloting.

Wider Range of Voter Choice

More third-party and independent candidates are likely to run under the two-round runoff system than under plurality voting rules, thus giving voters a wider range of choices at the polls. Under runoff rules, these candidates need not worry about being spoilers and they may be more confident of getting votes from their supporters in the first round.

This system does not make it any easier for these candidates to actually win office, but it does create a more welcoming electoral environment for their candidacies. However, some supporters of plurality voting would argue that this feature of two-round runoff voting is actually a disadvantage because it merely encourages frivolous candidates to crowd onto the ballot and thus serves to confuse voters.

Interparty Cooperation and Alliances

Experts have noted that this system fosters cooperation among political parties. In particular, it encourages larger parties to cooperate and form alliances with smaller parties. As the candidates of the larger parties go into the second round of voting, it makes sense for them to court the supporters of minor-party candidates who have been eliminated. Both sides can benefit from such alliances. The larger parties receive the support they need to win office and the smaller parties gain some leverage over these officials, because they can argue that their party made the difference in the candidate's victory.

Fewer Wasted Votes

Because a majority of votes is required to win office, the maximum number of wasted votes is 49.9%. Under plurality rules this number can be higher.

Disadvantages

Expensive to Administer

One of the main disadvantages of this system is that governments must often pay for two separate elections. This can make it much more expensive than one-round election systems such as plurality voting and instant runoff voting. It usually costs at least one to two dollars per resident to administer an election, so the costs of a second election can be considerable. In San Francisco, the cost of a runoff election for mayor can be nearly $1 million. In addition, runoff candidates have often spent nearly all their campaign funds, and so they are then forced to find added funds for another (albeit brief) campaign. However, advocates of this system maintain that these added expenses are a reasonable price to pay to ensure a majority winner.

Lower Turnout in Second Round

This runoff system can also be plagued by low voter turnout in the second and decisive round of voting. Often voter participation drops off considerably from that of the first round. Experts believe that this second-round drop-off is probably due to several factors, including voter fatigue and a decline in the excitement that originally surrounded the general election. In addition, supporters of candidates who do not make the runoff may also be less likely to vote a second time.

Since voter turnout is already low in American elections, any further drop in turnout can be a matter of concern. If turnout for the runoff falls from 50% to 30%, and the winner only garners a bit more than half of that, then that person only has the explicit support of less than 20% of the eligible voters. This situation again raises questions about the political legitimacy of the winning candidate and the validity of his or her mandate. It is not unheard of for the winner of the second round to garner fewer votes than the loser did in the first round. Does such a person really represent the majority of voters?

Some Discouragement of Sincere Votes

There are a few situations in which this system could discourage people from casting sincere votes for minor-party and independent candidates. For example, let's say that your preferred candidate on the ballot is Steadman, a Libertarian. But polls indicate that Steadman is likely to finish last and has virtually no chance of making the runoff. A vote for Steadman could then take a vote away from your next preferred candidate—say Martinez, the Democrat—and thus hurt Martinez's chances of making it to the runoff. In this case, it would make sense to abandon your first choice and vote for your second choice. But although this situation could occasionally occur, most experts do not consider it a very serious drawback, and it is clear that the two-ballot runoff system does not discourage sincere votes for minor-party candidates to the extent that plurality voting does.

Some Negative Campaigning

This system has a mixed impact on the quality of campaigns. In the first round of voting, candidates might be less likely to engage in negative personal attacks because they do not want to offend the other candidates' supporters, who might eventually become their supporters in a runoff. However, in the second round of voting, in a head-to-head runoff, the incentive to engage in negative campaigning would return because the previous political drawbacks have disappeared.

Elimination of Possible Winner

It is possible for this system to eliminate a candidate who might turn out to be the winner. This problem is most likely if the second and third-place candidates are relatively close, and the third is arbitrarily eliminated. Assume, for example, that in the first round of voting Martinez received 34%

of the vote, Chou 28%, Baylor 27%, and Steadman 11%. This system would eliminate Baylor and Steadman, even though it is conceivable that Baylor might beat Martinez in a runoff. Advocates of this system maintain that this is likely to be a rare occurrence, and so it should not be a large matter of concern. They also point out that such candidates would have lost in plurality voting as well.

Spotlight on the Debate 6.2:
How Often Do We Need Runoffs?

The appeal of two-round and instant runoff voting systems depends greatly on how often they are needed. So it would be helpful to know how often plurality voting produces winners with less than a majority of the vote. If this is a relatively rare occurrence, then there may be little need for these alternative voting systems. Unfortunately, there are as yet few systematic studies of this issue. One study done in Vermont found that over its history of statewide general elections, there have been 120 races with no majority winner—including 21 races for governor—and that in 37% of all election years at least one statewide office race produced a nonmajority winner. The report concluded, "Vermont has had frequent and serious problems with the failure to popularly elect constitutional officers by a majority vote."[1] This suggests that at least in Vermont nonmajority wins occur often enough to be a matter of some concern.

The frequency of nonmajority winners clearly depends on how many voters are interested in minor-party and independent candidates. This could vary from area to area. In jurisdictions with little such interest and only major parties on the ballot, plurality voting would seem to work fine. However, it is often unclear whether the lack of minor candidates on the ballot is actually a result of voter commitment to the two major parties or of the tendency of plurality voting itself to discourage support of minor-party candidates. The adoption of runoff systems may allow for the expression of previously stifled interest in nonmajor-party candidates.

Moreover, advocates of runoff systems note that some evidence suggests that Americans are becoming more likely to welcome minor-party and independent candidates. Recent polls indicate that two-thirds of voters would like to see other parties emerge to challenge the Republicans and Democrats. In addition, changes in campaign finance laws in some states are making it easier for such candidates to get funds and enter races. In 1998, 89% of U.S. voters received ballots containing at least one minor-party or independent candidate for office. As the number of these candidates increases, so too will the number of nonmajority winners, and this trend could fuel more interest in runoff voting systems.

INSTANT RUNOFF VOTING

Instant runoff voting is also known as *IRV*, the *alternative vote*, and *majority preferential voting*. This system is designed to remove the dilemma

Ballot 6.2
Instant Runoff Voting

<table>
<tr><td colspan="2" align="center">Official Ballot
Municipal Elections</td></tr>
<tr><td>DIRECTIONS TO VOTERS</td><td align="center">Candidates for Mayor</td></tr>
<tr><td rowspan="2">
1. Do not use X marks.
2. Mark your choices with NUMBERS only.
3. Put the figure 1 opposite your first choice, the figure 2 opposite your second choice, the figure 3 opposite your third choice, and so on. You may make as many choices as you please.
4. Do not put the same figure opposite more than one name.
</td>
<td>
Martinez, Richard (Democrat) |
Baylor, Susan (Republican) |
Chou, Thomas (Independent) |
Steadman, Peter (Libertarian) |
Write-In |
</td></tr>
<tr><td>
To Vote for a Write-In Candidate: Next to the name you have written in, put a number that represents your choice for that candidate.
</td></tr>
</table>

of having to choose between plurality voting (which might not produce a majority winner) and the two-round system (which is expensive and discourages participation). Instant runoff voting promises to produce a majority winner, while eliminating the major disadvantages of the two-round system.

IRV has been primarily used abroad, although it was first invented in the 1870s by a professor at the Massachusetts Institute of Technology. Currently it is used in the Republic of Ireland to elect their president, in London to elect its mayor, and in single-member districts in Australia to elect members of their lower house of parliament. IRV is also used by several private organizations in the United States, including the American Political Science Association and the American Psychological Association, to elect their officials.

How It Works

This system provides for a run-off without a separate election—hence the term *instant runoff*. Like plurality voting, all candidates are listed on the ballot. But instead of voting for only one candidate, voters can choose to rank the candidates in the order of their preference. This ranking process is illustrated in Ballots 6.2 and 6.3. On Ballot 6.2, voters simply write a 1 next to their first choice, a 2 next to their second choice, and so on. Ballot 6.3 is a ballot that is used with the scanning AccuVote machine, and the process of voting is similar to marking answers on the standardized tests

Ballot 6.3
Instant Runoff Voting (Scannable Version)

Official Ballot Municipal Elections		
INSTRUCTIONS TO VOTERS **Mark Your Choices by Filling in the Numbered Boxes Only** Fill in the number one ▯ box next to your first choice; fill in the number two ▯ box next to your second choice; fill in the number three ▯ box next to your third choice, and so on. You may fill in as many choices as you please. Fill in no more than one box per candidate. Fill in no more than one box per column.	**Candidates for Mayor**	*Only one vote per candidate* Only one vote per column
	Martinez, Richard (Democrat)	▯1 ▯2 ▯3 ▯4
	Baylor, Susan (Republican)	▯1 ▯2 ▯3 ▯4
	Chou, Thomas (Independent)	▯1 ▯2 ▯3 ▯4
	Steadman, Peter (Libertarian)	▯1 ▯2 ▯3 ▯4
	Write-In	▯1 ▯2 ▯3 ▯4
	To Vote for a Write-In Candidate: Next to the name you have written in, mark a numbered box to indicate your choice of number for that candidate.	
	Do Not Use Red To Mark Ballot	

used in schools. On this ballot, voters fill in numbered boxes to indicate their ranking of the candidates.

The counting of the ballots is also different from that in plurality voting. First, all the number-one preferences of the voters are counted. If a candidate receives over 50% of the first-choice votes, he or she is declared elected. If no candidate receives a majority, then the candidate with the fewest votes is eliminated. The ballots of supporters of this defeated candidate are then transferred to whichever of the remaining candidates they marked as their next preference. The votes are then recounted to see whether any candidate now has a majority of the vote. The process of eliminating the lowest candidate and transferring his or her votes continues until one candidate receives a majority of the continuing votes and wins the election.

This transfer process is illustrated in Table 6.3. In this hypothetical election, no candidate receives over 50% of the vote in the first round of counting. So the lowest candidate—Steadman—is eliminated and his ballots are transferred to each of his supporters' second choices. Of Steadman's supporters, 1,000 ranked Chou as their second choice, 5,000 indicated Baylor as their second choice, and 2,000 listed Martinez as number two. The new totals show that no one yet has a majority, so Chou is eliminated. Of Chou's votes, 6,000 are transferred to Baylor and 4,000 are given to Martinez. (If some of Chou's ballots had listed Steadman as the second preference, they would have been transferred to their third preference, since Steadman had been eliminated.) After this transfer it is clear that Baylor

Table 6.3
Transfer Process in Instant Runoff Voting

	First Count	Second Count		Third Count	
Candidates & Parties	Original First Choice Votes	Transfer of Steadman's Votes	New Totals	Transfer of Chou's Votes	New Totals
Martinez, Richard (Democrat)	43,000	+ 2,000	45,000	+ 4,000	49,000
*Baylor, Susan (Republican)	40,000	+ 5,000	45,000	+ 6,000	51,000
Chou, Thomas (Independent)	9,000	+ 1,000	10,000	-------	-------
Steadman, Peter (Libertarian)	8,000	-------	-------	-------	-------

*Winning candidate.
Note: Total electorate, 100,000; needed to win, 50,001.

now has over 50% of the vote and she is declared the winner. As this example illustrates, this system essentially operates as a series of runoff elections, with progressively fewer candidates each time, until one candidate gets a majority of the remaining votes.

Advantages

Majority Rule

Instant runoff voting shares many of the advantages of two-round runoff voting. Its main benefit is ensuring a majority winner and thus increasing the political legitimacy of elected officials and giving them a genuine mandate to govern.

More Sincere Votes

Supporters of minor-party candidates can cast their votes sincerely under IRV rules without fear that they will waste them. If their preferred candidate cannot win, then their ballot will likely be transferred to a candidate who has a better chance of victory.

Elimination of Spoilers

IRV also eliminates the possibility of third-party or independent candidates' acting as spoilers. In the race shown in the ballots, supporters of the independent candidate can vote for him without worrying that they will throw the election to the major party candidate they least prefer.

Fewer Wasted Votes

As with the two-round runoff system, IRV tends to produce somewhat fewer wasted votes than plurality voting. Experts note, however, that some votes in IRV may be wasted when they are "exhausted." Exhausted votes are those that cannot continue to be transferred, either because voters did not mark enough preferences or because their only remaining preference is for a candidate who was already eliminated.

Wider Range of Voter Choice

Because minor-party and independent candidates are more likely to receive votes under this system, they are more likely to run. So voters benefit from being able to choose from among a wider range of candidates and parties than would normally be available under plurality voting rules.

Cheaper Than Two-Round Runoff System

Supporters of IRV argue that one of its greatest appeals is that it addresses the problems of plurality voting while eliminating the disadvantages of the two-round runoff. For example, IRV avoids the higher expenses associated with holding a second election, so there is a significant cost savings for both governments and candidates. A recent runoff election for mayor in San Francisco cost that city almost $1 million.

No Drop in Turnout

Because it does not require a second runoff election held after the general election, IRV also prevents the drop in voter turnout that often occurs in the two-round runoff system. Higher voter turnout contributes to greater political legitimacy for elected officials.

Less Negative Campaigns

Some experts believe that IRV has the added benefit of discouraging negative campaigns and mudslinging. In this system, candidates can benefit from being the second choices of voters. Often these transfer votes can prove to be the margin of victory. But if they viciously attack their opponents, they risk alienating these possible supporters. In the preceding example, it would not be a good strategy for Baylor, the Republican candidate, to sling mud at Chou, the independent candidate, since it is likely that Baylor might otherwise receive some of Chou's transfer votes. So under IRV, it pays for candidates to spend less time on negative campaigning and more on explaining their own policies and values.

More Cooperative Politics

Some experts also believe that IRV may also be beneficial in situations in which there are deep political or racial divisions. Again this is due to its

tendency to encourage candidates to seek the votes of not only their supporters but also the second preferences of others. IRV requires that a winning candidate have a broad appeal in order to gain the majority of votes
needed to win. So instead of focusing on the narrow issues attractive to
only one group of voters, candidates could be moved to make broader,
more centrist appeals that would attract the maximum number of first- and
second-preference votes. One study of IRV use in Australia found that major parties have sometimes waged campaigns explicitly designed to increase
their attractiveness to supporters of particular minor parties.[2] In this sense,
IRV may foster more cooperative and less divisive politics.

Elimination of Primaries

Instant runoff voting can eliminate the need for primaries. In a mayoral
election, for example, all the candidates could run in the general election.
Those with the least support would be eliminated in the ballot transfer
process, much as they would have been in a primary. Voters who support
the least popular candidates would not have to worry about wasting their
vote. More importantly, all the expense, administrative burden, and low
turnout associated with primary elections could be avoided.

Disadvantages

Unfamiliar to Voters

One obvious drawback of IRV is its unfamiliarity to most American
voters. Since IRV would be a new and different system in most jurisdictions,
some critics argue that it would be confusing to many voters and cause
many spoiled ballots. Most experts believe, however, that Americans would
have little trouble using this voting system. Other countries that use this
system have not encountered voter confusion. With proper voter education,
American voters could easily master the process of ranking candidates.

Administrative Complexity and Expense

Administrators also will have to adapt to this new system and learn to
master the process of transferring the ballots. More importantly, this ranking process is difficult to accommodate on a number of current voting
machines. IRV advocates argue that the one-time expense of buying new
voting machines is not too high a price to pay for the advantages offered
by this system, and it is certainly less expensive in the long run than routinely funding separate runoff elections.

Guarantee of Majority of Continuing Votes Only

Some critics point out that instant runoff voting only guarantees that the
winner will receive a majority of the "continuing" votes, not a majority of

the votes that were originally cast. As seen earlier, IRV votes can be eliminated or "exhausted" if voters fail to mark enough preferences or if their only remaining preference is for a candidate who has already been eliminated. For example, if 1,000 of the voters who originally supported the independent candidate, Chou, did not mark any number-two preferences, then their ballots could not be transferred when Chou was eliminated. This would mean that a winning candidate would have to garner only a majority of the 99,000 continuing votes, not a majority of the original 100,000 votes that were cast.

Advocates of IRV maintain that this is hardly a major problem, and that even when it occurs, the winner still has more voter support than most nonmajority winners produced by plurality voting. They also argue that this possibility can be minimized by voter education campaigns that stress the importance of marking as many preferences as possible on the ballot. Australia has taken a somewhat different approach in its IRV elections: It requires voters to rank *all* the candidates running for office. This does help to minimize "exhausted ballots," but some reformers consider this too drastic a solution for what might be only an occasional problem.

Lack of Monotonicity

Some theoretically inclined critics of IRV point out that it can be non-monotonic, in that in some circumstances more first-place votes may hurt, rather than help, a candidate's chances of being elected. This complicated paradox involves a situation in which a candidate's receiving more votes can change the order in which other candidates are eliminated, with the result that their votes are transferred in ways that ultimately help a rival of the first candidate.[3]

It is undisputed that nonmonotonicity can theoretically occur in an IRV election, but most experts believe that the conditions needed for this paradox to occur are so special that it would be an extremely rare occurrence. One statistical study found that if IRV-like elections were held throughout the United Kingdom, a nonmonotonic result would occur less than once a century.[4]

NOTES

1. Vermont Commission to Study Preference Voting, *Final Report* (Montpelier, Vt.: Vermont House of Representatives, 1999), p. 7.

2. Clive Bean, "Australia's Experience with the Alternative Vote," *Representation* 34, no. 2 (1997): 106.

3. For a more lengthy description of this paradox, see David M. Farrell, *Comparing Electoral Systems* (New York: Prentice-Hall, 1997), pp. 134–136.

4. Crispin Allard, "Lack of Monotonicity—Revisited," *Representation* 33 (1995): 49.

CHAPTER 7

Making Your Final Choice

Now that you have come this far in your investigation of voting systems, you may be feeling a bit overwhelmed by all the information and arguments to which you have been exposed. You may also be more than a little confused by all the various options and their competing advantages and disadvantages. But be assured that some confusion at this point is natural. In fact, it may even be desirable. It is a sign that you have moved beyond your initial—and probably somewhat simplistic—views of voting systems and have begun to appreciate the complexity of these systems and their political implications. In any case, it is time to begin sorting out all of this information and to choose what you believe is the best voting system for your political circumstances.

The purpose of this chapter is to offer you some ways to think more clearly and systematically about that choice. The first part of this chapter describes some of the mistakes you should try to avoid in choosing among voting systems. I identify and discuss several of the most common mistakes that people make in thinking about and choosing among voting systems and suggest some ways to avoid these mental missteps. The second part of the chapter describes a simple yet systematic way to organize your thinking about voting system options—an approach that should help you a great deal in making your final decision.

SEVEN COMMON MISTAKES

Ironically, much of choosing a voting system in the right way involves *not* choosing one in the wrong way. There are many barriers to thinking clearly and rationally about voting system options. If you can avoid those mistakes, this will take you a long way toward making the best decision. What follows are the seven most common mistakes that people can make, along with some advice on how to avoid them.[1]

Unduly Limiting Your Options

Unduly limiting your options is one the most common mistakes made when selecting voting systems. If your range of alternatives is too narrow, you may inadvertently fail to consider the best voting system. It is impossible to choose the best system if it is not among the options you are considering. This may seem obvious, but many people nevertheless fall into this trap. In the past, reformers in the United States have often artificially restricted the range of alternatives they have considered. For instance, when city charter reform commissions have looked at alternative voting systems, invariably most have considered only single-member district or at-large systems. Or if they were being really creative, they also looked at a combined single-member and at-large systems. Rarely have they considered proportional or semiproportional systems. This is clearly a mistake that hampers the search for a good voting system.

The solution to this problem is simple. When looking for voting systems to examine, consider a wide variety of systems. Any adequate analysis should include systems not only from the plurality-majority family of systems, but from the other families as well. How many systems are included in the analysis will of course depend on the time and resources available to you or your group. An electoral reform commission with a year to produce a report could obviously consider many more options than a commission that must report in three months.

Keep in mind that the point here concerns not so much the number of systems you consider, but their variety. Considering a wide range of systems not only increases your chances of finding the best one, but the very process of comparing very different types of systems helps to illuminate the advantages and disadvantages of each and in that way contributes to a more informed decision.

Opting for the Comfortable Status Quo

Numerous psychological studies have shown that when faced with choices, people often have a strong bias toward sticking with the status quo.[2] This is understandable. The status quo often seems the most comfortable option, and it avoids the stress that accompanies any change. The problem, of course, is that the status quo may not be the best voting system, and automatically favoring it could mean that you retain an inferior system.

How do you know whether you are unfairly favoring the status quo? One common indication is a tendency to ignore or downplay problems with your current system. This is very easy to do. Often we become so used to the drawbacks of the prevailing system that we hardly notice them anymore. Take, for instance, the problem of wasted votes that is so common in the single-member plurality system we use in the United States. This problem is noticed immediately by most Europeans who observe an election in this country. Many are shocked at the high number of wasted votes in our elections. They are used to proportional representation voting systems in which there are few wasted votes and virtually everyone can win some representation in an election. But many Americans are so accustomed to our system that they rarely think of wasted votes as a problem. It is certainly not an issue raised by the media. Most people simply come to assume that it is normal for there to be winners and losers among voters, just as there are in every aspect of life. But this tendency to become accustomed to the problems of the prevailing system only serves to reinforce this inherent bias toward current arrangements.

How can you avoid this kind of knee-jerk preference for the status quo? One way is for you or someone else to play devil's advocate and raise arguments against the system currently in use. This will help to make sure that you are not unconsciously ignoring the problems inherent in this system. Another approach is to ask yourself whether you would favor your system if it weren't the current one. Would you choose your present system if you had to change to that system from another one? Finally, consciously try to make sure that you are not exaggerating the costs or efforts involved in switching voting systems. All political reforms involve some difficulties and awkward transitions, but these should not be allowed to discourage a change to a better voting system.

Black-and-White Thinking

It can be very tempting to fall into the trap of thinking of voting options in black-and-white terms—seeing a system as either good or bad. This approach can be appealing because choosing the best voting system is a complicated task, and thinking of your options as black or white can make that choice seem much easier. You can simply reject the bad systems and choose the good one. But this approach distorts the reality of the situation. None of the systems that we have looked at is all good or all bad; all have a combination of advantages and disadvantages.

Instead of seeing systems as either good or bad, think of them as existing along a scale from better to worse. For example, you may eventually decide that instant runoff majority voting is better than plurality voting for single-office elections. But that doesn't mean that the plurality voting is a bad system, only that you find that the instant runoff has more advantages and fewer disadvantages.

Selective Perception of the Evidence

As soon as you begin to look at different voting methods there is a tendency to find some of them more attractive than others. This is natural and is in itself not a large problem. It can become a problem, however, if you let this early preference affect the way you collect and consider evidence. The inclination is to seek out evidence that confirms your initial preferences and to ignore evidence that contradicts them. So if you are leaning toward PR, you seek out and focus on evidence of its advantages and ignore evidence of its problems. You might also focus on the problems of rival systems and disregard any evidence of their advantages. This selective perception often works in conjunction with black-and-white thinking. The tendency is to see all the good in one system and all the bad in the others, and that of course makes your decision much easier. Unfortunately, this comforting approach can interfere with thinking clearly about your options. It will give you a very distorted view of the evidence and lead to ill-informed choices.

If you keep several points in mind, you should be able to avoid this problem. First, you simply need to be aware of its existence and be on guard against its appearance. Recognizing when it is occurring is half the battle. Second, you should consciously try to be objective in collecting and considering evidence—something that is often easier said than done. One obvious step is to seek out evidence both for and against each system. If you have read the earlier chapters, then you have done much of that already. The problem then is not so much in gathering the evidence, but in which evidence you tend to focus on. Obviously, the more even-handed you can be in considering both the advantages and disadvantages of each system, the more accurate your understanding will be and the better your ultimate choice.

Being objective does not mean pretending that you aren't drawn to a particular system. It means acknowledging that attraction and yet trying to keep an open mind as you consider the evidence. In other words, you will inevitably form some initial impressions about voting systems, but try not to make any final decisions until you have considered all the relevant arguments and evidence.

Overreliance on Single-Country Examples

Another problem with evidence that can often get in the way of thinking clearly about voting system choices involves the use of single-country examples. There is sometimes a tendency to leap to conclusions about a voting system based on its use in one country. You may see a dramatic example of a country that has had serious political problems and use that to dismiss a particular method of voting from consideration. But this can be a mistake. As electoral scholars have pointed out, this kind of anecdotal evidence is notoriously unreliable. The political experiences of a single country using a voting system may be a very poor guide to the probable effects of that voting system somewhere else. Those experiences may not be typical of the countries that use that voting system, and the political problems of a single country may have more to do with other aspects of its political system or its political culture.

Nevertheless, you often see this focus on single-country cases in discussions about voting systems, and they are usually used to scare people away from even considering a particular system. Italy is a classic example. For years it was plagued by fragile parliamentary and cabinet coalitions that seemed to fall apart at the least provocation. It became notorious for its political instability. This led some critics of proportional representation to point to Italy as "proof" that PR would create unstable coalitions if we adopted it in the United States. You wouldn't want the United States to become another Italy, would you?

But the real question you should be asking is this: How reliable is Italy as an indicator of the stability of coalitions in PR systems? Not very, it turns out. Almost every European country using PR during the last several decades has enjoyed stable coalition government. Italy is a misleading example because it is not at all typical. Italy used an extreme form of PR that was unlike any of the more moderate forms that have been proposed for the United States. So it would be a mistake to use the problems of Italy as an excuse to eliminate all proportional representation systems from consideration.

New Zealand provides another example of the way a single country can be used to overgeneralize about a voting system. In single-member plurality elections there in 1978 and 1981, the party that came in second in the vote actually won the majority of the seats in parliament. These blatantly unfair results caused a great deal of political controversy. Some critics of plurality voting seized on these incidents as evidence that it is a terribly unjust and undemocratic system. But is this really a common outcome of plurality elections? The answer is no. It is a relatively rare occurrence and happens in less than 10% of these elections.

So it is important not to read too much into single-case examples—no matter how dramatic. Always ask yourself, Is this example typical of countries that use this voting system? More importantly, instead of drawing conclusions from experiences in a single country, try to find studies that have examined a large number of countries that use the same voting system. Many of the studies done by electoral scholars cited in this book and included in the Selected Bibliography take this approach, and they are a much more reliable guide to the probable political effects of these various voting systems.

Perfectionism

Another common problem that interferes with choosing a good voting system is that people often quickly reject a voting system option because of one major drawback. The unspoken assumption is that any new system that is adopted must be perfect—free of problems. So as soon as any major difficulty is encountered, that option is jettisoned. For example, someone might begin to look at a proportional representation system, discover that it would require new voting machines, and so quickly dismiss that option as impractical. This approach is clearly a mistake. It is unfair and irrational to dismiss a voting system simply because it has some disadvantages. As Kenneth Arrow demonstrated in the 1950s, no voting system can be perfect.[3] So the crucial question is not whether a voting system has any disadvantages—they all do—but whether the advantages of a system outweigh its disadvantages.

Often perfectionism signals a reluctance to change. In this sense, it can be another version of the status quo bias mentioned earlier. It is a way of rationalizing the quick rejection of alternatives to the present system. The logic usually goes something like this: Why change systems if you are simply going to get another flawed system? If all the systems have disadvantages, we might as well stick with the one we have. However, the mistaken assumption here is that because no system is perfect and all have flaws, they all must be equally desirable. And if they are all equally desirable, why not stay with the one we already have? But in reality, not all systems are equally flawed. Some systems have more flaws than others, and some flaws are worse than others. Depending on the criteria you have chosen as most important, you can and should make judgments about which systems are more desirable—flaws and all.

Being Blinded by Self-Interest

Self-interest is often one of the most persistent obstacles to choosing the best voting system. The temptation is for you to favor the system that gives you the most political advantage—it's only natural. If you are a member of a major party, for instance, you might be inclined to choose voting systems that make it difficult for minor-party candidates to win office. And if you are a member of a minor party, you would obviously lean toward systems that allow your party easier access to power.

But choosing the best voting system is about promoting the public interest, not your own private interest. There are many times in politics when it is entirely appropriate to pursue your own interests, but making election rules is not one of them. When choosing these rules, the point should be to find those that are fair to everyone, as in sports. In golf it is perfectly appropriate to seek a personal advantage by taking lessons, buying good equipment, and so on. But the rules of golf should be neutral and fair to everyone. Within the rules you can be as competitive as you want, but you shouldn't try to rig the rules in your own favor.

The same is true of elections. Parties and candidates should play to win and actively pursue their own interests, but the rules of elections should be fair to everyone. So in choosing voting systems, you should put your own interests on the back burner and use criteria such as fairness, openness, and representativeness to judge the worth of the voting system options. These goals and most of the criteria discussed in the second chapter of this book represent political values that presumably benefit everyone involved in elections, so they form the best basis for evaluating these voting systems.

So how can you avoid being blinded by your own self-interest? The first step is to be honest with yourself about your own motives. Acknowledge when self-interest is driving your judgments about voting systems. This kind of self-awareness can help you to avoid falling into this trap and to refocus your analysis on the appropriate criteria. Again the trick is not to try to deny that you have your own interests, but simply to recognize when those considerations are coloring your judgment.

There is also an intellectual exercise that can be helpful in trying to focus on what is fair rather than what is in your own interest. The philosopher John Rawls developed this exercise.[4] Rawls was interested in how people could transcend their own interests and devise fair and just political arrangements. He suggested that in choosing political arrangements—such as a voting system—people should imagine that they are operating in a "veil of ignorance." In a veil of ignorance, you do not know what your political position is in society. You pretend that you do not know whether you are a member of the majority or the minority, a Democrat or a Libertarian, a liberal or a conservative, a black or a white. In this position of uncertainty you will be unlikely to choose a voting system that unfairly favors one group over another, because you could never be sure that you wouldn't be a victim of these arrangements. It would be most rational and prudent for you to choose the voting system that is most fair to everyone. In other words, in a veil of ignorance, it is in your self-interest to promote what is good for everyone.

A familiar analogy can help to make the logic of this approach clear. Assume two people have a large piece of cake that they want to share by dividing into two pieces. They each naturally want as large a piece as possible. They agree that one of them is to cut the cake and the other is to choose one of the pieces. Since the person who is cutting the cake does not know which piece he or she will get, it makes the most sense to make the pieces as equal as possible—to create the outcome that is fair to both people.

It is easy to see the implications of this approach for choosing voting systems. For example, if you were looking at your options from within Rawls's veil of ignorance, it probably would not be rational to favor a voting system that made it easy for the dominant party in a state to gerrymander the voting districts and thus to "steal" legislative seats from other parties. Since you don't know your political position, you could be the victim of this gerrymandering scheme. It would make more sense to choose a system that made gerrymandering difficult because that would lessen your chances of being treated unfairly.

In this way, using Rawls's veil of ignorance can be useful for transcending your own particular interests. You always need to ask yourself whether you would choose this voting system if you weren't in your current political position. And this is not a purely hypothetical question. You can't always be completely sure of your political position, it may change over time. For instance, right now you may be a member of the largest party in your state and find it convenient to enjoy the advantages of gerrymandering. But over time, partisan shifts can take place—as has happened in the South—and your party may no longer be the largest one. You may then find yourself the victim rather than the beneficiary of gerrymandering, and you will probably wish the voting system were fairer.

Another example of how political positions are changeable can be found in the southwestern United States. Traditionally, white citizens in the cities of this region have favored plurality voting systems and as a result have enjoyed being overrepresented on their city councils. Hispanics have typically been underrepresented. But in some areas, rapidly growing Hispanic populations will soon become the majority—leading some whites to begin to rethink the desirability of their current voting system. As whites become more uncertain about their own political position, they will probably become more interested in voting systems that are fair to both whites and Hispanics. As these examples illustrate, in the long term it may be in everyone's interest to adopt Rawls's approach in choosing voting systems.

HOW TO DECIDE

So now that you know how *not* to think about choosing a voting system, how do you actually do it? As I mentioned in the introduction, the best approach to choosing a system involves a series of analytical steps, most of which you have already engaged in as you have read the previous chapters. The steps are as follows:

1. Establish your criteria for a good voting system.
2. Compile a broad range of alternative voting systems to consider.
3. Examine the alternatives and identify their political advantages and disadvantages.
4. Based on these political effects, determine which voting system best meets your criteria.

You addressed step one in the second chapter when you considered and prioritized the various criteria used to evaluate voting systems. In chapters three through six you looked at a broad range of alternative systems and examined their probable political consequences, both good and bad. This takes you to the fourth step. You now need to decide which system best meets your criteria for a good voting system. You have probably already developed some impressions about this as you have read about the particular systems. But it is best not to rely totally on these impressions, because in doing so you have a good chance of overlooking or forgetting important factors that may affect your decisions. You have looked at a large number of systems and considered a wide variety of advantages and disadvantages of each. The sheer volume of this information makes it very hard to keep all of these factors in mind as you try to make your choice. You need a more organized way to make sense of all the information you now have.

One useful approach is to construct a grid. This can help you to organize all the relevant information and systematically analyze which systems best meet your criteria. As shown in Figure 7.1, you list the systems you are considering along the top of the grid, and your criteria along the side. You then fill in the boxes to indicate how well a system fulfills each criterion. (A blank grid for you to photocopy and fill in is included as Appendix F.)

Here are some tips on how to construct the most useful grid. First, you need to limit somewhat the number of systems you consider. A grid that includes all the systems we have looked at would be unmanageably large and difficult to analyze. So you will want to list about four or five systems on the grid. Keep in mind, as mentioned earlier, that these alternatives should not all be from the same family of systems but should represent several different families. In the example shown here, the systems chosen—single-member plurality, instant runoff voting, mixed-member proportional representation, choice voting, and cumulative voting—represent all three families of voting systems.

Also, you want to list your criteria according to your priorities, with the most important ones at the top of the grid. If you did the exercises suggested in chapter two, this should not be hard. Prioritizing makes it easier to see which systems are best at fulfilling your most important guidelines. Do not be obsessive about the exact rankings—such as worrying whether "minority representation" is really your third or fourth priority. The basic idea is to make sure that your most important criteria are grouped near the top of the grid and your least important near the bottom. (The grid shown contains one possible ordering of priorities. You will of course want to construct your own.)

Obviously, filling in the grid is the most important step here. I recommend using a three-star system—it makes the grid easy to evaluate visually. One star indicates that a system is the least effective at fulfilling a criterion. Two stars mean that it is moderately effective at fulfilling a criterion. Three stars mean that a system is most effective at fulfilling a criterion. You need

Figure 7.1
Sample Voting System Evaluation Grid

	Single-Member Plurality	Instant Run-Off Voting	Mixed-Member Proportional	Choice Voting	Cumulative Voting
Majority Rule	*	**	***	***	**
Geographical Representation	***	***	***	**	**
Fair Party Representation	*	*	***	***	**
Racial Minority Representation	*	*	***	***	**
Political Stability	**	**	**	**	**
Voter Participation	*	?	***	***	?
Ease of Administration	***	*	**	*	**
Less Negative Campaigns	*	**	*	**	**
Effective Votes	*	**	***	***	**
Etc.					

Rating Scale	
*	Least effective at fulfilling the criterion.
**	Moderately effective at fulfilling the criterion.
***	Most effective at fulfilling the criterion.

to be careful about making these judgments and spend some time deciding how many stars each system gets in each category. It will probably be useful not to rely entirely on your memory, but to go back over the material in the previous chapters to confirm how well each system does in fulfilling particular criteria. Sometimes, because of lack of evidence or conflicting evidence and arguments, it may be unclear how well a system fulfills a particular objective. Two options are available in that situation: (1) Compromise and give the system the middle rating; or (2), when you really have no clue, simply put a question mark in that box.

ONE SET OF EVALUATIONS

Let's take a moment and go through some of the evaluations made in the grid. I will briefly explain my thinking about how to rate these voting systems according to the first seven criteria. That should be sufficient to give you an idea of how this process can work.

Majority Rule

The two PR systems, mixed-member PR and choice voting, do a good job of routinely ensuring majority rule, both at the district level and in the legislature, so they receive the highest rating: three stars. Instant runoff voting earns two stars because while it is explicitly designed to ensure majority rule at the district level, it does not necessarily do so at the legislative level. Plurality voting is the most likely to violate majority rule in district elections and especially in the legislature, where manufactured majorities are quite common. It gets one star. Where to place cumulative voting is a bit trickier. It is theoretically possible for it to violate majority rule, both on the district and legislative levels, but such occurrences seem rare in practice, so I gave it two stars.

Geographical Representation

In terms of geographical representation, plurality voting, IRV, and mixed-member PR all use small, single-member districts, so they certainly merit the three-star rating. Both choice voting and cumulative voting use larger multimember districts and so do not guarantee local geographical representation. On the other hand, if geographical representation is important to some voters, they can use these systems to vote for candidates from their local area. So I would give them the middle rating of two stars. If party list voting were on this list, it would probably get only one star because of its tendency to use very large multimember districts.

Fair Party Representation

Rating voting systems in terms of fair and accurate party representation is fairly straightforward. Since single-member district voting systems have the worst records of fair representation of parties, I give both plurality voting and IRV the lowest rating of one star. The two PR systems naturally have the greatest probability of producing proportional representation of parties, so they receive three stars. Cumulative voting, being a system that produces semiproportional representation of parties, logically receives the middle rating of two stars.

Minority Representation

Evaluating how systems represent racial and ethnic minorities is a bit more complicated. As a rule, single-member districts systems such as plurality voting and instant runoff voting do a very poor job of representing these minorities. On the other hand, it is possible to create special majority-minority districts to increase the representation of these groups; however, given the increasing hostility of the courts and legislatures to these districts, they have become a less viable option. Taking all of this into account, I am generally pessimistic about the ability of these systems to promote fair representation of minorities, and so I give them only a one-star rating—though this is certainly debatable.

Less disputable is the ranking of the two PR systems, which do the best job of representing these minorities. They receive the three-star rating. The cumulative vote receives a two-star rating because although it may often represent racial and ethnic groups accurately, its ability to do so is inconsistent and depends heavily on how many candidates they nominate and how they distribute their votes among them.

Political Stability

With the issue of political stability, we again enter a somewhat murky area. As the discussion in earlier chapters demonstrated, what exactly political stability is and how well voting systems encourage it are highly debated and controversial topics. So any ranking here is clearly going to be a complicated judgment call. But it must be attempted nevertheless.

Plurality, IRV, and the cumulative vote tend to produce single-party legislative majorities that are highly stable and are unlikely to fall apart. However, these may be manufactured majorities that do not enjoy the support of most of the electorate, and that result certainly does not enhance stability. In addition, alternating single-party majorities can lead to quick and dramatic shifts in political agendas, which undermine policy continuity. Because of this mixed score, I give these systems each two stars.

The two PR systems, MMP and choice voting, tend to lead to multiparty legislative majorities. These may be more difficult to form, and they are at least theoretically more likely to break up than single-party majorities. However, the evidence clearly suggests that this is rarely a problem in most PR countries. Moreover, multiparty coalitions are more likely to have a majority mandate and may encourage more policy continuity. I give them two stars as well. In essence, then, this category is a wash. No one system seems to have an overall advantage in terms of political stability.

Voter Participation

Numerous studies have shed a great deal of light on how voting systems affect voter turnout. Plurality voting is consistently the worst at encouraging turnout, so it gets one star. Both choice voting and MMP do a good job of encouraging voter participation, although in practice MMP has a better record. They both receive three stars.

The situations of IRV and cumulative voting are less clear. There are good theoretical reasons to believe that they would encourage more turnout than plurality voting. Both offer voters more viable choices of candidates and parties, allow voters to vote more sincerely, and waste fewer votes— all of which should raise participation levels. But since these two systems are rarely used on the national level, studies provide little systematic information on them. If forced to, I would probably rate them both as two stars, but given the lack of systematic evidence, I feel more comfortable putting a ? in their boxes.

Ease of Administration

Plurality voting clearly has the advantage here since it is typically the reigning voting system and administrators are quite used to it: three stars. All the other voting systems require some changes in vote accounting procedures and/or voting machines, which make them somewhat more difficult for administrators to cope with. MMP and cumulative voting are probably relatively easy to adapt to and so get two stars. IRV and choice voting, with their ranking systems and vote-transfer processes, are the most likely to require adjustments by administrators and perhaps new voting machines, so they get one star.

CLARIFING YOUR DECISION

As these examples illustrate, the evidence will often make it fairly simple to rate voting systems according to these criteria. But there will also inevitably be some areas of disagreement, as people weigh or interpret the evidence somewhat differently. In fact, you may have differed with some of my rating decisions. If you are exploring voting system options with a group, these differences can be used to provoke a useful political discussion. You could make copies of everyone's grid to share with the group. The existence of different ratings in some categories serves as a good opportunity for members of the group to question each other and demand justifications for people's ratings. As with the exercises in prioritizing criteria in chapter two, such discussions can give you some valuable insights into your own and other people's reasoning on these matters and perhaps even persuade you to change your mind on some of your judgments.

Once you've filled in the grid and discussed it with others, it should become more clear which system you should choose. No system will score the highest in all categories, but one or two of them should stand out as being generally better than the others in the categories that mean the most to you. If you want, you can add up the number of stars each system gets and put that at the bottom of the grid. This can be useful in getting a general sense of the overall performance of each system. However, don't rely completely on these totals, especially if you have a lot of question marks that would inadvertently count as zero stars in a category. Totals can also be a bit misleading because stars for fulfilling your least important criteria count the same as stars for achieving the most important ones. A system that meets only your least important guidelines—but does so very well—may thus get a very high total score. So it is probably best to focus your analysis more on the top of the grid and to take the total scores only as a rough indication of the desirability of each system.

SOME FINAL THOUGHTS

Choosing the best voting system is, of course, only part of the process of voting system reform. You still need to get your preferred system adopted. If the system you choose is the one in current use in your political jurisdiction, you are lucky and need do nothing to see it put into practice. However, if you choose a new system, then you have the job of convincing officials and the public that a change is warranted. The struggle for political reform (mobilizing the public, building alliances, developing political strategies, and so on) is obviously a complicated one and could easily be the subject of an entire other book. But the material in this book should prove useful in any effort at voting system reform. If you truly understand why your preferred voting system is the best—if you have a good grasp of all the arguments and evidence in support of your choice, if you can describe all the faults of the current system, and if you can anticipate and rebut the likely criticisms of your proposed voting system—then you will be in a very good position to convince others of the merits of your recommended change. Knowledge is power, and knowledge of voting systems increases your power to ensure that you and your fellow citizens enjoy the most effective, fair, and democratic voting system available.

NOTES

1. The book *Smart Choices* by John S. Hammond, Ralph L. Keeney, and Howard Riaffa (Boston: Harvard Business School Press, 1999) was the original inspiration for this section of the chapter and I have borrowed several of these mental pitfalls from that book.

2. Hammond, et al., *Smart Choices*, p. 194.

3. Kenneth J. Arrow, *Social Choice and Individual Values* (New York: Wiley, 1951).

4. John Rawls, *A Theory of Justice* (Cambridge, Mass.: Harvard University Press, 1971).

Seat Allocation Formulas in Proportional Representation

In party list proportional representation, the seats in the legislature are allocated in proportion to the party vote. A formula must be used to accomplish this allocation, and several of them are available. Three of the most common are described here. Tables are included to illustrate the operation of each formula and how the various formulas would allocate the seats, given the same distribution of votes among four parties. These formulas vary somewhat in how proportional their results are and whether they slightly favor certain sizes of parties over others.

LARGEST REMAINDER FORMULA

The largest remainder formula is one of the simplest. The first step is to calculate a quota. One commonly used quota is the *Hare quota*, which is determined by taking the total number of valid votes in a district and dividing it by the total number of seats at stake in the district. In Table A.1, voters have cast 99 votes, which are divided by 9 seats to produce a Hare quota of 11. Each party's vote is then divided by the quota, and the party receives a seat for each whole number produced. Thus party A received 36 votes, divided by 11, which yields 3 seats. As in most cases some votes are left over—3 votes for party A. The same process is followed for allocating seats to the other parties. If there are any seats left over after this process, they are allocated to the parties with the largest number of remaining votes. In this example, 1 seat is left to be allocated, and it is awarded to party D because it has the largest remainder.

One variation on this system uses a different quota, the *Droop quota*. This divides the total votes by the total number of seats *plus 1*. This slightly reduces the proportionality of the outcome.

D'HONDT FORMULA

The d'Hondt system is named after the Belgian lawyer Victor d'Hondt, although the same formula was also invented by Thomas Jefferson as a way to allocate congressional seats among the states. It is sometimes also called the *method of highest averages*. This system allocates seats by using what are called *divisors*. Each

Table A.1
Seat Allocation Using Largest Remainder Method

Parties	Votes	First Allocation Of Seats	Remaining Votes	Second Allocation of Votes	Final Seat Total
A	36	3	3	0	3
B	24	2	2	0	2
C	22	2	0	0	2
D	17	1	6	1	2

Note: Ninety-nine voters, 9 seats, quota of 11 votes.

Table A.2
Seat Allocation Using d'Hondt Formula

Parties	Votes/1	Votes/2	Votes/3	Votes/4	Final Seat Total
A	36 (1)	18(4)	12(6)	9(9)	4
B	24(2)	12(7)	8		2
C	22(3)	11(8)	7.33		2
D	17(5)	8.5			1

Note: Ninety-nine voters, 9 seats; number in parentheses indicates order in which seats are allocated.

party's vote is divided by a series of these divisors. In this formula the divisors are 1, 2, 3, 4, and so on. These divisions produce numbers called *averages*. Seats are allocated successively to the parties with the highest averages. Each time a party is allocated a seat, its vote is then divided by the next divisor to produce a new average for that party. In the example in Table A.2, party A has the highest average in the first round with 36 votes and so receives the first seat. Its votes are then divided by 2 to produce a new average of 18. Now party B has the highest average with 24 votes. It receives the next seat and its average is divided by 2 and reduced to 12. This process continues until all the seats are allocated.

The d'Hondt method is known for favoring somewhat the largest party at the expense of the smaller parties. In the example in Table A.2, it allocates 4 seats to party A, whereas the largest remainder system allocated only 3 seats to party A. Because of this tendency, other divisor formulas have been invented to try to minimize this large party bias. One of them, the Sainte-Lagüe formula, is described next.

SAINTE-LAGÜE FORMULA

The Sainte-Lagüe formula is another system that uses divisors. It uses the same basic approach as the d'Hondt method, allocating seats to the parties with the highest averages. But it uses a different series of divisors. Instead of 1, 2, 3, and so

Table A.3
Seat Allocation Using Sainte-Lagüe Formula

Parties	Votes/1	Votes/3	Votes/5	Votes/7	Final Seat Total
A	36 (1)	12 (5)	7.2 (8)	5.14	3
B	24 (2)	8 (6)	4.8		2
C	22 (3)	7.33 (7)	4.4		2
D	17 (4)	5.67 (9)			2

Note: Ninety-nine voters, 9 seats; number in parentheses indicates order in which seats are allocated.

forth, Sainte-Lagüe uses the odd numbers 1, 3, 5, and so on. This produces a more completely proportional allocation of seats. Note that the results of the Sainte-Lagüe formula shown in Table A.3 are the same as that for the largest remainder system. Both are considered more proportional than the d'Hondt method.

OTHER SYSTEMS

The preceding systems are only three of the most common ones; several others have been devised. The modified Sainte-Lagüe formula uses the divisors 1.4, 3, 5, et cetera, making it somewhat more difficult for the smallest parties to win seats and thus slightly favoring the midsize parties. The Imperiali formula uses the divisors 2, 3, 4, and so on, and this tends to favor the larger parties.

A Brief History of Proportional Representation in the United States

The United States has always had a tradition of single-member district, winner-take-all elections. So it is hardly surprising that few Americans are aware of our history of experimentation with proportional representation (PR) elections. Admittedly these experiments were few in number. During the first half of the twentieth century, two dozen American cities used for a time the single transferable vote (STV)—a form of proportional representation that is often called *choice voting* today. The story of how proportional representation came to be adopted and eventually abandoned provides some useful information about the history of this voting system, its political effects, and the politics of voting system reform.

THE HISTORICAL ROOTS OF PROPORTIONAL REPRESENTATION

The political roots of proportional representation in the United States originated in the Progressive movement of the early twentieth century. Besides such issues as child labor laws, antimonopoly legislation, and women's suffrage, Progressives were interested in government reform. Many were particularly concerned about the corruption in urban governments. Large cities often were dominated by party machines, of which Tammany Hall in New York City was the most infamous. Bribery, kickbacks, favoritism, and voting fraud were rampant in these cities. The Progressives wanted to clean up these cities and blunt the power of the party bosses.

Their urban reform program included such features as the nonpartisan ballot and replacement of elected mayors with appointed city managers. Some Progressives also added proportional representation to this reform agenda. They argued that winner-take-all, single-member district elections served to reinforce the power of urban political machines. It was not unusual for machines to win almost all the seats on city councils, on the basis of only 50%–60% of the vote. PR was seen as a way to end these one-party monopolies and to allow for the fair representation of a variety of political parties.

The Proportional Representation League of the United States was also instrumental in promoting the use of PR. Founded in 1893, the League soon followed the lead of English electoral reform groups and endorsed the single transferable

vote as the most preferable version of PR. The League eventually began to enjoy
some political success when it decided in 1912 that its most realistic goal would be
to promote the adoption of PR on the city level; cities presented the fewest legal
and procedural obstacles. Usually cities would need to change only their charters
to adopt PR elections. This change could be made by referendums that would be
voted on directly by citizens, thereby eliminating the need to convince government
officials to pass this reform.

Proportional representation received an important boost in 1914 when the National Municipal League, a leading proponent of urban reform, included PR elections in its model city charter. Soon afterward, in 1915, Ashtabula, Ohio, became
the first American city to adopt PR elections. Before long, Boulder, Kalamazoo,
Sacramento, and West Hartford followed suit. In the mid-1920s, the first large
urban areas, Cleveland and Cincinnati, adopted PR elections, and two other Ohio
cities, Toledo and Hamilton, soon joined them. The greatest victory of PR advocates
occurred in 1936, when voters in New York City approved the adoption of PR
elections by a large margin. Interest in PR jumped dramatically as a result, and was
eventually adopted in eleven other cities, including seven in Massachusetts. In all,
two dozen American cities joined the PR camp.

EFFECTS ON REPRESENTATION

What political effects did proportional representation have on the cities that
adopted it? In particular, did PR fulfill the political promises of its proponents to
reduce corruption, ensure fair representation, and increase voter participation? Or
did it confirm the fears of PR critics who predicted voter confusion, lower turnout,
and increased political divisiveness?

Scholars have begun to shed some light on these questions. The most extensive
research to date has been produced by Kathleen Barber and several colleagues. Their
study, *Proportional Representation and Electoral Reform in Ohio*, systematically
analyzed the political effects of PR in five Ohio cities. In many cases their findings
were also confirmed by results in other PR cities. For example, Barber found that
choice voting produced fairer and more proportional representation of political
parties. In particular, it eliminated the tendency of winner-take-all systems to ex-
aggerate the seats given to the largest party and to underrepresent the smaller parties. In the election before the adoption of PR in Cincinnati, the Republicans won
only 55% of the vote but received 97% of the seats on the council. In the first PR
election, the results were much more proportional: The Republicans won 33.3%
of the seats, based on 27.8% of the vote, and the rival Charter party won 66.7%
of the seats on 63.8% of the vote.

Similarly, in the last pre-PR election in New York City, the Democrats won
95.3% of the seats on the Board of Alderman with only 66.5% of the vote. During
the use of PR, the Democrats still had a majority of the seats, but it was a much
smaller one that more accurately reflected their strength in the electorate. In 1941,
proportional representation gave the Democrats 65.5% of the seats on 64% of the
vote. Moreover, it also produced representation for the Republicans and three
smaller parties in proportion to their voting strength. Similar results occurred in
the other PR cities, demonstrating that this system greatly improved the accuracy
of partisan representation.

Proportional representation also encouraged fairer racial and ethnic representation. It produced the first Irish Catholic elected in Ashtabula and the first Polish Americans elected in Toledo. In Cincinnati, Hamilton, and Toledo, African Americans had never been able to win city office until the adoption of PR. Significantly, after these cities abandoned PR, African Americans again found it almost impossible to get elected.

EFFECTS ON POLITICAL MACHINES

At times, proportional representation helped undermine the power of political machines and party bosses. In several cities, such as Cincinnati, the machines lost their majorities and their grip on power. After the transition to PR, Cincinnati went from a city with one of the worst reputations for corruption to one that won praise for the integrity and professionalism of its city government. Interestingly, even in cities where the dominant party retained its majority, PR sometimes helped to curb the power of the party bosses. It did so by allowing the election of independent Democratic and Republican candidates—candidates nominated by petition and not beholden to party bosses. PR proponents were correct, then, in predicting that this candidate-centered system would take power away from party leaders and give more of it to voters.

EFFECTS ON WASTED VOTES

Proponents of proportional representation also believed it would minimize wasted votes. They argued that the ballot transfer process would ensure that most people would cast effective votes—votes that actually elected someone to office. The evidence supports this claim. In Cincinnati, the number of effective votes improved dramatically, rising from an average of 56.2% in the three pre-PR elections to an average of 90% for the sixteen PR elections. Similar effects were found in other PR cities. In Cleveland, the number of effective votes increased from an average of 48.3% in the pre-PR period to an average of 79.6% during the PR period. And in New York City, the number of effective votes grew from an average of 60.6% to 79.2% with PR.

EFFECTS ON THE PARTY SYSTEM

How did proportional representation affect the size of the party systems in these cities? Did it subvert the traditional American two-party system, as some critics feared it would? Not always. In some cities, PR produced a stable two-party system. In Cincinnati, the PR elections were contested between the Republicans and the Charter Committee, with no minor-party candidates winning representation. Indeed, only once in all of the PR elections in the five cities in Ohio did a minor-party candidate win office—a Socialist in Ashtabula in 1915.

The situation was different in New York City—an intensely cosmopolitan area with a variety of political cultures. PR nurtured a vigorous multiparty system, in which at any one time the Democrats and Republicans were joined on the city council by three smaller parties, including the American Labor party, the Fusion party, and the Communist party. In general, however, PR did not seem automatically to favor a multiparty system over a two-party system; instead it tended to produce a party system that reflected whatever degree of political diversity already existed in particular cities.

EFFECTS ON VOTER TURNOUT

Proponents of proportional representation had predicted higher voter participation, reasoning that having fewer wasted votes and more choices at the polls would give citizens more incentive to vote. Opponents had forecast a drop in turnout, suggesting that voters would be discouraged by complicated ballots and incomprehensible vote-counting procedures. In reality, however, PR seemed to have little effect on voter turnout. Barber and her colleagues looked at turnout rates before, during, and after the use of PR in five Ohio cities and found little correlation between voting system and degree of voter participation. She concluded, "The emergence and disappearance of local issues and candidates appear to have had more to do with the act of voting than did the form of the ballot."[1] The scattered evidence from other PR cities seems to confirm the importance of local factors: Some cities saw increased turnout with the adoption of PR and others saw a decline.

EFFECTS ON POLITICAL STABILITY

Another common concern of PR critics was that it would increase political conflict and divisiveness. They worried that it would encourage so-called bloc voting along ethnic, racial, religious, and class lines, and that the resulting city councils would be paralyzed by conflict. In practice, PR often did result in substantial bloc voting. But as defenders observed at the time, so too did winner-take-all elections. As noted earlier, PR also produced some city councils that were more demographically and politically diverse. But there is no evidence that this increased political pluralism had any detrimental impact on the workings of these city councils. In the five Ohio PR cities, Barber and her colleagues found "no systematic evidence of greater dissension on PR elected councils, compared to councils elected by other means. . . . Indeed, striking decreases in conflict were found after PR/STV was implemented in Hamilton and Toledo."[2] This lack of increased conflict may have resulted from the ballot transfer process in choice voting, which may have encouraged politicians to be more civil to each other so as not to risk alienating potential supporters.

THE OVERALL EFFECTS OF PR

On the whole, from the available evidence, proportional representation seemed to have a beneficial effect on the cities that adopted it. It clearly produced more representative government and, where voters wanted it, a more diverse party system. Large increases in the number of effective votes were also enjoyed in these cities. It may not have resulted in the substantial increases in voter turnout that proponents predicted, but neither did it produce the increases in voter alienation that critics feared. And finally, even though PR city councils were often more diverse

politically, this makeup did not seem to impair their political efficiency or effectiveness.

THE ABANDONMENT OF PR

If proportional representation amassed such a generally favorable record, why
was it eventually rejected by all but one U.S. city, Cambridge, Massachusetts? The
answer to this question is complex, with a number of factors playing a role in the
abandonment of PR. Sometimes the reasons were primarily local. In a few cities
dissatisfaction grew over other elements of the reform charters, such as the city
manager system, and when the reform charter was thrown out, PR went with it.

However, there were several common factors at work in many of the cities that
abandoned proportional representation. For instance, this system universally came
under attack from the politicians and parties who lost power and privileges. In
Michigan and California, the dominant political parties mounted legal challenges,
and the courts in these states ruled that PR violated their constitutions. A more
common attack was the effort to repeal PR by popular referendum. The referendum
was a two-edged sword for PR—initially making it easier to adopt this reform, but
also making it easier for opponents to challenge it. In Cleveland, well-financed
opponents sponsored five repeal referendums in the first ten years of PR; the final
one succeeded. Similarly, PR opponents in Hamilton finally won their repeal effort
after four failed referendums in twelve years.

Another common factor contributing to the demise of proportional representation was the inability of supporters to defend it effectively. By 1932, the PR League
was losing steam. It was unable to finance an independent existence and had to
merge with the National Municipal League. In some cities, the progressive political
coalition that supported PR gradually disintegrated. Important reform leaders lost
interest over the years, moved to the suburbs, or died. Two exceptions to this trend
were Cincinnati and Cambridge, both of which had active and well-supported organizations dedicated to defending PR. In Cincinnati the Charter Committee ag-
gressively defended proportional representation, and it survived there for over thirty
years, despite repeated challenges. The Cambridge Civic Association has also
proved to be a energetic and capable defender of PR and has defeated every repeal
effort to date.

Another factor working against defenders of proportional representation in many
cities was the controversial nature of minority representation. Many Americans in
the early twentieth century were hostile to political and racial minorities—the very
groups aided by PR. Opponents of PR were not above fanning the flames of prej-
udice in their efforts to get rid of this reform. In particular, critics often played
upon two of the most basic fears of white middle-class Americans: Communists
and African Americans.

In Cincinnati, race was the dominant theme in the successful 1957 repeal effort.
The single transferable vote had allowed an African American to be elected for the
first time in the 1930s and two blacks eventually were elected to the city council
in the 1950s. The nation was also seeing the first stirrings of the civil rights movement and racial tensions were running high. PR opponents shrewdly decided to
make race an explicit factor in their repeal campaign. They warned whites that PR

was helping to increase black power in the city and asked them whether they wanted a "Negro mayor." Their appeal to white anxieties succeeded: Whites supported repeal by a two-to-one margin.

In New York City, fear of communism proved the undoing of proportional representation. Although one or two Communists had served on the PR-elected city council since 1941, it was not until the cold war that Democratic party leaders were able to exploit this issue effectively. As the historian Robert Kolesar discovered, the Democrats made every effort in their repeal campaign to link PR with Soviet communism, describing the single transferable vote as "the political importation from the Kremlin," "the first beachhead of Communist infiltration in this country," and "an un-American practice which has helped the cause of communism and does not belong in the American way of life."[3] This "red scare" campaign resulted in the repeal of PR by an overwhelming margin.

Just as the adoption of the single transferable vote in New York City prompted other cities to consider this reform, its well-publicized defeat there also encouraged repeal efforts in other PR cities. PR was abandoned in neighboring Long Beach and Yonkers in 1947 and 1948. Repeal campaigns also won in Boulder (1947), Toledo (1949), and Wheeling (1951). The PR movement never recovered from these defeats, and although supporters remained optimistic, the 1950s saw the repeal of PR in one city after another. By 1962, only Cambridge, Massachusetts, retained this system.

Although the repeal of proportional representation in these American cities is taken by opponents as evidence that this electoral system failed, proponents argue that it is more accurate to conclude that this system was rejected because it worked too well. They note that PR worked well in throwing party bosses out of government—bosses who never relented in their attempts to regain power—and it worked well in promoting the representation of racial, ethnic, and ideological minorities previously shut out by the winner-take-all system. For advocates of PR, then, it was the very political successes of this system that set the stage for a political backlash that was effectively exploited by its opponents and eventually led to the its demise in most of these cities.

NOTES

1. Kathleen L. Barber, *Proportional Representation and Election Reform in Ohio* (Columbus: Ohio State University Press, 1995), p. 295.

2. Barber, *Proportional Representation*, p. 305.

3. Robert J. Kolesar, "Communism, Race, and the Defeat of Proportional Representation in Cold War America" (University Heights, Ohio: History Department, John Carroll University, 1996), pp. 4–5.

Lesser-Used Voting Systems

The main text of this book covered all of the major voting systems commonly used in democracies around the world, and even a few that are not so common, such as limited voting. But people interested in elections have invented many other voting systems, most of which have seen very little use. This appendix describes four of these less common voting systems—ones that you may encounter as you read more about voting system reform.

APPROVAL VOTING

The approval voting system was developed in the 1970s by several analysts, the most prominent of whom is the political scientist Steven Brams. It is a variation of plurality-majority voting and can be used in single-office elections and single-member district legislative elections. In this system, the ballot resembles a standard plurality voting ballot. Voters can vote for, or approve of, as many candidates as they wish in multicandidate elections—that is, elections with more than two candidates. Each candidate approved of receives one vote and the candidate with the most votes wins.

Currently, approval voting is not used to elect a legislature in any democracy. It is used to elect the secretary general of the United Nations, and it is used to elect officials in several scientific and engineering societies, including the Mathematical Association of America and the Institute of Electrical and Electronics Engineers.

Advantages

For Brams, one advantage of approval voting is that it helps to prevent a situation in which three or more candidates battle it out and one of them winds up being elected with only a plurality of the vote. In these situations, he argues, the one who deserves to be elected is not the candidate with the plurality of the vote, but the candidate with the greatest overall support—the one most widely approved of by the voters. Approval voting would allow that candidate to win.

Another advantage of approval voting is that supporters of minor-party or independent candidates need not worry about wasting their votes, or inadvertently helping their least liked candidate get elected. If you vote for both a minor-party and a major-party candidate, and if the minor-party candidate cannot win, you have still helped the major-party candidate you most prefer get elected.

Approval voting may increase the range of parties and candidates on the ballot, and this could encourage more people to vote. Also, proponents argue that less negative campaigning would take place under this system, because candidates would try to woo voters who might have a different first choice. Throwing mud at other candidates would risk alienating their supporters and losing their approval.

Because approval voting is a form of plurality-majority voting, it has many of the advantages of that family of systems. When used for legislative elections, it promotes close constituency ties, good geographical representation, and stable single-party legislative majorities.

Disadvantages

Approval voting assumes that you support all the candidates you vote for equally. But in reality, most voters have one candidate they prefer over others, even if they approve of many. One major disadvantage of approval voting is that voting for more than one candidate may hurt the chances of your most preferred candidate. In a close three-way race, for instance, if you vote for two candidates, you may be helping your second-choice candidate to defeat your first choice. Understanding this problem, many voters probably would cast only one vote (a bullet vote) for their favorite candidate—especially since many candidates would ask their supporters not to cast more than one vote. The widespread use of bullet voting means that approval voting would revert to a standard plurality voting system and lose all of its unique advantages. In this situation, approval voting also would not be able to guarantee that the winner receives a majority of vote, as would be the case with the two-round runoff system and instant runoff voting.

Some critics of approval voting suggest that it gives an advantage to bland, centrist "smiley face" candidates who are likely to be approved by a wide cross section of the electorate. By avoiding taking strong stands on difficult issues, these inoffensive candidates run less of a risk of alienating voters and a better chance of gaining their approval vote.

Because approval voting is basically a form of plurality-majority voting, it also has most of its disadvantages. When used in single-member districts for legislative elections, approval voting will produce large numbers of wasted votes, deny minority representation, produce unfair party representation, and encourage gerrymandering.

FUSION VOTING

Fusion voting is a member of the plurality-majority family of voting systems and may be used in single-office elections or legislative elections using single-member districts. It is sometimes called *multiple nomination ballots*, and this phrase points to its unique feature. It is virtually identical to plurality voting except that candidates can be listed on the ballot several different times under different party labels. For example, the New party might nominate the same candidate nominated by the

Democratic party, and that candidate's name would appear twice on the ballot—first identified as a Democratic candidate and second as a New party candidate. Voters cast only one vote and have to choose under which party label they want to support their candidate. All the votes for each candidate, under all of his or her party affiliations, are added together to count toward his or her election.

Consider an election in which candidate A is running as a Republican, and candidate B is listed on the ballot as a candidate of both the Democratic party and the New party. A receives 46% of the vote. B receives 40% of the vote as the Democratic candidate and 14% as the New party candidate. Candidate B wins the election with 54% of the vote.

History

Fusion voting was a common feature in many midwestern and western states during the golden age of minor parties in the United States, the late nineteenth century. It provided a way for supporters of such minor parties as the Progressives, Grangers, and Populists to participate effectively in elections and to make their concerns heard by candidates elected to office. As one historian has concluded: "Fusion helped maintain a significant third party tradition by guaranteeing that dissenters' votes could be more than symbolic protest, that their leaders could gain office and their demands might be heard. Most of the election victories normally attributed to the Grangers, Independents, or Greenbackers in the 1870s and 1880s were a result of fusion between those third-party groups and Democrats."[1] Eventually the Republican party, fearful of the advantage that fusion gave to the Democrats, led an effort to abolish this voting system, and thirteen states passed bans on fusion between 1897 and 1907. Eventually it was banned in forty-one states. Currently New York is one of the few states that use fusion, and the Liberal and Conservative parties there attribute much of their longevity to the option of fusion voting.

Interest in this voting technique resurfaced in the 1990s with the emergence of several new third-party efforts. In 1994, a small progressive party called the New party brought suit to overturn the ban on fusion voting in Minnesota. That year it had chosen as its candidate for state representative a person who was already the incumbent candidate for a major party, the Democratic-Farm-Labor party. The candidate accepted the New party's nomination and signed an affidavit of candidacy for the New party. However, state officials refused to accept the affidavit on the grounds that Minnesota state law banned the use of fusion voting. Members of the New party took Minnesota to federal court, asserting that the ban on fusion voting violated their associational rights under the First and Fourteenth Amendments to the U.S. Constitution—in particular, their right to nominate the candidate of their choice. The federal district court ruled in favor of the state, but the appellate court ruled in favor of the New party. The case finally ended up before the Supreme Court as *Timmons v. Twin Cities* in 1996. In a controversial and highly political decision, the Court ruled that the ban on fusion voting is constitutionally valid because states have an interest in preserving the two-party system, and the use of fusion voting would threaten that interest. In Chief Justice William Rehnquist's words: "The States' interest permits them to enact reasonable election regulations that may, in practice, favor the traditional two party system and that temper the destabilizing effect of party splintering and excessive factionalism. The Constitution permits the Minnesota Legislature to decide that political stability is best served through a healthy two party system."[2] Naturally this decision has undermined efforts in other states to revive this voting system.

Advantages

The basic advantage of this system is that it allows minor parties to nominate candidates who have a good chance of winning. Most third-party candidates are unlikely to be elected to office under plurality rules. But under fusion voting the third-party candidate also has the support of one of the major parties (more likely it is vice versa), and this often allows that candidate to gain enough voter support to be victorious in a plurality system.

In most plurality voting systems, votes for minor-party candidates are almost inevitably wasted. But in fusion voting, these votes can easily contribute to the victory of a candidate and are less likely to be wasted. This could encourage more turnout by supporters of the third-party candidates.

Fusion voting offers another advantage for minor parties: It gives them a source of political leverage over the legislative behavior of a candidate they helped to elect. They can argue that their supporters played a key role in electing that candidate and therefore the candidate should promote some of the policies preferred by those minor-party supporters.

In addition, supporters point out that fusion gives minor parties a better chance to remain viable organizations. Parties that never win elections often quickly disappear from the political landscape. Fusion gives these parties at least partial victories and enhances their ability to attract additional members and donations.

Finally, when used in single-member districts, fusion voting has most of the advantages associated with those arrangements, including close constituency ties and good geographical representation.

Disadvantages

Some critics contend that fusion voting undermines our traditional two-party system and leads to a multiparty system. It is true that it often results in the inclusion of more parties on the ballot. But it doesn't necessarily result in the presence of more parties in the legislature. Under fusion voting, everyone elected to the legislature may still represent one of the two major parties—although some have also been endorsed by other parties. So although there is a change in the ballot, there may be little change in the partisan makeup of the legislature.

The fact that fusion doesn't usually result in the election of real third-party candidates (or any other political minorities) is seen as a drawback by advocates of proportional representation. PR, they argue, does what fusion cannot do: It allows minor parties and racial minorities to elect their own members to the legislatures. This allows their views to be directly represented in the political process.

Proponents of PR also point out that fusion voting suffers from most of the other common political drawbacks that afflict all single-member plurality voting systems.

It can produce large numbers of wasted votes, unfair party representation, violations of majority rule, gerrymandering, and other effects.

SINGLE NONTRANSFERABLE VOTE

Despite its name, the single nontransferable vote (SNTV) is not closely related to the single transferable vote; it is actually a variation of the limited vote and it belongs to the family of semiproportional systems. In this system, there are multiple seats at stake in the district, but voters are limited to one vote. In a four-seat district, for instance, voters have one vote to cast for a candidate. The candidates with the highest vote totals win the seats. This system is rarely used today. It is most famous for being used in Japan for forty-five years, until it was abandoned for a parallel voting system in the 1994. Currently SNTV is in use in Jordan, Taiwan, and Vanuatu.

Advantages

The main advantage of SNTV, as with other semiproportional systems, is that it can allow for the representation of political minorities. In a four-seat district, for instance, the threshold of exclusion is 20%, so any minority group that can muster this proportion of the vote is assured of a seat. As the number of seats in the district goes up, this threshold goes down and makes it easier for minorities to get elected. In addition, SNTV tends to waste fewer votes and produce more proportional results than plurality-majority voting systems. It is also relatively easy to use and to administer.

Disadvantages

Because the single nontransferable vote is a semiproportional system, it shares many of the disadvantages of those systems. Unlike fully proportional voting systems, SNTV cannot be relied on to always produce proportional results or minority representation. If parties do not run the optimal number of candidates or do not distribute their votes in the most effective way, SNTV can produce manufactured majorities and majority sweeps. Attempts by the parties to control nominations strictly and to manage the distributions of votes may produce some resentment among voters.

In addition, many voting system experts who have studied SNTV are highly critical of it. They argue that in practice, as in its use in Japan, it primarily has served to privilege current power holders and fragment the opposition.

CONDORCET VOTING

There is a long history of scientists and mathematicians who dabbled in election theory and invented voting systems. They include Jean-Charles de Borda, the Marquis de Condorcet, and C. L. Dodgson—better known as Lewis Carroll, the author of *Alice's Adventures in Wonderland*. These men were interested in developing a

Table C.1
Voter Preferences in Condorcet Vote

Four Voters	Three Voters	Two Voters
A	B	C
C	C	A
B	A	B

mathematical theory of elections and improving voting methods. Their voting systems were often accused of being overly complicated and have rarely been used in practice. However, you often encounter their theories in scholarly works on voting systems. I focus on only one example of these systems: the Condorcet method.

Marie Jean Antoine Nicolas Caritat, Marquis de Condorcet, was an eighteenth-century French mathematician, philosopher, economist, and social scientist. Among students of elections, he is most famous for devising the *Condorcet criterion*, which can be applied to single-winner elections in which there are three or more candidates. This criterion describes which candidate should be elected in these circumstances. For Condorcet, the candidate who deserves to be elected is the one whom the voters, on average, hold to be superior to the others. Or to put it more in his terms, the winning candidate is the one who defeats all the others in pairwise elections, using majority rule. To understand exactly what this means, it is helpful to look at a hypothetical election to which we can apply the Condorcet voting method.

Assume that nine voters are trying to elect one person from a field of three candidates, A, B, and C. The first step in the Condorcet method is for voters to list their preferences among these candidates, as in choice voting. Their distribution of preferences is summarized in Table C.1. Four voters prefer candidate A first, C second, and B third. Three voters prefer candidate B first, C second, and A last. And two voters prefer C first, A second, and B third.

Which candidate should win the election? If we used the standard plurality criterion, A would win the election with four first-place votes, with three for B and two for C. But Condorcet argued that candidate C should win. And if you use the Condorcet voting method, C would indeed be the victor. After establishing the voters' preferences, these votes are tallied by computing the results of separate pairwise elections between all the candidates; the winner would be the one who wins a majority of all of the pairwise contests. So in this case, each voter's list is used to simulate how he or she would have voted in three pairwise elections: A versus B, A versus C, and B versus C. In the first election, six voters prefer A to B and three prefer B to A, so A wins. In the second election, four voters prefer A to C and five prefer C to A, so C wins. In the last election, three voters prefer B to C and six prefer C to B, so again C wins. Since C wins a majority of the pairwise elections—two out of three—that candidate is declared the winner.

Advantages

For Condorcet, the main advantage of his voting method is that it allows the candidate most highly rated by the majority of voters to win. This would not necessarily be the case with majority or plurality voting. Some supporters of this method also argue that this system has the advantage of favoring candidates and parties of the center over those on the extreme. This is because it punishes candidates whom many people put last.

Other Condorcet supporters argue that ranking the candidates allows voters to avoid the lesser-of-two evils problem that plague majority and plurality systems. People can vote sincerely for the candidates they prefer most without having to consider whether they are wasting their vote.

This voting technique is most often proposed for single-office elections, such as mayor, but it can also be used in single-member district legislative elections. In the context of legislative elections, it would share many of the same advantages of plurality and majority systems, including close constituency ties and good geographical representation.

Disadvantages

One disadvantage is that this method will not always produce a winner. If, in the example, the first four voters had instead listed A first, B second, and C third, then the pairwise contest would not have produced a majority winner. Each candidate would have won one election. Some critics also argue that this system tends to favor the most bland and least offensive candidate instead of the best candidate.

If this voting system were used in single-member district legislative elections, it would share the many of the usual disadvantages of winner-take-all systems such as plurality and majority voting. It would produce large numbers of wasted votes, deny minority representation, produce unfair party representation, and encourage gerrymandering.

NOTES

1. Argersinger, Peter H., "A Place on the Ballot: Fusion Politics and Antifusion Laws," *American History Review* 85 (1980): 288–89.
2. *Timmons v. Twin Cities Area New Party*. 1996. 137L. Ed. 2nd, p. 603.

Statutory Language for Choice Voting, Cumulative Voting, and Instant Runoff Voting

The following are three model statutes for adopting choice voting, cumulative voting, and instant runoff voting. They can serve as rough models for drafting this kind of legislation, but keep in mind that they may have to be modified to fit various local situations.

CHOICE VOTING STATUTE

First: Definition and Principle

(a) DEFINITION: "Choice Voting" shall be defined as a voting system that achieves proportional representation by allowing voters to rank candidates for city council in the order of their choice.

(b) PRINCIPLE: Choice Voting tabulates votes based on the principle that any vote cast that would not otherwise help elect a voter's most preferred candidate(s) shall be used to help elect that voter's next-most preferred candidate(s). Thus, if a voter's first choice among the candidates receives more than enough votes to win, the surplus proportion of that vote will be transferred to that voter's second or succeeding (next-highest ranking) choice. Alternatively, if a voter's first choice candidate is eliminated, that vote instead will be cast for the voter's second or succeeding (next-highest ranking) choice.

Second: Ballot Specifications and Directions to Voters

Ballots shall be simple and easy to understand. Sample ballots illustrating voting procedures shall be posted in or near the voting and included in the instruction packet of absentee ballots. Directions provided to voters shall conform substantially to the following specifications.

Directions to Voters

CITY COUNCIL: Vote for up to 9 council candidates in your order of choice. Indicate your first choice by marking an "X" in column 1 next to that candidate's name, your second choice by marking an "X" in column 2, and so on. Do not assign any two candidates the same choice. Note that ranking additional candidates cannot affect a higher-choice candidate's chance to win.

Third: Tabulation of Votes

Ballots shall be counted by election authorities according to the following rules:

(a) DETERMINATION OF VICTORY THRESHOLD: For any given election, the number of votes necessary for a candidate to guarantee an elected position shall be termed the *threshold*. The threshold is used to determine transferable surpluses as defined in (b)(1). The threshold shall be the fewest number of votes that can be obtained only by the winning number of candidates. This threshold is determined by dividing the number of valid votes by 1 plus the number of seats, and then adding 1 to that number: (valid votes cast/1 + seats) + 1.

(b) RULES REGARDING TRANSFER OF VOTES: The following rules regarding vote transfer shall apply to all stages of the tabulation:

(1) Votes acquired by a candidate in excess of the threshold for that election shall be termed his or her *surplus*. A candidate's votes shall be transferred according to the following rule: Transfer a portion of each vote determined by dividing the surplus of the candidate by the total number of votes for that candidate. For example, if a candidate receives 15,000 votes in an election threshold is 10,000, that candidate has a surplus of 5,000 votes and one-third (5,000/15,000 = .3333) of a vote from each of those 15,000 ballots is transferred to those voters' next choices.

Votes cast for candidates who are eliminated (as described in (c)(3) below) shall be transferred at their full current value to those next choice(s).

(2) Votes may not be transferred to candidates who have already met the threshold, nor may votes be transferred to candidates who have been eliminated. When a voter's next choice is not eligible for receipt of transferred votes, that vote (or portion of a vote) shall be transferred to the voter's next indicated choice until all choices on that ballot have been exhausted.

(3) If a voter omits or mistakenly designates any choice on his or her ballot, the vote shall be transferred to that voter's next clear choice.

(4) Any votes cast for eligible write-in candidates shall be tabulated in the same manner as those for candidates whose names are printed on the ballots, provided that the voter assigns any such candidate a choice in relation to other candidates appearing on the ballot for that office.

(c) STAGES IN THE TABULATION:

(1) Vote counting shall start with a tabulation of first-choice votes and with the transfer of a proportion of all surplus votes according to the rules specified in (b). Transfer of surpluses shall commence with the candidate having the largest surplus and proceed successively to the candidates with the next largest surplus.

(2) If the transfer of surplus votes to voters' next-choice candidates creates a new surplus, then a proportion of these votes shall be transferred to those voters' succeeding choices, until all surpluses have been transferred or all declared choices on a ballot have been exhausted.

(3) When all surplus votes have been distributed in this manner, a tally shall be taken. All candidates with less than 0.5% of votes shall be eliminated simultane-

ously. Votes for these candidates shall be transferred at their current value to the next-choice candidates named on these ballots. If a next-choice candidate already has been elected or defeated, then the ballot goes to the succeeding choice.

Any surpluses created by this transfer shall once again be transferred, and a new tally taken, until all surpluses have been transferred. Then the remaining candidate with the least number of votes shall be eliminated.

This process of transferring surpluses followed by eliminating candidates with the least numbers of votes shall continue until the number of candidates remaining matches the number of positions to be filled. Votes of the candidate last eliminated shall be transferred, and the election shall be at an end.

(d) DETERMINATIONS IN THE CASE OF A TIE: For ties between candidates occurring at any stage in the tabulation, the tie shall be resolved in accordance with the general election laws of (insert state name here).

(e) FILLING A CITY COUNCIL VACANCY: Any vacancy of an elected City Council member shall be filled by recounting the ballots from the general election that elected that member, in the manner specified herein for general elections, except that the vacating member's name shall be deleted from all ballots. The candidate accruing the most votes in the recount who was not elected to office in the original count shall fill the vacancy. For the purpose of filling City Council vacancies, all general election ballots shall be retained by election authorities for at least four years.

Fourth: Provision for Change of Voting Method

The council or election authorities may provide for the use of mechanical, electronic, or other devices for marking, sorting, and counting the ballots and tabulating the results and may modify the form of the ballots, the directions to voters, and the details with respect to the method of marking, sorting, counting, invalidating, and retaining of ballots, and the tabulating and transferring of votes, provided that no change shall be made that will alter the intent or principles embodied in this subsection.

Fifth: Severability Clause

If any part of this subsection is declared unconstitutional by a court of competent jurisdiction, the remaining parts shall survive in full force and effect. If a conflict arises between this amendment and any other provision of law, the policies and purposes of this amendment shall govern.

CUMULATIVE VOTING STATUTE

Relating to elections in the town/city of _____; providing for elections by a method known as cumulative voting; describing and defining such election method.

BE IT ENACTED BY THE LEGISLATURE OF (insert state here):

Section 1. Elections for the town/city council of _____ shall henceforth be elected by the method known as cumulative voting.

Section 2. The council shall consist of five members who shall be elected at large by the voters of the town/city. Each voter shall cast five votes and may distribute them among candidates in any manner the voter chooses, including casting more than one vote for a candidate. The five candidates receiving the most votes shall be elected. There shall be no runoff. Ties shall be broken by lot.

Section 3. Ballots shall be simple and easy to understand. Sample ballots illustrating voting procedures shall be posted in or near the voting booth and included in the instruction packet of absentee ballots. Directions provided to voters shall conform substantially to the following specifications: "You may cast up to five (5) votes. Your may distribute your five votes in any way among the candidates: all for one candidate, three for one and two for another, one for each of five candidates, etc."

Section 4. Ballots with five or fewer votes shall be counted. Ballots with more than five votes shall be considered void. Electronic voting systems and voting machines shall be set up to reject ballots with excess votes, so that the voter shall be prevented as far as possible from spoiling his or her ballot. The statement of canvass and the recapitulation sheet shall show the number of ballots rejected because of excess votes cast.

Section 5. In all other respects, the election laws usually applying to municipalities shall apply to the elections in the town/city of _____.

Section 6. All laws or portions of laws inconsistent with this act are repealed to the extent of their inconsistency.

Section 7. This act shall take effect immediately upon its approval by the governor or upon its otherwise being enacted into law.

INSTANT RUNOFF VOTING STATUTE

Section 1: Ballot Specifications and Directions to Voters

Ballots shall be simple and easy to understand. Sample ballots illustrating voting procedures shall be posted in or near the voting booth and included in the instruction packet of absentee ballots. Directions provided to voters shall conform substantially to the following specifications:

"Vote for candidates in order of preference. Indicate your first choice by marking the number 1 beside a candidate's name, your second choice by marking the number 2, your third choice by the number 3, and so on, for as many choices as you wish. You may choose only one candidate, but ranking additional candidates will not affect your first-choice candidate. Do not mark the same number beside more than one candidate. Do not skip numbers."

Section 2: Ballot Counting

Ballots shall be counted by a method known as the instant runoff. The instant runoff tabulates votes based on the principle that any cast for a last-place candidate shall be transferred to the next-choice candidate on the ballot until one candidate has a majority of votes. The ballot-count duplicates what would occur if all voters participated in a graduated series of runoff elections. Vote counting shall start with a tabulation of first-choice votes. If a candidate receives a majority of the first-choice votes, then that candidate shall be declared elected. If no candidate receives such a majority, then the candidate with the fewest first choices shall be declared defeated.[1] Ballots cast for this defeated candidate shall be transferred at full value to the next-choice candidate marked on each ballot. Last-place candidates are eliminated and their supporters' ballots transferred to next-choice candidates who are still in the race in a similar manner until a candidate receives a majority of votes that have not been exhausted.

If a ballot has no more available choices ranked on it, that ballot shall be declared "exhausted." Ballots skipping a number shall be transferred to that voter's next clearly indicated choice. Ballots with two of the same number shall be declared exhausted when such double numbers are reached.

Section 3: Provision for Change of Voting Method

The legislative body or election authorities may provide for the use of mechanical, electronic, or other devices for marking, sorting, and counting the ballots and tabulating the results and may modify the form of the ballots, the directions to voters, and the details with respect to the method of marking, sorting, counting, invalidating, and retaining of ballots, and the tabulating and transferring of votes, provided that no change shall be made that will alter the intent or principles embodied in this law.

Section 4: Determinations in the Case of a Tie

Any ties between candidates occurring at any stage in the tabulation shall be resolved in accordance with the general election laws of the state of _____.

NOTE

1. For large elections with numerous voters, it is recommended that write-in candidates with fewer than ten first-choice votes be declared defeated and all their votes transferred at full value to next choices as indicated on each ballot.

Transfer of Ballots in Choice Voting

The unique attribute of choice voting (otherwise known as the *single transferable vote*) is that it utilizes the transfer of ballots so that votes will not be wasted. The method by which ballots are transferred is a bit complex and deserves some detailed description. Two types of ballot transfers take place: (1) Once a candidate is elected, all of his or her surplus votes—those in excess of the quota or threshold needed to be elected—are transferred to other candidates, and (2) a candidate in last place is eliminated and his or her ballots are transferred to the voters' second choice.

The second kind of transfer is very straightforward. The ballots of excluded candidates are transferred directly to the next available candidate on the ballot, passing over any candidate already elected or excluded. Any ballots with preferences that have been exhausted are set aside.

The transfer of surplus votes from candidates already elected is more complicated. The simplest approach would be to take the last ballots that come in over the threshold and transfer them to the next-preferred candidates. Thus if the threshold were 100 votes and candidate A received 200 votes, the last 100 votes would be transferred. But this approach is faulty because the next preference for the last 100 voters may not be representative of all the ballots for that candidate. To prevent this problem another mode of transfer is often used: All 200 ballots are transferred at a fraction of their value. The number of surplus votes (100) is divided by the total number of ballots (200) to produce the fraction of ½. Then all the second-choice votes for each candidate are added up and multiplied by ½ to determine the actual number of ballots transferred to each. Thus if candidate B receives 120 second-preference votes and candidate C receives 80, these vote totals would be multiplied by ½ to get 60 and 40 ballots, respectively—equaling the total of 100 surplus ballots to be transferred. This method ensures that all surplus ballots are transferred in proper proportion to the other candidates.

Blank Grid for Comparing Voting Systems

Criteria	Voting Systems				

Rating Scale	
*	Least effective at fulfilling the criterion.
**	Moderately effective at fulfilling the criterion.
***	Most effective at fulfilling the criterion.

Glossary of Terms

Additional member system (AMS). Another term for a *mixed member proportional* voting system.

Alternative vote. Another term for *instant runoff voting*.

Approval voting. A voting system used in single-member district systems and single-office elections in which voters can vote for, or approve of, as many candidates as they wish. Each candidate approved of receives one vote and the candidate with the most votes wins. The winner need not garner a majority of the votes.

At-large system. Another term for a *multimember plurality* voting system.

Bullet voting. The term used when a voter votes for only one candidate, when he or she had the option of voting for more than one.

Choice voting. A *proportional representation system* in which voters rank the candidates on the ballot, putting a 1 next to their first choice, a 2 next to their second choice, and so on. Candidates receiving votes beyond the *quota* needed to get elected are declared winners. Voters' ballots are reallocated to their next preferences when their first candidate is eliminated or when there are surplus votes for an elected candidate.

Closed list. A type of ballot found in *list proportional representation*, in which votes are cast for a party and its list of candidates. The order of the candidates on the list is fixed and is determined by the party, usually in a convention, caucus, or primary. Voters cannot express a preference for any particular candidate within that list.

Compensatory seats. The list PR seats in a *mixed-member proportional system* that are allocated to parties on the basis of their proportion of the vote. These seats are designed to compensate for any disproportionality in representation resulting from the *single-member district* portion of the elections.

Cumulative vote (CV). A system that uses multimember districts and in which voters have the same number of votes as there are seats being contested. Voters may allocate their votes among the various candidates in any way they see fit—including giving more than one vote to a particular candidate. In a three-seat district, a voter may give two votes to one candidate and one to another, or one vote each to three candidates, and so on. Considered a *semiproportional system.*

Districts. The geographical regions into which a city, state, or country is divided for election purposes. Single-member districts elect one member of the legislature. Multimember districts elect two or more members.

District magnitude. The number of seats elected in a district.

First-past-the-post system (FPTP). A British term that refers to *single-member district plurality* elections.

Gerrymandering. The manipulation of district boundary lines in order to advantage or disadvantage a candidate or political group unfairly. Typically used to create a district that is favorable to an incumbent, or a series of districts that allow a particular party or political group to receive more seats than it deserves in terms of its proportion of the vote.

Instant runoff voting (IRV). A *majority voting system* used in *single-member district* systems and *single-office elections.* Voters mark their preferences on the ballot by putting a 1 next to their first choice, a 2 next to their second choice, and so on. A candidate who receives over 50% of the first-preference votes is declared the winner. Otherwise, the weakest candidate is eliminated and his or her votes are reallocated to the voters' second choices. This reallocation process continues until one candidate receives a majority of the votes.

Invalid votes. Another term for *spoiled ballots.*

Limited vote (LV). A system that uses multimember districts and in which voters have more than one vote, but fewer votes than the number of seats being contested. The candidates with the most votes are declared the winners. Considered a *semiproportional system.*

List proportional representation (List PR). A system that uses multimember districts and in which voters choose between lists of candidates offered by political parties. The seats in the district are distributed among the parties according to their proportion of the vote. The two basic forms are *closed list* and *open list* PR.

Majority system. A single-member district system or single-office election system that tries to ensure that the winning candidate receives an absolute majority of the votes. Examples include the *two-ballot run off system* and *instant runoff voting.*

Majority sweep. An election result in which the party with the majority of votes wins all the seats in a district.

Manufactured majority. A situation in which a single party wins less than 50% of the vote but receives over 50% of the seats in the legislature.

Minority rule. An election result in which the party that comes in second in the voting wins the majority of seats in the district or the legislature.

Mixed-member proportional (MMP). A PR system that combines *list PR* and *single-member plurality* districts. In the German variant, one-half of the legislators are elected in single-member districts. The other half of the seats are filled from the party lists, and they are added on to the number of district seats that a party wins so that their total share of the legislative seats is equivalent to the proportion of the votes won by that party on the list portion of the ballot.

Multimember district. A district in which more than one member is elected to the legislature.

Open list. A type of ballot found in *list proportional representation* in which voters can express a preference for a candidate within a party list as well as vote for that list. Votes for individual candidates improve their chances of being elected.

Parallel system. A mixed system in which some legislative seats are filled in *single-member district* contests and others from a *list PR* election. Unlike in the *mixed-member proportional* system, however, there is no effort to use the list seats to produce an overall proportional outcome in the legislature. Since the list seats do not fully correct the disproportionality caused by the single-member district contests, this is considered a *semiproportional system*.

Plurality system. Voting system that uses single-member or multimember districts and in which the winner is the candidate or candidates with the most votes. The most common in the United States is the *single-member district plurality system*.

Preference voting. Another term for *choice voting*.

Proportional representation. A group of voting systems whose major goal is to ensure that parties and political groups are allocated seats in legislative bodies in proportion to their share of the vote. A party receiving 30% of the national vote should receive 30% of the seats in the national legislature.

Quota. Another term for *threshold*—the minimum proportion of the vote needed to receive any seats in a PR system.

Semiproportional system. Voting system that may produce more proportional representation than plurality/majority systems but usually falls short of the fully proportional results produced by PR systems such as *list PR, choice voting*, and *mixed-member proportional* systems. The three most common kinds of semiproportional systems are *cumulative voting, limited voting*, and *parallel voting*.

Sincere voting. When voters are able to cast their votes for their most preferred candidate, they are voting sincerely. This contrasts with insincere or strategic voting, in which voters must cast a vote for a candidate other than their first preference in order to best pursue their political interests.

Single nontransferable vote (SNTV). A variation of the *limited vote* and a member of the family *of semiproportional systems*. In this system, there are multiple seats at stake in the district, but voters are limited to one vote.

Single-member district. A district in which only one member is elected to the legislature.

Single-member plurality voting (SMP). A system in which candidates are elected in single-member districts, with the winner being the one with the most votes—the plurality of the votes.

Single transferable vote (STV). Another term for *choice voting*, usually found in the academic literature.

Single office election. An election to choose the occupant of a single office, such as mayor or governor—in contrast to elections that choose entire legislatures.

Spoiled ballots. Ballots that, as a result of accidental or deliberate errors in the marking process, are declared invalid and are eliminated from the count.

Spoiler. A phenomenon of plurality/majority voting systems in which an independent or third-party candidate takes away enough votes from one major-party candidate to ensure the victory of the other major-party candidate, who would not have won otherwise.

Threshold. In a *proportional representation* system, the minimum portion of the vote that a party must receive in order to receive any seats in the legislature. Known technically as the *threshold of exclusion* because if a party reaches this threshold, it cannot be excluded from winning a seat.

Two-round system (TRS). A *majority voting system* that is used in single-member district systems and single-office elections to ensure that the winner has the support of the majority of the voters. If no candidate receives a majority of the vote in the first round of voting, a second election is held a short time later. In this second election, the top two candidates face off and one of them usually wins with a majority of the vote. Sometimes also called the *runoff system* and the *second-ballot system*.

Wasted votes. Votes that do not ultimately contribute to the election of a candidate. Votes that are cast but that do not actually produce any representation.

Winner-take-all system. Another term for a *plurality* or *majority* voting system that produces one winner in each district.

Selected Bibliography

BOOKS

Amy, Douglas J. *Real Choices/New Voices: The Case for Proportional Representation Elections in the United States*. New York: Columbia University Press, 1993.

Barber, Kathleen L. *The Right to Representation: Proportional Election Systems for the Twenty-first Century*. Columbus, Ohio: Ohio State University Press, 2000.

Blair, George S. *Cumulative Voting: An Effective Electoral Device in Illinois Politics*. Urbana, Ill.: University of Illinois Press, 1960.

Bogdanor, Vernon. *What Is Proportional Representation?* Oxford: Martin Robertson, 1984.

Bogdanor, Vernon, and David Butler. *Democracy and Elections: Electoral Systems and Their Political Consequences*. New York: Cambridge University Press, 1983.

Brams, Steven J., and Peter C. Fishburn. *Approval Voting*. Boston: Birkhauser, 1983.

Carstairs, Andrew McLaren. *A Short History of Electoral Systems in Western Europe*. London: George Allen and Unwin, 1980.

Center For Voting and Democracy. *Voting and Democracy Report 1995*. Washington, D.C.: The Center for Voting and Democracy.

Farrell, David M. *Comparing Electoral Systems*. New York: Prentice Hall, 1997.

Grofman, Bernard, and Arend Lijphart, eds. *Electoral Laws and Their Political Consequences*. New York: Agathon, 1986.

Guinier, Lani. *The Tyranny of the Majority: Fundamental Fairness in Representative Democracy*. New York: Free Press, 1994.

Hallett, George H. *Proportional Representation: The Key to Democracy*. New York: National Municipal League, 1940.

Hermens, Ferdinand A. *Democracy or Anarchy? A Study of Proportional Representation*. South Bend, Ind.: Notre Dame, 1941.

Katz, Richard S. *A Theory of Parties and Electoral Systems*. Baltimore: The Johns Hopkins University Press, 1980.

Lakeman, Enid, and James Lambert. *Voting in Democracies*. London: Faber and Faber, 1959.
LeDuc, Lawrence, Richard Niemi, and Pippa Norris, eds. *Comparing Democracies: Elections and Voting in Global Perspective*. Thousand Oaks, Calif.: Sage Publications, 1996.
Lijphart, Arend. *Patterns of Democracy: Government Forms and Performance in Thirty-Six Countries*. New Haven, Conn.: Yale University Press, 1999.
Lijphart, Arend, and Bernard Grofman, eds. *Choosing an Electoral System: Issues and Alternatives*. New York: Praeger, 1984.
Loenen, Nick. *Citizenship and Democracy: A Case for Proportional Representation*. Toronto: Dundurn Press, 1997.
Rae, Douglas W. *The Political Consequences of Electoral Laws*. New Haven, Conn.: Yale University Press, 1971.
Reynolds, Andrew, and Ben Reilly. *The International IDEA Handbook of Electoral System Design*. Stockholm: International Institute for Democracy and Electoral Assistance, 1997.
Richie, Robert, and Steven Hill. *Reflecting All of Us: The Case for Proportional Representation*. Boston: Beacon Press, 1999.
Rule, Wilma, and Joseph F. Zimmerman, eds. *United States Electoral Systems: Their Impact on Women and Minorities*. New York: Greenwood Press, 1993.
Rule, Wilma, and Joseph F. Zimmerman, eds. *Electoral Systems in Comparative Perspective: Their Impact on Women and Minorities*. Westport, Conn.: Greenwood Press, 1994.
Straetz, Ralph A. *PR Politics in Cincinnati*. New York: New York University Press, 1958.
Taagepera, Rein, and Matthew Soberg Shugart. *Seats and Votes: The Effects and Determinants of Electoral Systems*. New Haven, Conn.: Yale University Press, 1989.

ARTICLES

Cohen, Frank. "Proportional versus Majoritarian Ethnic Conflict Management in Democracies." *Comparative Political Studies* 30 (October 1997): 607–30.
Cole, Richard L., Delbert A. Taebel, and Richard L. Engstrom, "Alternatives to Single-Member Districts." *Western Political Quarterly* (March 1990): 191–99.
Engstrom, Richard L. "Modified Multi-Seat Election Systems as Remedies for Minority Vote Dilution." *Stetson Law Review* 21, no. 3 (Summer 1992): 743–770.
Lind, Michael. "Alice Doesn't Vote Here Any More." *Mother Jones* 23, no. 2, (March/April 1998): 52–55.
Norris, Pippa. "Women's Legislative Participation in Western Europe." *West European Politics* 8 (1995): 90–101.
Pildes, Richard, and Kristen Donoghue. "Cumulative Voting in the United States." *The University of Chicago Legal Forum* (1995): 241–313.
Richie, Robert, Caleb Kleppner, and Terril Bouricius. "Instant Run-Offs: A

Cheaper, Faster, Better Way to Conduct Elections." *National Civic Review* 89, no. 1 (Spring 2000): 95–110.

Rule, Wilma. "Electoral Systems, Contextual Factors, and Women's Opportunity for Election to Parliament in Twenty-Three Democracies." *Western Political Quarterly* 33: 477–98.

Weaver, Leon. "The Rise, Decline, and Resurrection of Proportional Representation in Local Government in the United States." In *Electoral Laws and Their Political Consequences*. edited by Bernard Grofman and Arend Lijphart, 139–53. New York: Agathon, 1986.

Zeller, Belle, and Hugh Bone. "The Repeal of PR in New York City: Ten Years in Retrospect." *American Political Science Review* 42 (December 1948): 1127–48.

Zimmerman, Joseph F. "Alternative Local Election Systems." *National Civic Review* 79, no. 1 (January-February, 1990): 23–36.

Additional Resources

WEB SITES ON VOTING SYSTEM REFORM

PR Library: Readings in Proportional Representation
A source of information on proportional representation voting systems—including beginning readings, in-depth articles by scholars and activists, an extensive bibliography, and a guide to related web sites.
http://www.mtholyoke.edu/acad/polit/damy/prlib.htm

The Center for Voting and Democracy
A nonprofit educational organization located in Washington, D.C. The center is the leading organization in the United States dedicated to educating the public about alternative election systems.
http://www.fairvote.org

The International Institute for Democracy and Electoral Assistance
Located in Sweden, this organization strives to promote sustainable democracy worldwide. It has a particular interest in improving electoral systems. Has particularly good information about women's representation and voter turnout worldwide.
http://www.int-idea.se/

A Comparison of Municipal Election Methods
A study conducted by the League of Women Voters of Seattle that examined the advantages and disadvantages of various systems that can be used for town and city elections.
http://www.scn.org/civic/lwvseattle/comp.html

Reflecting All of Us: A Debate on Proportional Representation
A series of articles for and against proportional representation published in the *Boston Review*. The lead article is by Rob Richie and Steven Hill of the Center for Voting and Democracy, with eight responses from political scientists, voting rights attorneys, the New party, Congresswoman Cynthia McKinney, and others. Now also available as a book, *Reflecting All of Us*, from Beacon Press.
http://www-polisci.mit.edu/bostonreview/BR23.1/

ORGANIZATIONS PROMOTING VOTING SYSTEM REFORM

United States

The Center for Voting and Democracy
Mail: 6930 Carroll Ave., Suite 901, Takoma Park, MD 20912
Phone: (301) 270–4616
Fax: (301) 270–4133
E-mail: cvdusa@aol.com
Web Site: http://www.fairvote.org

Northern California Chapter of Citizens for Proportional Representation
Phone: (415) 221–4575, (408) 759–9147, (510) 527–8025
E-mail: info@fairvotencal.org
Web Site: http://fairvotencal.org

Fairvote Minnesota
Mail: P.O. Box 19440, Minneapolis MN 55419–0440
Phone: (612) 724–5540
E-mail: solga002@tc.umn.edu
Web Site: http://www2.bitstream.net/~gabeo/

Illinois Citizens for Proportional Representation
Mail: PO Box 14314, Chicago, IL 60614
Phone: (773) 508–4890
E-mail: proportionalrepresentation@msn.com
Web Site: http://www.prairienet.org/icpr/

Washington Citizens for Proportional Representation
Mail: P.O. Box 20534, Seattle, WA 98102
Phone: (206) 233–8509
E-mail: washington@fairvote.net.
Web Site: http://fairvote.net/washington/

International

Electoral Reform Society
   Founded in England in 1884, the ERS is the longest continuous PR organization.
   This site contains particularly good information about the single transferable
   vote—the society's preferred form of PR. They also have an excellent analysis of
   the report issued by the Jenkins Commission that recommends a new voting sys-
   tem for British parliamentary elections.
   Mail: 6 Chancel Street, London SE1 OUU, United Kingdom
   Phone: +44 (0)171 928 1622
   Fax: +44 (0)171 401 7789
   E-mail: ers@reform.demon.co.uk
   Web Site: http://www.electoral-reform.org.uk/

Proportional Representation Society of Australia
   Like the Electoral Reform Society, this organization is a long-established proponent

of proportional representation, especially the single transferable vote (called *Hare-Clark quota preferential voting*).
Mail: Bogey Musidlak, 14 Strzelecki Crescent, Narrabundah, ACT 2604
Phone: +61 6 295 8137, +61 6 249 8546
E-mail: lee@cs.mu.oz.au.
Fax: +61 3 9589 1680
Web Site: http://www.prsa.org.edu

Canadians for Proportional Representation
This organization favors a party list or a mixed-member system of proportional representation over STV.
Mail: Post Office Box 24026, Winnipeg, Manitoba, R3N 2B1
E-mail: mycolog@pacificcoast.net
Web Site: http://www.ualberta.ca/~dbailie/C4PR/

Index

Access to political representatives, 17; choice voting and, 101; type of district representation and, 31, 75–76, 83–84, 89–90

AccuVote system, 96

Adams, John, 15

Additional member system (AMS), 201. *See also* Mixed-member proportional systems

Administration of elections: ease or complexity of, 20, 143, 149, 155, 156; expenses associated with, 42, 47, 53, 54; in plurality-majority systems, 31, 42, 54; in proportional representation systems, 85, 103, 171; in semiproportional systems, 125, 127–28, 137, 171. *See also* Election procedures

Africa, emerging democracies in, 7

African American political representation, 6, 40, 111, 113, 121, 181. *See also* Racial and ethnic minority representation

African National Congress (South Africa), 89

Alabama, cumulative voting in, 111, 116, 121, 123

Albania, parallel system in, 132

Alternative vote (AV), 201. *See also* Instant runoff voting (IRV)

Amarillo, Texas, cumulative voting in, 116

American Labor Party, 179

American Political Science Association, 152

America. *See* United States

Andrae, Carl, 96

Approval voting, 183–84, 201

Ashtabula, Ohio, proportional representation system in, 178

Asian American political representation, 6, 111. *See also* Racial and ethnic minority representation

At-large voting, 27, 28, 55, 201; advantages of, 57–58; ballots for, 50, 51, 57, 61; disadvantages of, 58–60. *See also* Multimember districts

Australia, proportionality and choice voting in, 54, 95, 156; proportional representation system group in, 210–11

Austria, runoff voting in, 28, 147

Azerbiajan, parallel system in, 132, 133

Balkanization, 82–83

Ballots: for at-large voting, 50, 51, 57, 61; for closed party list voting, 86; for cumulative voting, 117; "exhausted," 157; for instant runoff voting, 50, 51, 152, 153; for limited voting, 126; for mixed-member voting, 91; for open party list voting, 87; for parallel voting, 133; for

About the Author

DOUGLAS J. AMY is Professor of Politics at Mount Holyoke College. He has written extensively about voting systems and voting system reform. Among his earlier books are *Real Choices/New Voices: The Case for Proportional Representation Elections in the United States* (1993) and *The Politics of Environmental Mediation.*